Charlie's Fly Box

Charlie's Fly Box

SIGNATURE FLIES FOR FRESH AND SALT WATER

Charlie Craven

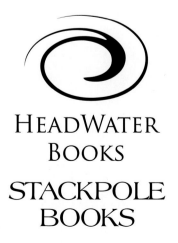

HEADWATER
BOOKS

STACKPOLE
BOOKS

Published by
STACKPOLE BOOKS
5067 Ritter Road
Mechanicsburg, PA 17055
www.stackpolebooks.com

Printed in China

First edition

All photos by the author unless otherwise noted.

10 9 8 7 6 5 4 3 2 1

Library of Congress Cataloging-in-Publication Data
Craven, Charlie.
    Charlie's fly box: signature flies for fresh and salt water.—1st ed.
      p. cm.
   ISBN-13: 978-0-8117-0732-9 (hardcover)
   ISBN-10: 0-8117-0732-6 (hardcover)
   I. Title.

SH451.C66 2010
688.7'9124—dc22

2010018937

For Mom and Dad

Contents

Acknowledgments ix

Introduction xi

ONE   Jujubee Midge   1

TWO   Jumbo Juju Chironomid   12

THREE   Jujubaetis   23

FOUR   Poison Tung   33

FIVE   Two Bit Hooker   43

SIX   Caddistrophic Pupa   57

SEVEN   Charlie's Mysis   69

EIGHT   Wiggle Damsel   77

NINE   Soft Hackle Emerger   86

TEN   Mole Fly   96

ELEVEN   Mugly Caddis   104

TWELVE   Charlie Boy Hopper   111

THIRTEEN   Baby Boy Hopper   127

FOURTEEN   GTH Variant   139

FIFTEEN   Lead Eyed Gonga   154

SIXTEEN   Bonefish Junk   167

SEVENTEEN   Ragin' Craven   182

Index 204

Acknowledgments

I would like to thank the many people who came together in one way or another to make this book possible.

My friend and editor, Jay Nichols, first and foremost for staying on me to get this thing written and for his never ending encouragement and professionalism in making my work look so much better than it really is.

My dear wife, Kristi, for her utter patience and unending encouragement. They say behind every good man there is a great woman, and in this case it couldn't be more true.

My three children, Charlie, Julie, and Jack, for an almost endless supply of fly pattern names, the laughter, and their innate ability to keep their father in check.

Ross Bartholomay and Matt Prowse, my two favorite fishing buddies, for indulging my pattern developments even when they fail, voicing a sometimes hard-edged opinion, and thinking of those things that never occur to me.

My Mom and Dad, for introducing me to the outdoors, giving me free rein to explore and wander and the chance to find my way in this world.

And finally, to all the fly tiers of the world, for your work and innovative ideas that keep me on the edge of my seat year after year.

This was one of the many cutthroat that fell for the same yellow Charlie Boy Hopper. I try to design flies that are durable so I can spend more time fishing than changing flies.

Sitting down at the vise, while sometimes a chore, is more often an escape for me into a realm of development and creativity. Each day spent on the water is not only a hunt for fish but also a hunt for the perfect fly. Anglers are always looking for flies that float better or sink faster, last longer, or combine more attractive attributes, and I consider it my job to search these things out. Some fly tiers can sit down and develop a fly to match a particular hatch or insect stage from start to finish in a few hours or days, but this is rarely the way things happen for me. I am experimenting endlessly, and the ability to recognize a single useful facet of any off-the-wall bug that falls from my vise is one of my favorite tools. I am engulfed by the "what-ifs" and "how-coulds" of fly tying. What if I use this material to make a body rather than a wing? What other applications might this material be good for? Questions like this keep me tying and experimenting in the quest for an answer to a question that may have never been asked.

Every fly you tie will open your eyes to new techniques and materials . . . if you let it.

When you fill up a fly box, the best course of action is to buy another and start filling it up too.

In this new book, I will be covering the patterns that I have developed over the past decade or so, walking through the step-by-steps with as much detail as I can get away with. I have purposely made these tutorials a bit (but *just* a bit) more succinct than those in my *Basic Fly Tying* book in the hopes that I (and you) will be able to move forward from those basic techniques and branch out more into the development of patterns and the thought processes behind them. The techniques in this book are a bit more advanced than those in *Basic Fly Tying*, and I hope that this book will improve your skills. I have always considered myself more of a "technique" kind of guy rather than one ruled by pattern, and I hope that the patterns I show here will adequately highlight the methods to tie them. It doesn't matter if you live and fish in the northern, southern, eastern, or western United States; the patterns herein will produce fish for you, and the techniques will help you tie patterns of your own creation. My goal in this book is not to popularize my own patterns, but rather to show new techniques and how I develop my ideas.

As you will see, very few of the flies presented here were developed individually; instead they're part of a body of work with common themes throughout. For instance, the Jujubee Midge and Jujubaetis are obviously close relatives. The technique of wrapping the abdomen with Superhair was perfect for creating a slim-bodied midge with smooth segmentation and transferred beautifully over to creating the tapered abdomen of a *Baetis* nymph. Adding in a final body-shaping overcoat of epoxy to the Jujubaetis series separated the patterns further, yet the common lineage remains clear. The fact that the ragged nature of the Mugly Caddis is present in the Caddistrophic Pupa is no accident either, in spite of my own proclivities to tie neat, clean flies. Sometimes ragged is called for, and I am getting better at letting it sneak in where appropriate.

My fly design aesthetics revolve around durability and problem solving. I like flies that hold together just like everyone else, but to me durability also involves some utilitarian features as well—dry flies that float longer and better require less maintenance. Functional features like these are every bit as important to me as how a fly looks. Weighted nymphs that can retain a slim, accurate profile sink more quickly and stay in the strike zone longer, keeping me from having to constantly fiddle with additional weight on my leader. Let's face it—lots of flies will catch fish. Well-designed flies do it over and over again in a variety of circumstances.

I also strive to tie my flies well. Aside from being durable, well-tied flies are repeatable. Mastering the techniques to tie any given pattern allows me to tie more of them that are exactly the same. I know many tiers and fishermen who pick through their flies looking for a "good one." Sloppy variations are not acceptable to me, and when I lose a fly in a streamside bush or on a rock, I want to reach back into my fly box and pick out another just like it. This nonsense of the "one fly that worked then I lost it" drives me nuts. Consistency comes from practice. Tie lots of flies and don't be satisfied with adequate.

I have spent a lot of time explaining the thought processes that went through my head as I developed each of these patterns. I hope this will encourage you to take a look at your own tying and to learn to keep your eyes open for problem-solving opportunities. Some of my flies have a good story behind them; others just happened to fall into place. But none of them came easily or without at least a bit of tweaking.

New tying techniques and uses for materials are as much a part of my tool box as are feathers and fur. I am lucky to have stumbled upon as many new tricks and techniques as I have over the years, and while they often are the results of what I like to call "happy accidents," I think that experimenting and tinkering leads to far more discoveries than simply tying standard patterns. Every fly I tie is a chance to discover a new twist or develop a different technique or application, no matter how mundane the pattern. The ability to keep my eyes and mind open to these developments has served me well over the years.

I am not yet at the level of great fly-tying minds like John Barr and Mike Mercer who can depend on the exclusive use of their own patterns to match nearly any insect they might encounter. While I do prefer to use my own patterns, using others' flies often helps spur my own creative process. Determining a weakness or room for improvement in a pattern is something on which I pride myself, and I often consider much of my tying to be more of pattern improvement than solely development.

Well armed for a day fly fishing. While I do prefer to use my own patterns, using others' flies often helps spur my own creative process.

That being said, nothing makes me happier than stumbling upon a truly new pattern, although in this day and age it is really tough to come up with anything that honestly fits the description.

Fly tying is a simple collection of techniques, and given enough time and practice, anyone can become adequate. What separates adequate tiers from really good ones is the ability to solve a problem. Sometimes, the hardest part is recognizing the problem in the first place. The first thought in my mind with every fly I fish or tie is, how can I make it better? It doesn't matter if the pattern is one of my design or a common everyday favorite. The quest for "better," if not "perfect," is what keeps me twisting thread around a hook.

Simple variations on a theme generally don't work any better than the original, but if you can change something in a pattern to make it more durable, more accurate, or fish better, then you are really onto something. Take the ubiquitous Pheasant Tail Nymph. While it is a wonderfully popular pattern with an accurate mayfly nymph profile, it is, unfortunately, not very durable. Its saving grace is that it is cheap and easy to tie, so if it comes apart after a few fish, you can simply replace it. Creating a more durable fly that has the same kind of profile, perhaps with some weight and a strip of flash down the back, might get you something like my Two Bit Hooker. Sure, it takes a bit longer to tie, but having a more durable fly that can be fished on a dropper without additional weight is worth the effort. So sit down, go through the book, and pick out what you like. I urge you to pay attention to the techniques themselves as well as the patterns as you tie—you are certain to pick up a helpful little tidbit here or there. I know from my commercial tying experience that even the most unexciting or least-applicable patterns have always taught me some useful technique or use for a material. I hope that in this book you find your next great epiphany.

My goal in this book is not to popularize my own patterns but rather to show new techniques and how I develop my ideas. Hopefully you will take some of these themes and apply them to your own tying.

ONE

Jujubee Midge

Super Hair provides a beautifully segmented abdomen in a plethora of color combinations for the Jujubee Midge.

Many years ago, I was feverishly tying up a last-minute batch of barracuda flies for an upcoming trip to Belize. It was late at night and my desk was piled high with all sorts of crazy materials. Flash, Super Hair, stick-on eyes, and epoxy all cluttered my work space. I had tied a long hank of chartreuse Super Hair to the bend of a 3/0 saltwater iron to create the elongated body of a needlefish in hopes of luring some poor, overly aggressive barracuda into making a mistake.

To this day I clearly remember quickly wrapping the threaded bobbin forward over the hook shank when a single strand of that Super Hair tail caught up in the thread and got twisted up the shank along with it. What was at first an annoyance with my sloppy technique quickly became something to give me pause. As I looked at the wound Super Hair, an idea popped into my head that changed both the rest of my evening and, in many ways, my life. I had accidently stumbled upon using an old material in a new way. Though Super Hair

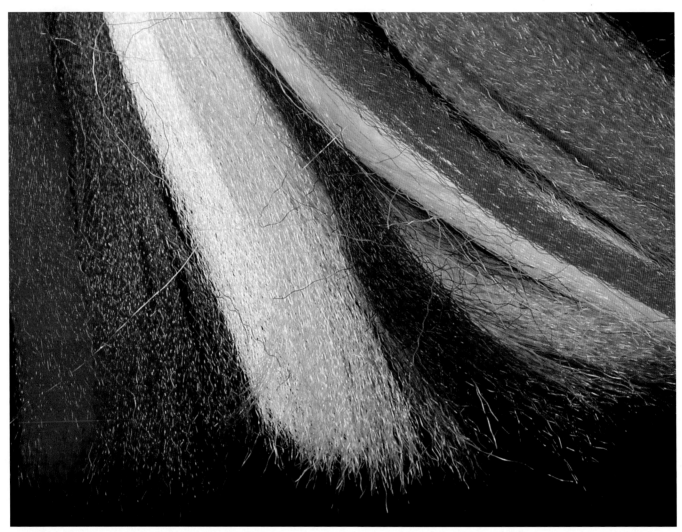

Super Hair has become one of my favorite materials. It is tough, cheap, and commonly available in a variety of colors.

has been a staple in saltwater and baitfish patterns for years, it occurred to me that I could wrap it around the hook to create a near perfect midge body. I swept all the saltwater materials to the side of my desk with my arm, dug into my hook drawer for some curved scud hooks, and ventured forth with this new idea perched on my fingertips.

At first, I simply tied in a single strand of Super Hair to the shank behind the eye, wrapped over it to the bend, and proceeded to wrap the Super Hair in abutting turns forward to the hook eye. I quickly discovered that using a dark thread killed the translucent properties of the Super Hair. I switched to the smallest white thread I could find (the now-no-longer-available 40-denier Gudebrod 10/0) and found that the Super Hair wrapped over a white thread base made a beautifully segmented body with translucence unlike anything else I had seen. I

finished this simple larva pattern off with a black thread head and thought that I just might be on to something.

Over the course of the next few weeks I continued to play with the Super Hair. Finally, at some point, I decided to add another color for a contrasting rib. Using one strand in each color made for a fly that was a little too busy for me, and I finally smartened up and used two strands of the primary color along with one strand of a contrasting rib color. By mixing and matching the colors, I found I could create bodies that mimicked the natural's ribbing and segmentation. Using more subtle colors together, like brown and olive, created a muted "camo" type body, while the contrasting colors like chartreuse and black made for much more prominent segmentation.

Moving on to the wing case and wing buds where I originally used Antron, I later used a then-new material from Umpqua Feather Merchants called Fluoro Fibre. Fluoro Fibre is essentially organza in its raw form. Rather than being woven into a sheet like organza, Fluoro Fibre comes in a hank and is much easier to use. The fiber-optic and light-gathering nature of the Fluoro Fibre made it a perfect choice for the Jujubee's wing case. The parts were all laid out and the construction was simple from there.

At the time the Jujubee was being put together, I was guiding on the South Platte River for my daily bread. I stashed my secret pattern in my box and had clients unknowingly field-test the pattern for me on the notoriously tough Cheesman Canyon trout. The fish loved it and I attribute their zeal for the pattern to its prominent segmentation and slightly shiny wing case. It ain't easy keeping a good thing secret and eventually, my little "SuperMidge" (this is what I called the fly at that time, for lack of a better name) crept out to the other guides. Luckily, the lack of detailed tying tricks that I have now described here kept the others from tying it for their own boxes. I had my little secret pattern all to myself and my friends for the most part for several years.

It was when Van Rollo convinced me to submit my Charlie Boy Hopper and a few other patterns to Umpqua Feather Merchants that my little midge really got moving. I had tied up a couple dozen sample patterns for the boys at Umpqua to peruse and had lined them up neatly in a large foam fly box for their inspection. There was some space left on one side of the foam box and I felt like I needed to fill it all up, so I went into my midge box and pulled out a few of my secret weapons and stuck them in with the rest. I really thought this pattern was too simple to sell very well, and I included it in the submissions more to fill out the box than from any notion that it would be picked up.

Turns out I was wrong again. Umpqua's "Fly Czar," Bruce Olson, loved the fly and insisted that it, along with my Charlie Boy Hopper, become part of the Umpqua catalog. The only catch was the name of the fly had to be changed to something less generic. "SuperMidge" just wasn't unique enough, and Bruce asked that I try to come up with something better. I figured that if I were ever to have something this cool happen to me, I ought to share it with those I love and so I named the fly the Jujubee Midge in honor of my daughter Julie. We have called her "Jujubee" since she was born and the name was kind of catchy . . . so the fly became known as the Jujubee Midge. As it turns out, mistakenly wrapping a few strands

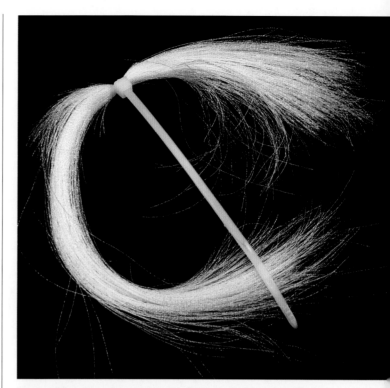

Fluoro Fibre has shine without flash and picks up light well, making it perfect for wings, tails, wing cases, and wing buds. It is available in a host of useful colors.

of Super Hair around the hook may have been the best idea I have ever had.

TYING TIPS

I have had perhaps a hundred different tiers come to me over the years with the same question and problem: "How do you keep all three strands of Super Hair even and together as you wrap them up the hook shank?" If you tie in the three strands of Super Hair to the bend and then try to wrap the three strands together at a right angle to the hook shank, the fibers *will* separate as you approach the apex of the hook bend. The solution is not terribly intuitive, but it is simple. The Super Hair strands must be wrapped at a right angle to the tabletop or floor, regardless of the hook's orientation. The first turn, placed at a right angle to the floor, leaves a tiny gap at the hook bend but also allows the fibers to lie neatly next to each other as you wrap them forward up the hook shank. I elaborate on this technique in the tying steps.

Tying the wing case and wing buds with too much Fluoro Fibre results in a fly with too much bulk and an overbearing amount of shine. I typically use twelve strands of Fluoro Fibre for the wing cases on a #18 Juju, drop down to ten fibers for a #20, and use eight fibers for the #22s. I encourage you to actually count out a dozen strands of Fluoro Fibre for at least the first few batches of flies. Twelve fibers isn't a whole lot, and it appears to me that most tiers seem to mistake 40 to 50 fibers for a dozen.

Using the 2X short-shanked Tiemco 2488 hook makes the nominal length of the #22 plenty small enough for my waters, but for those of you that enjoy fishing with flecks of dust, I suggest using Unique Hair for the smallest of the fly bodies. Unique Hair and Super Hair both come from Best Way Products and are exactly the same, except that the Unique Hair fibers are even thinner than the Super Hair fibers. Unique Hair is too fine for the average size range of #16-22 but works beautifully for the smaller #24-30 versions popular on a certain tailwaters. On these smallest of the small Jujus, I cut the wing case fibers down to about six to keep the fly properly sparse.

While my very first Jujubees were tied on the Tiemco 2487 scud and light midge hook, I later made the permanent change to the Tiemco 2488. The 2488 has a ring eye that just seems to fit this pattern a bit better and to be honest, other than my own taste in the look of the fly, there is really no reason that either hook wouldn't work well. I do try to avoid using the Tiemco 2488H, as its heavier wire makes the fly too fat for my eye. I have had requests to tie Jujus on these heavier hooks for folks who fish some of the western tailwaters known for larger than average-sized fish, and while it can be done, I think the fly loses its diminutive and delicate profile. I am in no way conceding that the 2488 is a weak hook, but modern fluorocarbon tippets and fast-action rods allow for much more pressure to be put on a fish these days, and one must keep in mind that the hook has in many cases become the weak link in the system.

FISHING THE JUJUBEE

I find the Jujubee imitates midge larvae and pupae equally well and can be fished successfully from the top of the water column to the bottom, depending on where the fish are feeding. Midge larvae and pupae are the most commonly available food on most trout waters, particularly so during the leaner shoulder seasons of fall through spring. Having a pattern like the Jujubee that can mimic either the larval or pupal form in several color combinations has proven to be a tremendous asset to me over the years.

I most commonly fish the Jujubee on a 9-foot leader with a 5X or 6X tippet in a multiple fly rig, often behind a heavier fly like a Poison Tung. The heavy front fly keeps the Juju down but allows it to find its place in the currents and react as the naturals would. I usually attach a small foam indicator about 1½ times the water depth above the first fly. I generally try to get away with just the heavier fly as a weight, as I have become a true believer in the stealthier approach of using a weighted fly rather than split shot to get the fly down, but I resort to using split shot and lead putty to seal the deal if need be.

I fish the Jujubee in tailouts and deep pools during colder months, as the fish tend to congregate in these areas. As the water temperatures rise in the spring, the fish move up into the riffles and the heads of pools, and I'll target them there as well.

My typical approach begins with scanning the area for signs of visibly feeding fish. Depending on the water depth, I may be looking for an entire fish, the flash of a fish turning to feed, or even just the white inside of a trout's mouth. It is not uncommon in the winter and early spring to find several fish together in a good seam, picking off emerging pupae. I always try to sight-fish rather than blind-cast, because to me there is just about nothing as boring as watching an indicator drift through slow water. I'm not saying I won't do it, and I'm not saying I haven't done it, but given a choice and the prospect of even one visible, feeding fish, I will take the one I can see over the ones I can't any day. That's just me.

I try to cast above and slightly beyond the fishes' feeding lane so the flies have time to sink both down to their feeding level as well as into their lane. Watch the spot where your flies hit the water when you cast as compared to where they are when you pull them up at the end of the drift. The flies will end up much closer to you than they started because they are tethered to the leader, which is, in turn, tethered to you. Casting beyond the fishes' lane will allow the flies to drop through the water column to both the proper depth as well as into the proper lane. High-sticking by lifting the rod tip up, slightly above horizontal to the water, will help you to keep track of the drifting flies while also allowing for minor adjustments in the directing of the drift. Keeping the leader and tippet as vertical as possible in the water, without creating drag, will also help them to cut through

Jujubees are my go-to midge pupae pattern, and I carry them in a variety of colors and sizes. Ten dollars worth of materials will tie a lifetime supply.

the water more easily and get down faster than if the line goes through the water at an angle.

I typically use the small white pinch-on indicators on the leader, more to help me direct the cast and control the drift than to actually indicate a strike. I then watch the fish closely as the flies drift into their zone for any signs of a take. Over the years I have become convinced that the big yawning takes that are so noticeable when watching a trout eat your artificial are really the fish trying to spit the fly out. By the time you see the fish chomping and showing the big white inside of its mouth, it already has the fly and is trying to get rid of it (this is where sticky-sharp hooks become a clear advantage). Waiting for the indicator to twitch can be too little, much too late. Strike gently at any indication of an eat; most often it can be foretold by a more animated movement from the fish or a change in its body language.

JUJUBEE MIDGE
(OLIVE)

Hook:	#16-22 Tiemco 2488
Thread:	White 74-denier Lagartun
Abdomen:	Two strands of olive Super Hair and one strand of black
Thorax:	Black 8/0 Uni-Thread
Wing Case:	White Fluoro Fibre

TYING THE JUJUBEE MIDGE

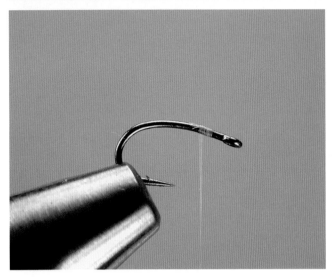

1. Place the hook in the vise and start the white thread about an eye length back from the hook eye. Do not move the thread back to the bend yet, just let it hang one eye length back for the time being. You do not want to build a thread base, because the final fly is slender.

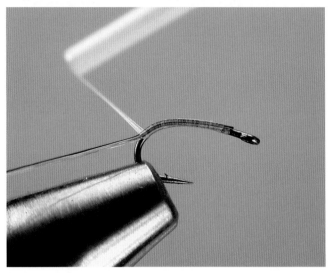

3. Bring the thread up and capture all three strands with a loop of thread along the near side of the shank. Pull the long front ends down as close to the hook as you can and continue wrapping back over the three strands all the way back to about halfway down the bend, taking care to keep them aligned along the near side of the shank.

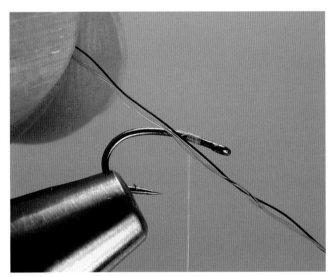

2. Grab two strands of olive and one strand of black Super Hair and pull them out of the clump. Line the Super Hair strands up and draw them between your fingers, stretching them just slightly to remove some of the kinkiness of the fibers and make them a bit easier to work with. Clip all three strands so their ends are even and lay them across the near side of the hook shank.

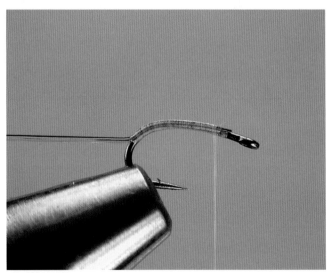

4. Return the thread to the starting point, taking care to make a smooth thread base as you go. I try to make abutting turns of thread here as I move forward to keep the underbody smooth and flat and to completely cover the shank with a smooth layer of white thread.

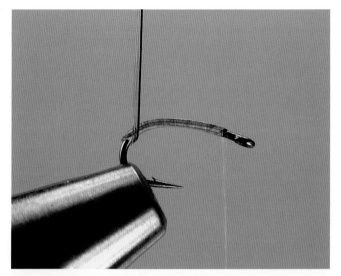

5. Bring all three strands of Super Hair around the hook bend and up on the near side of the shank. Make sure to pull directly up on the three strands to align them perpendicular to the tabletop. Pull hard on the Super Hair and perhaps even rock the fibers back and forth a bit so they line up in a neat little row. You want the three strands lined up and not twisted at all.

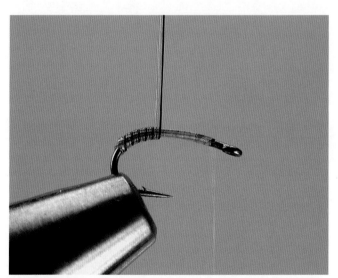

6. Begin wrapping all three strands forward, taking care to keep the wraps parallel to each other as you go.

7. Continue wrapping the strands of Super Hair forward up to the starting point and tie them off with three tight turns of thread. Clip the excess Super Hair flush with the shank.

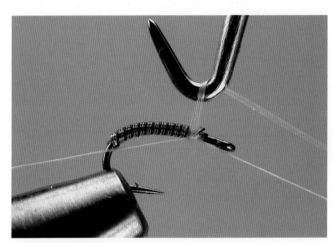

8. Whip-finish and clip the white thread.

9. Start the black 8/0 thread right on top of the tie-off point. Make a turn or two over the front edge of the abdomen to assure that everything overlaps nicely.

10. Separate ten strands of Fluoro Fibre from the clump and cut them loose. Cut one end so all the fiber tips are square and tie them in to the top of the front edge of the abdomen with two turns of thread.

11. Pull the long end of the Fluoro Fibre back to shorten the front end so it is just short of the thread wraps holding it down.

12. Build a thorax with the black thread in the shape of an elongated oval, ending just short of the hook eye. Be sure you have a bit of bare shank just behind the eye to complete the rest of the fly.

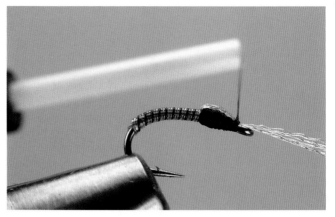

13. Pull the Fluoro Fibre forward over the top of the thorax and tie it down with two turns of thread just behind the hook eye.

14. Divide the front ends of the Fluoro Fibre in half (five strands per side).

15. Pull half the Fluoro Fibre strands back along the near side of the hook, just slightly below the shank. Hold this side a bit below the shank and make a thread wrap over them to pin them along the side of the hook. The thread torque will pull the fibers up from below the shank to the side of the shank as you wrap over them.

16. Pull the other half of the fibers back along the far side of the shank, but this time hold them slightly above the shank, so that the thread torque will pull them down and in line with the shank as you tie them down.

17. The wing buds should now be lined up perfectly along the sides of the hook shank as shown here. Build a small but prominent thread head.

18. Whip-finish and clip the thread.

19. Trim the wing buds just a touch longer than the wing case, taking care to keep both sides even as you trim them.

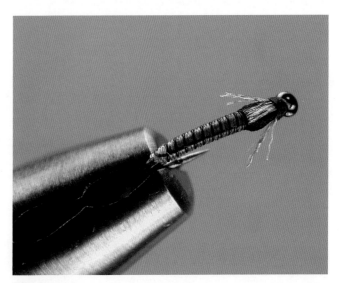

20. Top view.

JUJUBEE MIDGE (OLIVE)

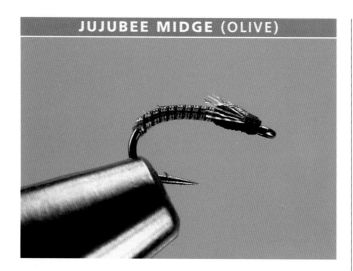

Hook:	#16-22 Tiemco 2488
Thread:	White 74-denier Lagartun
Abdomen:	Two strands of olive Super Hair and one strand of black
Thorax:	Black 8/0 Uni-Thread
Wing Case:	White Fluoro Fibre

JUJUBEE MIDGE (ZEBRA)

Hook:	#16-22 Tiemco 2488
Thread:	White 74-denier Lagartun
Abdomen:	Two strands of black Super Hair and one strand of white
Thorax:	Black 8/0 Uni-Thread
Wing Case:	White Fluoro Fibre

JUJUBEE MIDGE (BROWN)

Hook:	#16-22 Tiemco 2488
Thread:	White 74-denier Lagartun
Abdomen:	Two strands of dark brown Super Hair and one strand of white
Thorax:	Camel 8/0 Uni-Thread
Wing Case:	White Fluoro Fibre

JUJUBEE MIDGE (RED)

Hook:	#16-22 Tiemco 2488
Thread:	White 74-denier Lagartun
Abdomen:	Two strands of red Super Hair and one strand of white
Thorax:	Red 8/0 Uni-Thread
Wing Case:	White Fluoro Fibre

JUJUBEE MIDGE (CHARTREUSE)

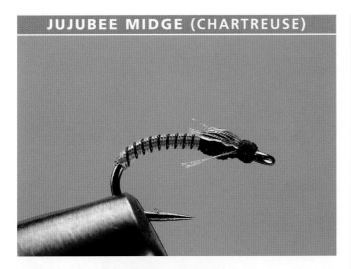

Hook: #16-22 Tiemco 2488
Thread: White 74-denier Lagartun
Abdomen: Two strands of green chartreuse Super Hair and one strand of black
Thorax: Black 8/0 Uni-Thread
Wing Case: White Fluoro Fibre

JUJUBEE MIDGE (BLUE)

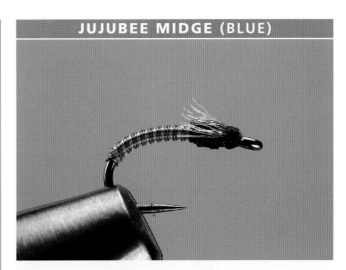

Hook: #16-22 Tiemco 2488
Thread: White 74-denier Lagartun
Abdomen: Two strands of navy blue Super Hair and one strand of green chartreuse
Thorax: Black 8/0 Uni-Thread
Wing Case: White Fluoro Fibre

TWO

Jumbo Juju Chironomid

Over the last several years, Colorado anglers have gotten on the stillwater train as a way to start their season a bit earlier in the year and in some cases avoid some of the more crowded early season tailwaters. What these anglers found is that some of the best fishing in the state, both in fish size and numbers, occurs in our shallow, high country reservoirs. Many other states have reservoirs and lakes like ours and we Coloradoans might just have been the last to recognize this opportu-nity. Oregon and Washington anglers have been clued in to the stillwater fishing angle for many years now, and their record on pattern and technique development speaks for itself. I love discovering anything new to me in the fly-fishing realm, and the stillwater opportunities available here in Colorado are sure to get any fisherman's blood pumping. Large lakes and reservoirs are home to some of the biggest fish but are often overlooked by fly anglers who disdain the usual approach of throwing out a

I developed the Jumbo Juju to imitate the larger midges found in lakes and reservoirs throughout the country.

Woolly Bugger and stripping it back in. Both the size and numbers of fish available in these impoundments can be astonishing and should not be overlooked, particularly early in the season.

A Chironomid (pronounced "ker-on-uh-mid") is a large, lake-dwelling midge pupa that emerges in our high-altitude reservoirs early in the year and remains all summer. These giant midges can grow as large as a #8 3XL hook, and get down as small as about #18. These are the first active insects of the year in most lakes, and the trout feed heavily on them right from the get-go.

Chironomids themselves are not so funny, but the pronunciation of that word by customers coming into our shop has been butchered in so many ways it's sometimes hard to keep a straight face. Chrominoids, sheronamids, kernamids, shamwows, chironowiches, humanoids, and chironomidges are just a few of the flies we've been asked for, and it becomes pretty easy to decipher this strange code after a few weeks in the spring and early summer.

I thought I knew a lot about fishing these midges in lakes until I watched Ralph and Lisa Cutter's DVD called *Bugs of the Underworld: The Natural History of Aquatic Insects*. While most of the secondhand information I have gleaned over the years from a variety of different books has suggested that these insects work their way feebly toward the surface to hatch, the Cutters' DVD shows them in a whole different light. Filmed almost entirely underwater, this video has changed the way I think about more than one insect hatch and has made me reconsider what I thought I knew about most of them. Of particular note in this film is the footage of a large Chironomid pupa emerging toward the surface. Where I expected to see a bug being slowly and gently buoyed to the surface with the oft-mentioned gas bubble, I instead witnessed the pupa vigorously whipping its back end to and fro and swimming like a minnow to the top. This motion was not at all delicate or slow and the bug seemed in complete control of its path to the surface. After all my years in this game, I still love learning new things. This video will change the way you look at insects and certainly challenge what you have been led to believe. Watch it and you'll be a better angler for it.

As the name implies, the Jumbo Juju is a variation of the Jujubee Midge. At first I simply tied an oversized version of the standard Juju on a long-shanked hook, but I found that the closely striated ribbing sort of lost its effect on the larger fly. I turned to using a few strands of each color rather than the 2 to 1 ratio in the smaller sister pattern, and with a bit of tweaking found a technique that creates a beautifully barred body with great segmentation and translucence.

Some of the first patterns I tied with the new body technique had poly-yarn bow tie heads, common on many midge patterns, to imitate the natural's prominent gills. Somewhere along the way someone came up with the idea of using a painted white bead for the head on flies like this, and given my propensity and attraction to heavy flies, I jumped right on this idea. For a while I tied my new Chiro with a bow tie *and* a white bead until an expert lake fisherman friend of mine mentioned, almost in passing, that he liked the white beads on his midges because he could skip the white tufts at the head of the fly. It struck me like a ton of bricks that adding both was redundant. So I sheepishly took the bow tie off and proceeded with just a simple white bead head.

The train of thought that led to the addition of a Thin Skin wing case and opal tinsel flashback came when I was sitting in my float tube one day staring at a million midge shucks floating on the surface of the water. Their iridescence was overwhelming, and I figured the trout *had* to be able to pick up on this farther down the water column. The corresponding flashback was added to the top of the wing case of my rapidly developing pattern, and I filled in the thorax with a bit of fine dark dubbing to round out the prominent thorax. When I tied the first version of this new pattern it struck me that leaving the flashback exposed across the top of a Thin Skin wing case was just asking for trouble. I had learned this lesson many years back when I got lazy and reasoned that skipping the epoxy top coat on a batch of Copper Johns would make no difference. I was quickly slapped in the face by the fact that no matter how tightly you tie that flash in, it *will* pull out when you fish and handle the fly, leaving a short, flashy stub hanging off the top of the fly. Of course the solution to this was to just take the time to coat the wing cases with epoxy, so I bit the bullet and added this somewhat time-consuming step to my new fly, although I later stretched that epoxy coat all the way down the dorsal surface of the fly, both to create an emergent halo of light around the fly and to add overall durability to the pattern.

The last part I added to the fly came after a year or two of fishing the Jumbo Juju. I tied a small nub of thread at the bend of the fly and colored it with a red permanent marker. This nub's purpose was twofold: it helped keep the Super Hair strands from sliding down around the bend, and with the little hot shot of color (the marker will bleed up into the thread underbody as well, adding a bit of subtle color to the whole rear end of the fly), the fly matched the natural's glowing red butt brought on by the super oxygenated hemoglobin they produce upon emergence. After several years and variations, I felt I finally had this pattern ready enough to share with others, and it has turned out to be a killing pattern for many of my friends and customers alike.

Given the rainbow of colors that the natural midges come in, I thought it prudent to tie up several color variations of this fly. This spectrum includes a black and white version tied with three strands of black Super Hair and two strands of white, a blood-colored version tied with three strands of burnt orange and two strands of dark brown (these colors blend together nicely to create a reddish-brown hue), and an olive version tied with three strands of olive Super Hair and two strands of black. These three versions seem to match most of the bugs I cross paths with, although I have also tied the "Bleeder" version of three strands of black, one strand of red, and one strand of white to accentuate the reddish tones the naturals sometimes take on. Of course an all-red version is quite valuable to have hanging around in the box too—you know, just in case.

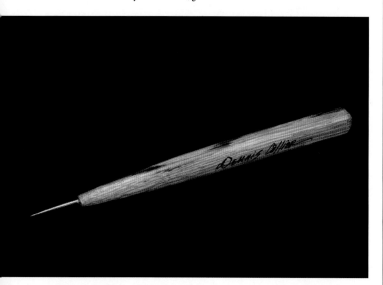

Dennis Collier and I developed the Collier Fine-Tipped Bodkin. The short, fine tip makes applying delicate and precise coats of epoxy much easier than with the traditional long-needle bodkins.

FISHING THE JUMBO JUJU

My usual method of fishing the Jumbo Juju involves a floating line and a slip indicator designed to break loose and slide down the line when a fish is hooked. I start by attaching my fly or flies as described below, but most importantly by determining the depth of the water. Some guys have depth finders these days to help with this step, but I am sort of old school in that I pinch my forceps onto the bend of the bottom fly and drop them in the water. When they stop sinking, I move the indicator a foot closer to them so the flies will hang just over the bottom (or the top of the weeds) and then gingerly retrieve my forceps. Some smarter guys carry a small bundle of bell sinkers to serve this same purpose, and I know at least one guy who uses a spark plug. Smarter.

To the end of my floating line I attach a long length of 2X fluorocarbon tippet. The length of this piece will vary depending on water depth, but it is generally 5 to 12 feet long. To the end of this heavier line I attach a piece of 3X or 4X fluorocarbon tippet that is about two feet in length, and I'll attach the first fly to that. I have been known to fish three of the same color fly if the fish have really shown a preference for one tone, but I generally try to mix the sizes and colors up a bit until the fish decide which one they like. The more I fish the more I have come to believe that the depth of the fly is far more critical than the exact pattern, as even the best pattern on earth can't do its job if the fish are always swimming well under or over it.

I'll usually add a second fly tied to a section of 4X fluoro off the bend of the first with a clinch knot and drop it down another 12 to 18 inches. One handy and fly-saving consideration to keep in mind, and much to the contrary of my sometimes greed-driven multi-fly rigs, is that once you've figured out the depth at which the fish are cruising, it's a good idea to pare the rig down to the single fly that is at the right depth. Cutting things back like this makes the rig much easier to handle and keeps you from losing three flies at a time on a hot fish.

Many lake fish are broad-shouldered steelhead replicas that rip off 50 yards of line before you even realize you have them on. Broken tippets and straightened hooks are part of the game, but a few considerations will help minimize these issues. I fish with a light drag on my reel and depend on the drag of the line in the water to create all the tension I need on these larger fish.

Generally just hanging a Chironomid at the right depth under an indicator is all it takes to draw the attention of fish during an emergence, and any wave action can bounce your indicator enough to impart some up-and-down action to the fly. Recalling that big midge in the Cutter video has prompted me to experiment with a steady sweep of the rod trip to draw the flies steadily toward the surface on calmer waters or when the bite seems to go off a bit. I draw the rod up with a smooth lift and then slowly pick up the slack line with a hand twist retrieve. I've had some rod-bending takes at the start of this lift and even more super-subtle eats as the fly starts descending back down after the lift. It pays to change up the technique and depth more often than changing patterns, as getting the fly in front of the fish is more than half the battle.

I am the absolute most impatient fisherman on the planet and can get incredibly bored if left to simply watch an indicator, but luckily for me, lake fishing at the right time and place can pay off with obscene numbers of fish, any number of which could turn out to be the biggest fish you land all season.

JUMBO JUJU CHIRONOMID
(BLOOD)

Hook:	#10-16 Tiemco 2302
Bead:	White brass or tungsten, slightly undersized
Thread:	Fluorescent white 70-denier Ultra Thread for the abdomen and black 8/0 Uni-Thread for the thorax
Abdomen:	Three strands of dark brown and two strands of orange Super Hair
Flashback:	Opal Mirage Tinsel (medium)
Wing Case:	Black Thin Skin
Thorax:	Black Superfine dubbing
Coating:	Five-minute epoxy

TYING THE JUMBO JUJU CHIRONOMID

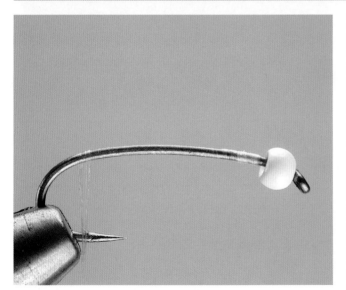

1. Place the bead on the hook, slide it up to the eye, and clamp the hook in the vise. Start the thread behind the bead and wrap a thin thread base back to the hook bend. Try to keep the thread flat and smooth as you wrap back, without any lumps or bumps.

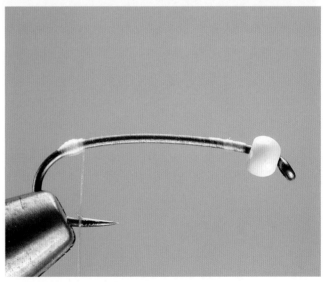

2. Build a small nub of thread at the hook bend right above the barb. I try to make the center of this nub line up with the hook barb and extend equally back and forward of that point. This nub should not be too big and ultimately should match up to the body diameter.

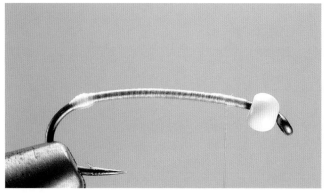

3. Return the thread to the starting point, taking care to keep the thread laying flat along the shank. You may need to spin your bobbin to untwist the thread as you wrap.

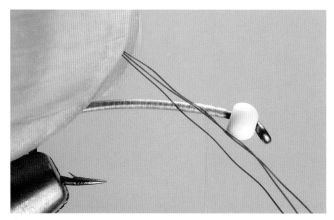

4. Cut three strands of the dark brown Super Hair from the clump and pull them between your fingertips to straighten them a bit. Clip the ends so they are all even.

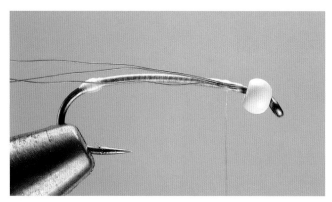

5. Lay the Super Hair strands in at an angle and capture them with two firm wraps of thread. I try to tie the first three strands of Super Hair in squarely along the near side of the hook shank. Pull the long ends of the hair back along the shank to shorten the front ends so they are just in front of the first turn of thread with which you tied them down.

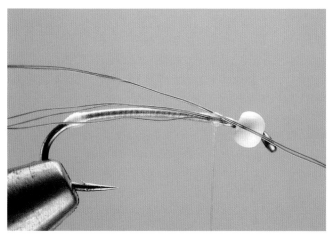

6. Cut two strands of the orange Super Hair and straighten them as you did with the brown ones. Cut the ends so they are even and lay the strands at an angle across the near side of the hook shank. Capture the orange Super Hair with two turns of thread, taking care to keep these two strands separate from the brown ones. I try to tie the second clump in above the first, more on the top of the hook than on the side, although the strands should all line up in order from the bottom to the top with little space between them.

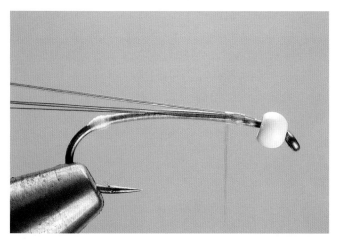

7. Draw all five Super Hair strands taut and toward the rear of the hook. I use the pad on the tip of my index finger to keep the strands slightly divided here so they don't intermix as you wrap back over them. Be sure that you have two separate bunches of hair: three brown strands and two orange.

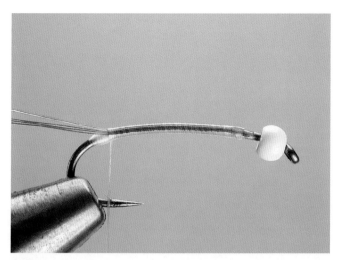

8. Wrap the thread smoothly back over the five strands of Super Hair all the way to the front end of the thread nub at the bend. Be sure to keep the thread as flat as possible as you wrap (untwist it if necessary) and that the strands of Super Hair remain separate bunches stacked vertically on top of one another.

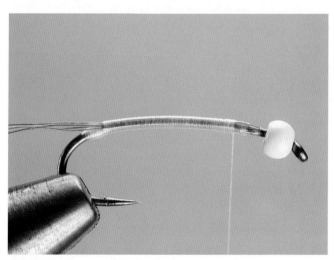

9. Return the thread to the starting point once again. For this final layer of thread from the bend forward to the front, be sure the thread lies flat and smooth. If you allow the thread to twist and cord up, the underbody will have ridges that make it nearly impossible to wrap the Super Hair over smoothly. The ridges created by twisted thread create high and low spots that will separate the individual strands of Super Hair.

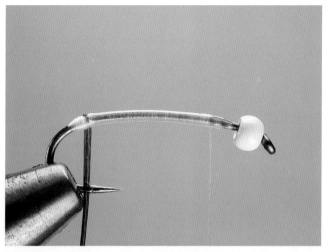

10. Grasp all five strands of Super Hair so they remain aligned and flat like a ribbon. While holding all the strands taut, fold the bunch over the top of the hook and pull them straight down, at the immediate front edge of the thread nub. Note that the five strands are still aligned, with the two orange strands now leading, the three brown strands following.

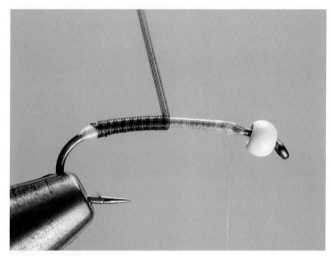

11. Continue wrapping all five strands forward up the shank as one unit. Each turn should result in the aligned Super Hair lying flat on the shank, creating a ribbed effect. Note that the order is still the same, two orange followed by three brown, as in that first turn.

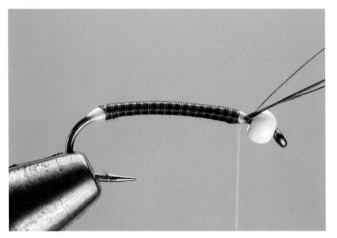

12. Continue wrapping the Super Hair strands forward to just behind the bead. Tie the Super Hair off with a few firm wraps of thread. Make sure they are secure because if the strands slip out from under these wraps you'll have to start over again.

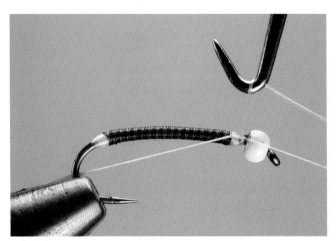

13. Clip the excess Super Hair strands flush and whip-finish the white thread over the butt ends.

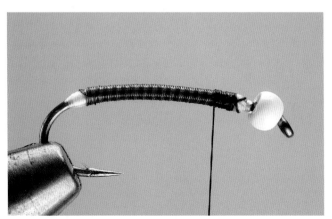

14. Start the black 8/0 thread over the front end of the abdomen. Wrap back to about the 80 percent point.

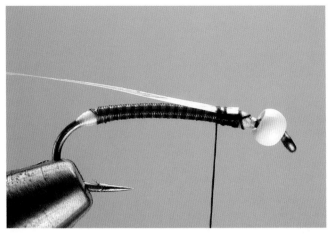

15. Tie in a single strand of medium Opal Mirage Tinsel at the 80 percent point so it lies flat on the top of the abdomen. Make sure the flash is centered on the shank. You can tie the flash in with two soft turns and then manipulate the long end to square it up on the fly. Anchor the flash in place with two more tight wraps.

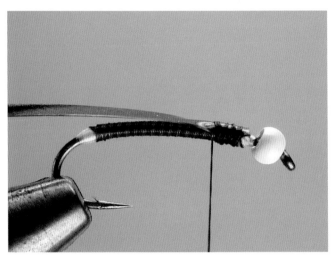

16. Cut a strip of Thin Skin that is about half as wide as the gap of the hook. Remove the paper backing and tie in the Thin Skin with the side that was attached to the paper facing up at the 80 percent point, right on top of the flash. With the paper side facing up, the Thin Skin curls away from the area where the rest of the tying process takes place and doesn't bounce around in the way while you tie the rest of the fly.

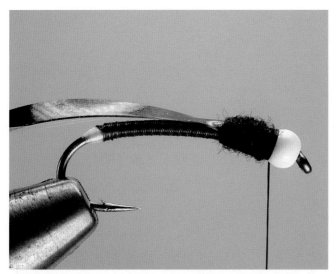

17. Apply a thin strand of tightly twisted Superfine dubbing to the thread and build an elongated egg-shaped thorax up to the back edge of the bead. The thorax should be about the same diameter as the bead itself. Make a few turns of thread between the back of the bead and the front of the dubbing to create a firm base for the wing case tie-down to come.

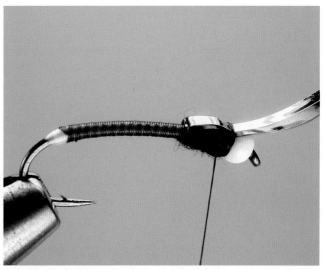

19. Pull the flash forward over the top of the Thin Skin, taking care to keep it centered. Use two firm wraps of thread to tie it down behind the bead.

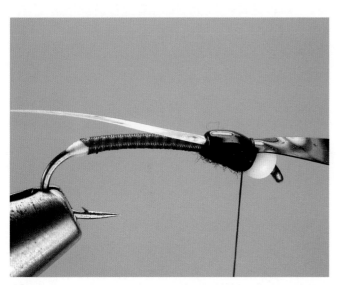

18. Pull the Thin Skin strip forward over the dubbed thorax and anchor it down with two tight wraps just behind the bead. Be sure that the Thin Skin buckles around the thorax, creating the tight, smooth wing case you see here.

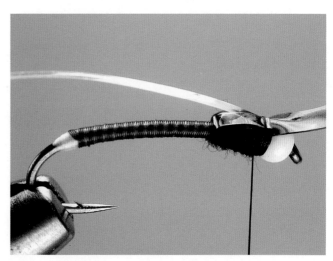

20. Pull the long end of the flash back once again, folding it over just behind the bead. Make two more tight wraps of thread over the fold to secure the flash in place.

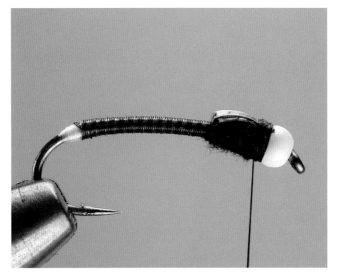

21. Pull the Thin Skin tightly forward and reach in with the tips of your scissors and trim it off as close to the bead as you can. If you stretch the Thin Skin just slightly you can get a much closer cut. Lift the long end of the flash and make a small cut at the near edge with the tips of your scissors. Pull the flash toward the far side of the hook and it will tear off cleanly and even with the thread wraps, leaving no stub end.

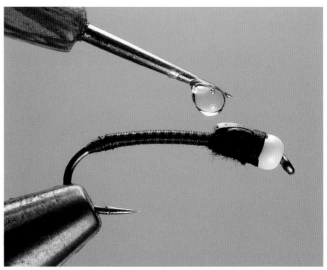

23. Mix a small batch of five-minute epoxy. Try to mix the epoxy gently so as not to create too many bubbles. You can use a cigarette lighter to heat the epoxy by waving the flame across the top of the puddle. This will help to pop some of the bubbles and also makes the epoxy dry a bit faster. Pick up a drop of epoxy with the end of your finest-tipped bodkin.

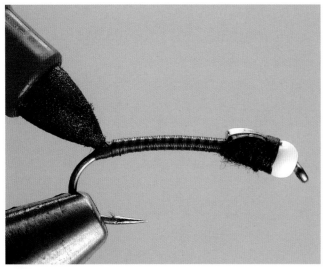

22. Build up a few turns of thread to cover the butt end of the Thin Skin wing case and whip-finish the thread. Use a red marker to color the thread nub at the hook bend. If you simply press the tip of the marker onto the thread here, the ink will run through the thread and even bleed slightly up the underbody beneath the abdomen, creating a realistic red butt on the fly.

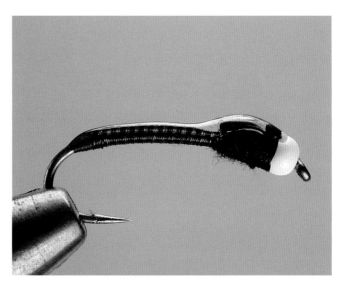

24. Place the drop of epoxy down on the top of the wing case and then use the bodkin to smear the epoxy back to the hook bend all the way to the end of the thread nub. Continue the epoxy coat up to the back of the bead, getting some of it on the bead itself. Continuing the epoxy coat from the bead to the bend makes for better adhesion and creates a more durable fly.

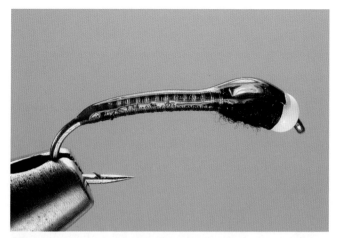

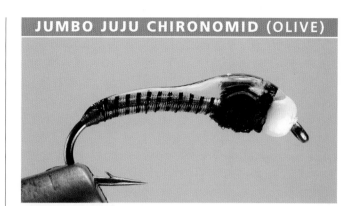

25. The epoxy should only be on the top and just slightly down the sides of the fly. The Thin Skin wing case should be covered entirely with epoxy.

JUMBO JUJU CHIRONOMID (ZEBRA)

Hook:	#10-16 Tiemco 2302
Bead:	White brass or tungsten bead, slightly undersized
Thread:	Fluorescent white 70-denier Ultra Thread for the abdomen, and black 8/0 Uni-Thread for the thorax
Abdomen:	Three strands black Super Hair and two strands white Super Hair
Flashback:	Opal Mirage Tinsel (medium)
Wing Case:	Black Thin Skin
Thorax:	Black Superfine dubbing
Coating:	Five-minute epoxy

JUMBO JUJU CHIRONOMID (OLIVE)

Hook:	#10-16 Tiemco 2302
Bead:	White brass or tungsten bead, slightly undersized
Thread:	Fluorescent white 70-denier Ultra Thread for the abdomen, and black 8/0 Uni-Thread for the thorax
Abdomen:	Three strands olive Super Hair and two strands black Super Hair
Flashback:	Opal Mirage Tinsel (medium)
Wing Case:	Black Thin Skin
Thorax:	Black Superfine dubbing
Coating:	Five-minute epoxy

JUMBO JUJU CHIRONOMID (BLUE)

Hook:	#10-16 Tiemco 2302
Bead:	White brass or tungsten bead, slightly undersized
Thread:	Fluorescent white 70-denier Ultra Thread for the abdomen, and black 8/0 Uni-Thread for the thorax
Abdomen:	Three strands dark blue Super Hair and two strands dark brown Super Hair
Flashback:	Opal Mirage Tinsel (medium)
Wing Case:	Black Thin Skin
Thorax:	Black Superfine dubbing
Coating:	Five-minute epoxy

JUMBO JUJU CHIRONOMID (RED)

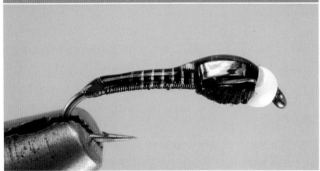

Hook:	#10-16 Tiemco 2302
Bead:	White brass or tungsten bead, slightly undersized
Thread:	Fluorescent white 70-denier Ultra Thread for the abdomen, and black 8/0 Uni-Thread for the thorax
Abdomen:	Five strands red Super Hair
Flashback:	Opal Mirage Tinsel (medium)
Wing Case:	Black Thin Skin
Thorax:	Black Superfine dubbing
Coating:	Five-minute epoxy

JUMBO JUJU CHIRONOMID (BLEEDER)

Hook:	#10-16 Tiemco 2302
Bead:	White brass or tungsten bead, slightly undersized
Thread:	Fluorescent white 70-denier Ultra Thread for the abdomen, and black 8/0 Uni-Thread for the thorax
Abdomen:	Two strands black Super Hair, one strand red Super Hair, and two strands white Super Hair
Flashback:	Opal Mirage Tinsel (medium)
Wing Case:	Black Thin Skin
Thorax:	Black Superfine dubbing
Coating:	Five-minute epoxy

JUMBO JUJU CHIRONOMID (CAMO)

Hook:	#10-16 Tiemco 2302
Bead:	White brass or tungsten bead, slightly undersized
Thread:	Fluorescent white 70-denier Ultra Thread for the abdomen, and black 8/0 Uni-Thread for the thorax
Abdomen:	Three strands olive Super Hair, one strand black Super Hair, and one strand dark brown Super Hair
Flashback:	Opal Mirage Tinsel (medium)
Wing Case:	Black Thin Skin
Thorax:	Black Superfine dubbing
Coating:	Five-minute epoxy

THREE

Jujubaetis

I hate to admit how many times I've come up with a good idea completely by mistake, and fear I may be blowing my own cover with all these stories, but this is really how these flies came about. I always say the trick to all this is to tie lots of flies and keep your eyes and mind open, and the Jujubaetis is a perfect example of what can happen.

I first started playing with a more specific *Baetis* imitation after fishing a standard olive or black Jujubee

Midge during *Baetis* emergences and having pretty good luck. I will often fish a *Baetis* nymph like a Barr Emerger, Pheasant Tail, or RS2 in tandem with a small Jujubee to cover my bases in the spring and fall. When I realized that I was catching more fish on the slim Jujubee than the other patterns, I finally thought maybe I ought to try to make a more specific, yet still related, *Baetis* pattern.

I started by simply adding a tail to the Jujubee Midge to match the natural's rear appendage. This

My Jujubaetis series can be tied in many colors. Shown here are (from top, clockwise) the Juju PMD, the original Jujubaetis, and the purple Jujubaetis. Experiment with the body colors and see what you can come up with. The possibilities are endless!

The Jujubaetis has become many trout anglers' favorite pattern. The slim silhouette and tapered profile both contribute to its effectiveness.

pattern worked well enough—or to be more honest, it worked exactly as well as the Jujubee Midge did during *Baetis* hatches. I then added a strip of pearl Flashabou to the wing case to brighten the fly up and perhaps draw the attention of some cynical trout, and changed the colors up a bit to match the dark-brown nymphs in Colorado waters. This version seemed to work a bit better, and since it was a bit more specific, I had the confidence to fish it more. The combo of a small Jujubee Midge and the hot-off-the-press Jujubaetis turned out to be a tough pair to beat in the fall. I fished this little pattern for several years but never really got too excited about it because it was, after all, just a minor variation of the existing Jujubee.

Then one day I was at my bench coating a few wing cases on some Copper Johns and ended up with a some leftover epoxy. I grabbed my nymph box and quickly perused it to see if there were any flies in there in need of a little top coat. Most of the bugs in the box looked pretty good, so I just reached in and decided to sacrifice

a little Jujubaetis. I clamped the fly in the vise and ran a smooth bead of the now-drying and goopy epoxy onto the wing case. When I lifted the tip of my bodkin the congealed epoxy didn't let go and a thin strand stretched out off the wing case and back over the top of the fly. In a botched attempt to save the fly, I pinned the end of the epoxy strand to the base of the body just at the front of the tail, creating a smooth shellback over the entire topside of the fly. While I had only planned on coating the wing case, the whole fly was now coated, from the eye to the bend. The resulting epoxy shellback added a bit of shine and an accurate taper. My mind flashed back to all the *Baetis* nymphs I had scrounged from under rocks and from stomach pump samples over the years and their diminutive teardrop shape. The epoxied Jujubaetis mirrored this silhouette perfectly. Real *Baetis* (and most other mayfly nymphs for that matter) are slimy looking, slim, and tapered smoothly from head to tail. The epoxy top coat smoothed out the shape of the body, eliminating the gap in diameter between the thorax and abdomen and produced the most accurate overall profile I had ever seen on an artificial. Yahtzee! I had finally added that extra little bit that would make this fly stand out from the crowd.

As I later sat down to really dial the pattern in, I realized the Fluoro Fibre wing case would all but disappear when coated in epoxy, leaving only the thin strand of Flashabou visible. The Flashabou was too thin to replicate the natural's wide wing case, so I swapped it out for a wider strand of medium Mirage Tinsel. Mirage Tinsel is an opalescent Mylar similar to pearl tinsel, but with a bit more "fire" and color that I have really grown to like on some patterns. The wider tinsel also covered the Fluoro Fibre well yet let me use the butt ends as legs in an easy tying maneuver. While the Fluoro wing case disappears under the flash, I found it was a worthwhile part to keep because I could easily use the butt ends for the legs. I did finally change the color of the Fluoro Fibre from the white used on the Jujubee to a gray to perhaps better match the emerging wings of our fall *Baetis*. The Fluoro Fibre also helped to hump the back of the thorax a bit, better imitating the natural's prominent wing case. These changes coupled with my newfound epoxy overcoat created a durable fly with a more realistic silhouette and an edge I had been hoping for.

The beauty of the Jujubaetis is that it can be fished in so many different ways. I usually fish the Jujubaetis in a two-fly rig with a Jujubee Midge, as I mentioned before, or sometimes behind a Soft Hackle Emerger during a heavy hatch. When I do fish with an indicator, these combinations are usually tied on my tippet. I'll attach the required amount of split shot or soft lead about 12 inches above the top fly and tie an additional 15-inch length of tippet to the bend of the first fly to trail the dropper. I have had great success with this rig in fast-moving shallow riffles as well as long, slow-moving pools, just letting the flies dangle and drift under the indicator. The takes can be alarmingly subtle, so I always try to sight-fish where I can, or at the very least I keep my eyes open for any flashes or glints to betray the fish taking my flies. Subtle yet attractive, the Jujubaetis has repeatedly proven my theory that fish are more prone to eat small, slender, and more realistic patterns late in the season, and this little fly seems to catch fish even on the slowest of days.

As it turns out, the Jujubaetis has become a hugely popular commercial pattern and may even rival the Jujubee for numbers sold. The durability and unusually natural profile of this pattern has clearly been a hit with anglers and fish alike. When I think that I almost let this fly slip into oblivion, I cringe. I'm glad I try some of these weird little experiments sometimes.

TYING THE JUJUBAETIS

JUJUBAETIS

Hook:	#16-24 Tiemco 2488
Thread:	White 74-denier Lagartun (for abdomen)
Tail:	Mottled brown India hen saddle fibers
Abdomen:	One strand black and two strands dark brown Super Hair
Flashback:	Opal Mirage Tinsel (medium)
Wing Case/Legs:	Gray Fluoro Fibre
Thorax:	Black 14/0 Gordon Griffith's
Coating:	Five-minute epoxy

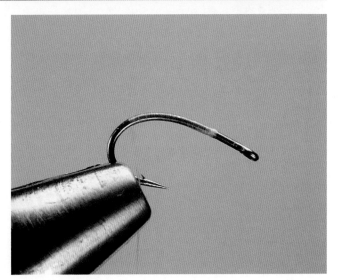

1. Clamp the hook in the vise. Start the thread about two eye lengths back from the eye and wrap a smooth layer of thread back to about halfway down the hook bend.

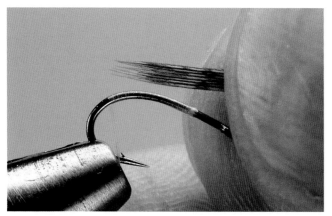

2. Even the tips of a small clump of hen saddle fibers and peel them from the stem. Measure these fibers against the hook so they are about a half shank long.

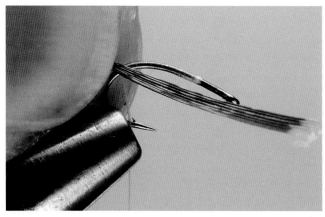

3. Lay these fibers in at the hook bend with the butt ends angled down on the near side of the hook shank.

4. Bring the thread up and over the fibers to let the thread torque pull the fibers to the top of the hook shank as you bind them down. Make two more wraps right in front of this first turn to anchor the tails in place.

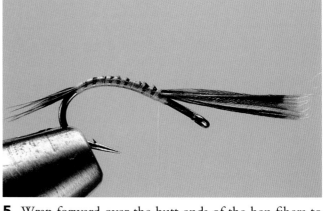

5. Wrap forward over the butt ends of the hen fibers to the starting point, making sure to keep them on top of the shank.

6. Clip the excess hen fibers flush at the front.

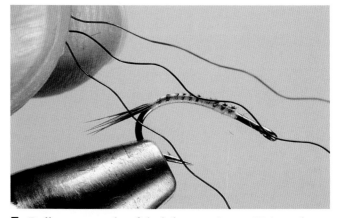

7. Pull two strands of dark brown Super Hair and one strand of black from their bundles. Super Hair has a slightly wavy texture to it, which you can eliminate by simply pulling the fibers between your fingertips like you would to straighten a leader. Straightening the fibers really makes no difference in the finished fly, but it does make it slightly easier to wrap the fibers up the shank and keep them flat.

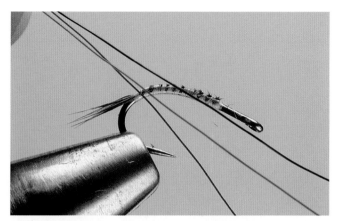

8. Here's what the straightened Super Hair looks like. Much better.

9. Cut the ends of the Super Hair square and tie in all three strands at the front of the fly on the near side of the shank with two firm wraps of thread. Pull the fibers to the rear of the hook until the front ends butt against the thread wraps.

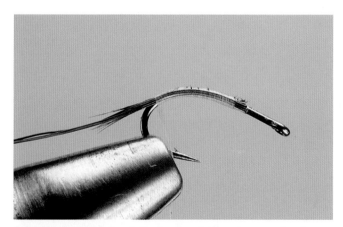

10. Wrap a single tight layer of thread over the Super Hair to the base of the tail. Try to keep the fibers lying flat on the side of the hook. The order of the fibers makes no difference.

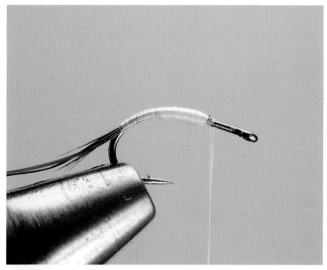

11. Bring the thread back to the starting point, building a smooth and slightly tapered underbody as you work to the front. The underbody should *not* be as thick as you ultimately want the body to be, as you still have yet to wrap another layer of Super Hair on top of it. Keep the underbody as thin as you can while maintaining an obvious taper.

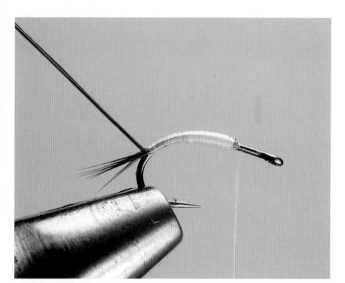

12. Here's where everyone seems to go awry. The first turn of the Super Hair needs to be made at a right angle to the table top or floor, not at a right angle to the hook shank like I've illustrated here. If you start your wraps like this, with the fibers perpendicular to the hook shank at the bend, the fibers will separate from each other as you approach the apex of the hook bend and leave gaps as you wind forward. You don't want gaps.

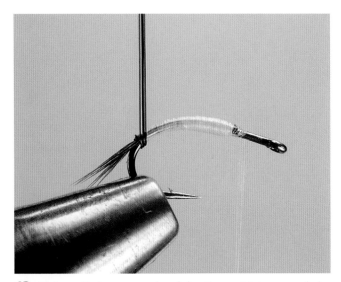

13. Bring all three strands of the Super Hair around the hook shank and *straight up* on the near side of the hook. Rock the fibers back and forth while pulling them tight above the shank to line them all up side by side. Treat all three fibers as one unit, keeping them flat on the shank like a ribbon.

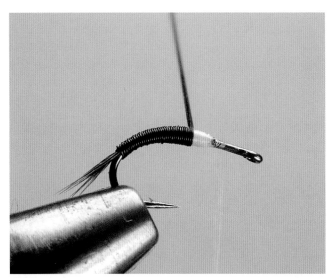

14. Continue wrapping all three strands forward up the hook shank, keeping them as upright as possible as you go. Note that the strands of Super Hair on this body are all parallel to each other as they travel up the hook. I find it helps keep the fibers from spreading apart if you hold them close to the hook as you wrap, rather than letting your fingers slide up and away from the shank.

15. Wrap the strands of Super Hair to the end of the thread underbody and tie them off with several firm wraps of thread. If the thread breaks now, the whole fly will explode and you'll have to start all over, so be careful not to let things blow up. This has never actually happened to me, but I heard about a guy that it happened to once and he was just never the same.

16. Clip the ends of the Super Hair fibers flush. Whip-finish and clip the white thread. Save the remaining Super Hair for the next fly. Run the three remaining strands through your mouth, wetting them a bit. They will be stuck together right where you left them when you get to the next fly.

17. Start the black 14/0 thread right over the front edge of the abdomen and wrap back to just in front of the hook point. I usually shoot for about a 60 percent abdomen and 40 percent thorax configuration.

18. Tie in a single strand of Opal Mirage Tinsel on top of the abdomen just ahead of the hook point. Be sure the tinsel is centered and is lying flat on the top of the fly.

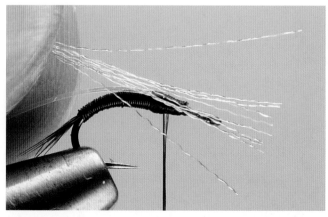

19. Cut ten strands of Fluoro Fibre from the hank and clip the ends so they're all square. Note that I said "ten fibers" and nothing like "thirty-five fibers." This fly should be sparse.

20. Tie the Fluoro Fibre in on top of the hook with a few soft turns of thread. Pull the front ends down flush with the first wrap of thread and continue wrapping back over them to the base of the Mirage Tinsel.

21. Wrap the thread forward, covering the butt ends of both the flash and the Fluoro Fibre as you build a smooth roundish thorax. Be sure to leave a bit of bare space behind the hook eye to complete the fly. I do make a single layer of thread in this area (one eye length behind the hook eye) after I have built up the thorax to give the hook some texture to further secure the Fluoro Fibre wing case.

22. Pull the Fluoro Fibre forward over the top of the thorax and hold it taut above the hook eye. Bring the thread up over the Fluoro Fibre and bind it down just behind the eye with two turns of thread. Make sure the Fluoro Fibre wing case is centered on the top of the hook shank.·

23. Pull the Mirage Tinsel forward over the top of the Fluoro Fibre and hold it taut. Bind the flash down as you did the Fluoro Fibre, using only two wraps and making sure that it is centered across the top of the fly.

24. Pull the long end of the flash back over the top of the fly, folding it at the tie-down point. Put two more taut wraps of thread over the folded flash here just behind the hook eye. Folding the flash and binding it down like this assures that it will never pull out.

25. Divide the Fluoro Fibre into two equal bunches (five strands per side). Roll each bundle in your fingertips to get them to twist together into nice neat bunches on each side of the fly.

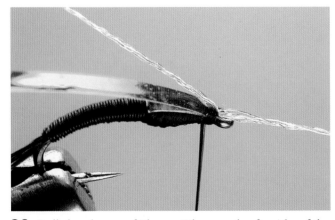

26. Pull the clump of Fluoro Fibre on the far side of the hook back along the side of the hook shank. Bind the far clump down with two turns of thread.

27. Pull the clump on the near side of the hook back along the near side of the shank. Bind the near side down as you did with the first clump, using just two turns of thread.

28. Build up a smooth yet prominent thread head that continues the thorax taper and whip-finish the thread. A tiny head is not desirable on this fly, as the thread helps anchor the epoxy overcoat at the end.

29. Clip the flash as close to the front of the wing case as you can. Trim the legs so that they're just a touch longer than the wing case.

30. Set the fly upright in the vise and mix up a small batch of five-minute epoxy. I typically tie a dozen or so flies and then coat them all at once to keep the tying process going smoothly. I find that with a small single batch of five-minute epoxy I can comfortably coat ten, maybe eleven flies, but never a whole dozen before the epoxy starts to goop up. Better to mix another small batch of epoxy than to goober up a few finished flies with snotty epoxy.

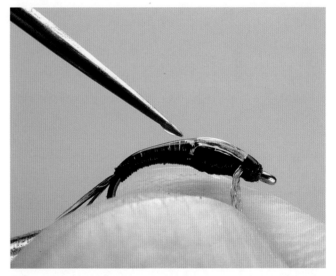

31. Pull the legs down out of the way and place the drop of epoxy directly on top of the wing case. Use the tip of a fine dubbing needle to draw the epoxy back to the base of the tail, coating the entire upper surface of the fly with a smooth, slightly tapered epoxy overcoat. Bring the needle back to the front and draw the epoxy forward from the wing case onto the thread head, terminating the coating right at the hook eye.

32. Finished fly, quarter top view. Let the flies dry upright in a block of foam. There is no need to rotate them as they dry since the epoxy is only on one side.

JUJUBAETIS (PURPLE)

Hook:	#16-24 Tiemco 2488
Thread:	White 74-denier Lagartun for abdomen, black 14/0 Gordon Griffith's for the thorax
Tail:	Mottled brown India hen saddle fibers
Abdomen:	One strand dark blue and two strands purple Super Hair
Flashback:	Opal Mirage Tinsel (medium)
Wing Case/Legs:	Brown Fluoro Fibre
Thorax:	Black 14/0 Gordon Griffith's
Coating:	Five-minute epoxy

JUJU PMD

Hook:	#16-24 Tiemco 2488
Thread:	White 74-denier Lagartun for abdomen, black 14/0 Gordon Griffith's for the thorax
Tail:	Mottled brown India hen saddle fibers
Abdomen:	One strand dark brown and two strands burnt orange Super Hair
Flashback:	Opal Mirage Tinsel (medium)
Wing Case/Legs:	Brown Fluoro Fibre
Thorax:	Brown 14/0 Gordon Griffith's
Coating:	Five-minute epoxy

FOUR

Poison Tung

The Poison Tung was expressly developed as a slim, heavy midge pattern to be fished with the Jujubee Midge. Honestly, this fly started off as nothing more than a slightly stealthier version of a split shot because I wanted a fly that wasn't as large or obtrusive as a Copper John or Jack Flash but would still drag the Juju down. Fishing a big, heavy fly like these with the small, delicate Juju behind it was often like throwing a whole hot dog cart in the river and then trying to sell hot dogs—the cart scared 'em all away!

As I fish a lot of Jujubee Midges during the shoulder seasons, usually in low, clear water, I felt that fishing a split shot and indicator rig was sometimes a bit more conspicuous than I really wanted. Of course, the Jujubee Midge has no weight of its own, and there is really no place to add any without changing the whole profile of the fly, so additional weight is needed in one form or another to keep the fly down.

Out here in Colorado, it isn't uncommon to see fish on the more popular tailwaters move out of the way

The Poison Tung can be tied in a wide range of insect-matching or attractor colors.

My Poison Tung pattern was developed as a point fly to help drag down the lighter and skinnier Jujubee Midges. I wasn't the only one surprised by how well they caught fish!

when they see your split shot drift by. (Apparently, they have learned that the little round ball of lead means bad things can happen.) In instances like this, it doesn't really matter how good your imitation is, because you just can't get the fish to hang around long enough to see it. This can be some of the most frustrating fishing to be had and has left me sitting on the bank with steam coming from my ears more than once. It seems that the fish don't enjoy our little game as much as we do, because sometimes they just won't play.

It was after a couple days like this that I decided to try to put a little something together that would be small, thin, and inconspicuous, yet sink well. It really didn't make a big difference to me if it caught fish or not because I really just wanted to use it as a weight.

I sat down at the vise and picked out a #18 heavy wire scud hook, reasoning that the heavier-wired hook would be a good start. I added a black tungsten bead thinking that the heavier bead would be an advantage

and the dark color would keep the fly from being too flashy. I mean, there's got to be all sorts of little black stuff drifting along the bottom of a river, right?

I considered making the body out of thread to keep it thin, but I realized that I had already done that with a pattern—one whose name rhymes with "Mebra Zidge." I needed heavier. And duller. It occurred to me to wrap the body with thick wire, thicker than would normally be used on a fly of this size. I pulled out a spool of black UTC Ultra Wire in Brassie size and tied it down the shank. When I wrapped it forward, it created a fat body that was way out of place on a small chassis like this and was lumpy and bumpy to boot. I wanted a fly that was thin so it would sink readily, not something that looked like I wrapped an old sock around a hook.

I cut the wire from the hook and went back to work, thinking maybe I could just wrap the wire around the shank without tying it down. I cut a length of wire from the spool and wrapped it around the bare shank in tight spirals from the back of the bead to the bend. I got a small-diameter body with nice, prominent segmentation. This was more like it. To secure the wire in place, I started the thread behind the bead and tied it down tightly over the front end of the wire. I dubbed a small black head to finish off the fly and was pretty happy with what I had come up with: a flat black, thin-bodied, yet heavily weighted little midge larva.

Fished ahead of the Jujubee, this little bomb of a fly did just what I had hoped. Mostly. It dragged the Juju down, didn't raise any fish eyebrows as it drifted by them, and was pretty sneaky about getting its job done. The only catch was, sometimes the fish would eat it instead of the hallowed Jujubee. If only I could have such problems with every fly I tie.

In the years since I tied up that first little experimental fly, it has turned out to be a much more remarkable pattern than I had ever expected. The success of the all-black version led me to branch out into some other colors more closely matching a variety of midge larvae and pupae. I think it even crosses over to a caddis larva in some of the larger sizes as well, and any fly that can be taken for more than one type of bug is a winner in my book. Black and olive, wine and silver, and all red are some of the more popular variations of this fly, and their weight and subtlety have produced spectacular results for anglers as far away as New Zealand. I have had some busy days on stillwaters with this little fly as well, casting it under a small foam indicator and just letting it bob along the waves. Evidently, the Poison Tung is an OK Chironomid pattern too.

I have made two simple changes to this pattern over the years, one in an effort to make it a bit more durable and the other to make it a bit more practical. It seems that sometimes in my haste to tie the fly on, I would hold the body of the fly while I pulled the knot tight . . . and I would slide the wire body back down the hook shank and around the bend, rendering the fly useless. I never had a fly come apart if I could get it tied to the tippet first, but more often than not, I would ruin the fly when I tied it on. I decided something had to be done and added a thread base under the wire to help it adhere to the shank without building up any bulk. This simple thread layer has worked wonders and has significantly improved the sturdiness of the fly. Now all I have to worry about is the fish wearing the colored coating off the wire, and that I can live with.

I also changed the hook from the heavy-wired Tiemco 2457 to the lighter-wired, ring-eyed 2488. My reasoning behind this is that it was easier for me to bury the point of the finer wire hook in the fish's mouth than the heavier wire, and I didn't need the stoutness of the heavy hook because I was fishing this fly on relatively light tippets anyway. The tippet should break long before the hook straightened. The ring eye also sets the bead up and away from the hook point, leaving a tiny bit more exposed gap. In retrospect, the idea of the heavy hook really adding much to the sink rate is inconclusive.

The last alteration to the Poison Tung came about one winter after reading an article written by Ed Engle on the efficacy of blue flies. It seems Ed had been doing a bit of research regarding the color blue and found that it, being a short-wavelength color, stayed visible further underwater than other colors. This article intrigued me, and I decided to twist up a couple of blue wire Poison Tungs to try the next time I was out. Of course, when I sat down at the bench I went off on all sorts of tangents, tying some flies completely out of the darker blue UTC wires, some with just the darker blue wire rib, and some with a finer wire from Lagartun. The Lagartun wire was

Tungsten beads add weight and flash to my nymph patterns. Copper and black have become my favorites, but sometimes the extra flash given off by the brighter gold and silver beads are what's needed to catch a fish's eye.

Lagartun's peacock blue fine wire lends the perfect amount of color and segmentation to my Deep Blue Poison Tung.

much finer than UTC's, and was a much more brilliant shade of light blue.

I tied up a few of these flies with a black bead head and black dubbing, a few with a silver bead and some bright blue Antron dubbing, and finally a few more with just a light blue wire rib over gray thread and a more subtle UV gray Ice Dub head. I stashed these all in my box and took them along the next time I went out. I was excited about the prospect of having a new little trick up my sleeve, and I remember walking quickly into the canyon that overcast winter morning anxious to see what was to come.

As it turned out, there is such a thing as a fly that's too blue. The flies I had tied with an entirely bright blue body made fish run like I had thrown rocks at them. I was beginning to wonder if Ed's article was some kind of a mean joke. I could plainly see the blue color of the flies glinting along the bottom of the deep run I was fishing, clearly signaling "Stay Away" in Morse code to the trout. The darker blue flies I had tied with the UTC wire seemed about as effective as the original all-black version, but no more or less so.

The brighter blue Lagartun wire was surprisingly visible in the water, but perhaps was a bit too much for the fish. I finally dug one of the last two new pattern variations from my box and tied it on. This fly was tied with a simple blue Lagartun wire rib wrapped sparsely over a pale gray thread underbody. A dubbed head of UV gray Ice Dub (I had selected this dubbing color because it was sort of blue-gray, but not too blue) and a small silver tungsten bead completed the fly. This fly was much more subtle than the others, with just a hint of blue accented along a plain gray body.

I cast the fly upstream of a visible rainbow, lifted the line to allow the fly to sink straight down, and did my best to high-stick the fly right into his mouth. It felt like my cast was off a bit, and I saw the fish make a sudden hard move to his left. I thought I must have bumped him with the line. I lowered the rod tip to let the fly slide by unnoticed when I saw the fish shaking his head like he was suddenly very unhappy with something. My brain hesitated a moment before it sent the signal to my hand to set the hook. In the meantime it sent the message to my brain that the fish had actually charged over three feet to eat the little blue fly and threw in a couple of unprintable insults while it was at it.

I was astonished.

The fly was much farther away from the fish than I had planned, and yet not only was he able to see it, he actually went out of his way to eat it. When I saw that fish turn to his left, there was no doubt in my mind that something went awry and he was running away from either me or the fly. The move was definitive and composed, and it totally blew me away that he was actually turning so hard on the fly. I'm glad this happened so visibly that day because now I pay a lot more attention to any sudden subtle and not so subtle moves fish make when this fly is anywhere near them. I had inadvertently struck upon a near-perfect blend of colors for a wintertime fly like this, and I was glad that I hadn't stopped with the plain, dark-blue wired versions when I sat down at the bench the week before. Experimenting pays off.

It has since become clear to me that the deep blue Poison Tung seems to work best in low light situations. Cloudy, overcast days in the spring and summer or winter and fall days when the light is at a lower angle seem to be more productive when coupled with this unusual fly. Maybe it has something to do with just how well that blue color shows up, and maybe that's just another one of those things in my head, but I've never had a great day with this fly under bright clear skies. However, any day with some cloud cover or a storm overhead will find me sight fishing a deep blue Poison Tung to every available fish. My latest addition to this game has been to see just exactly how far I can get a fish to move for it. Would you believe my record is somewhere around four feet? Hard to believe, but it's true.

Incidentally, the unusual name of this fly came courtesy of my Uncle Mike Giambrocco. When I was a kid, he had a big chow dog with a black tongue. He'd always scare us little kids by yelling, "Don't let that dog lick you! He has a poison tongue!" That sight of that dog scared the daylights out of me and that phrase never left my head, so when I came up with that first little black fly with a TUNGsten bead, well . . . there you go.

POISON TUNG
(DEEP BLUE)

Hook:	#16-22 Tiemco 2488
Bead:	Silver tungsten (2 mm)
Thread:	Gray 8/0 Uni-Thread
Rib:	Peacock blue Lagartun wire (fine)
Head:	UV gray Ice Dub

TYING THE POISON TUNG

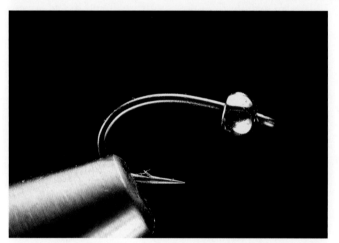

1. Place the bead on the hook with the small hole closest to the hook eye and slide it up to the eye of the hook. Clamp the hook in the vise.

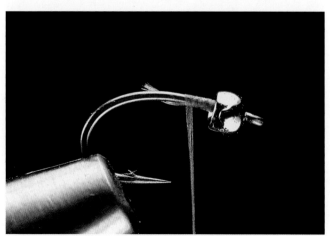

2. Start the thread right behind the bead with as few turns as possible.

3. Lay a piece of the fine Lagartun wire across the shank right behind the bead on the near side of the hook, as shown here.

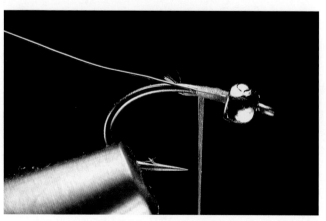

4. Trap the wire with the thread along the near side of the hook shank. Pull the front end of the wire down to length so the front end slides under the first turn of thread.

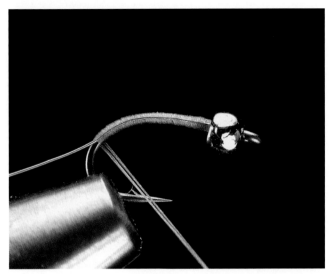

5. Hold the wire along the near side of the shank as you wrap back over it to about halfway down the hook bend. I try to keep the wire in line with the near side of the shank as I wrap back over it to create a smooth thread underbody.

6. Return the thread to the back of the bead, forming a smooth, level thread body as you travel. The wire almost shows through the thread where it is tied down, as the body should be very thin and slender. Keep in mind that these photos are greatly enlarged so the effect is far more subtle than seen here.

7. Spiral wrap the wire forward with about six or seven evenly spaced turns to the back of the bead. Tie the wire off with a couple firm wraps of thread and break off the excess. This fine wire can be snapped off easily by popping it back toward the hook bend with a firm tug. Be sure to brace the eye of the hook with your fingertip as you do this to prevent pulling the hook from the vise.

8. Pull a tiny amount of Ice Dub from the package. Tear the fibers a bit with your fingers to both shorten the individual strands as well as to stretch them out into even finer strands. Ice Dub is relatively coarse and long, so tearing the dubbing will make it a bit more proportional to the small size of this fly.

9. Twist the torn dubbing onto the thread and build a small ball just behind the bead. The dubbed head should be about the same diameter as the bead, or just slightly bigger.

10. Whip-finish the thread, letting the wraps fall tightly in between the bead and the dubbed head. Clip the thread.

11. Finished deep blue Poison Tung.

POISON TUNG (BROWN)

Hook:	#16-22 Tiemco 2488
Bead:	Copper tungsten bead (2 mm)
Thread:	Camel 8/0 Uni-Thread
Rib:	Copper Lagartun wire (fine)
Head:	Brown Superfine

POISON TUNG (PURPLE)

Hook:	#16-22 Tiemco 2488
Bead:	Silver tungsten bead (2 mm)
Thread:	Purple 70-denier UTC thread
Rib:	Peacock blue Lagartun wire (fine)
Head:	Holographic purple Ice Dub

TYING THE WIRE BODIED POISON TUNG

As mentioned above, there are essentially two versions of the Poison Tung: the wire ribbed variety and the version with a body made entirely of wire. The blue and copper versions have a thread body ribbed with wire, and all the others are composed entirely of wire wraps.

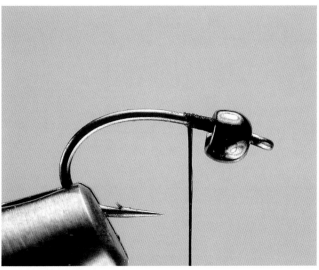

1. Place the bead on the hook, clamp the hook in the vise, and start the thread immediately behind it.

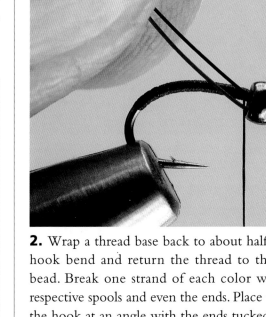

2. Wrap a thread base back to about halfway down the hook bend and return the thread to the back of the bead. Break one strand of each color wire from their respective spools and even the ends. Place the wire across the hook at an angle with the ends tucked into the back of the bead.

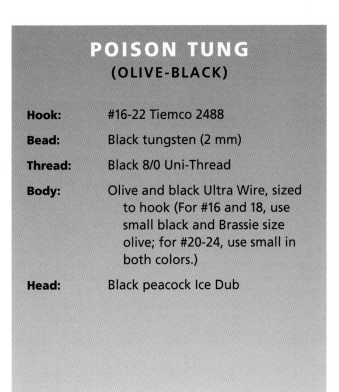

POISON TUNG
(OLIVE-BLACK)

Hook:	#16-22 Tiemco 2488
Bead:	Black tungsten (2 mm)
Thread:	Black 8/0 Uni-Thread
Body:	Olive and black Ultra Wire, sized to hook (For #16 and 18, use small black and Brassie size olive; for #20-24, use small in both colors.)
Head:	Black peacock Ice Dub

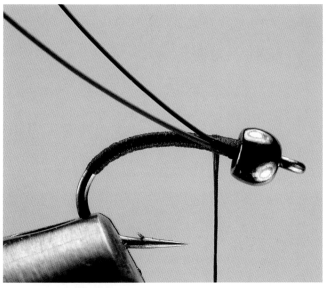

3. Capture the ends of the wire with several tight wraps of thread, forming a band to anchor them in place just behind the bead.

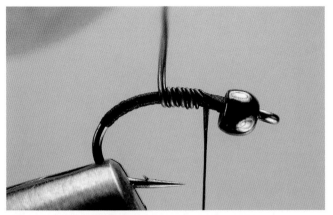

4. Leave the thread hanging just behind the bead and begin wrapping both strands of wire as one unit back to the end of the hook. Take care to make sure the wire strands lay one right next to the other as you wrap.

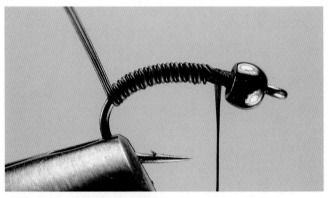

5. Continue wrapping the wire all the way back to the end of the thread base at halfway down the hook bend. Helicopter the ends of the wire by twisting them at a right angle to the hook shank until they break off. Hold the wires as close to the hook as you can as you twist them to break them off flush.

6. Tear a bit of the black Ice Dub into finer shorter strands and twist it onto the thread. Build a small ball of dubbing immediately behind the bead.

7. Whip-finish the thread at the back edge of the bead and clip.

POISON TUNG (ZEBRA)

Hook:	#16-22 Tiemco 2488
Bead:	Black tungsten (2 mm)
Thread:	Black 8/0 Uni-Thread
Body:	Black (Brassie) and silver (small) Ultra Wire
Head:	Black peacock Ice Dub

POISON TUNG (TIGER)

Hook:	#16-22 Tiemco 2488
Bead:	Black tungsten (2 mm)
Thread:	Black 8/0 Uni-Thread
Body:	Black (Brassie) and copper (small) Ultra Wire
Head:	Black peacock Ice Dub

POISON TUNG (WINE/SILVER)

Hook:	#16-22 Tiemco 2488
Bead:	Black tungsten (2 mm)
Thread:	Black 8/0 Uni-Thread
Body:	Wine (Brassie) and silver (small) Ultra Wire
Head:	Black peacock Ice Dub

POISON TUNG (RED)

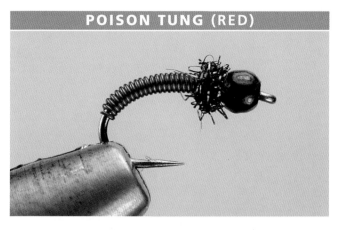

Hook:	#16-22 Tiemco 2488
Bead:	Black tungsten bead (2 mm)
Thread:	Black 8/0 Uni-Thread
Body:	Red Ultra Wire (Brassie)
Head:	Black peacock Ice Dub

POISON TUNG (BLACK)

Hook:	#16-22 Tiemco 2488
Bead:	Black tungsten bead (2 mm)
Thread:	Black 8/0 Uni-Thread
Body:	Black Ultra Wire (Brassie)
Head:	Black peacock Ice Dub

FIVE

Two Bit Hooker

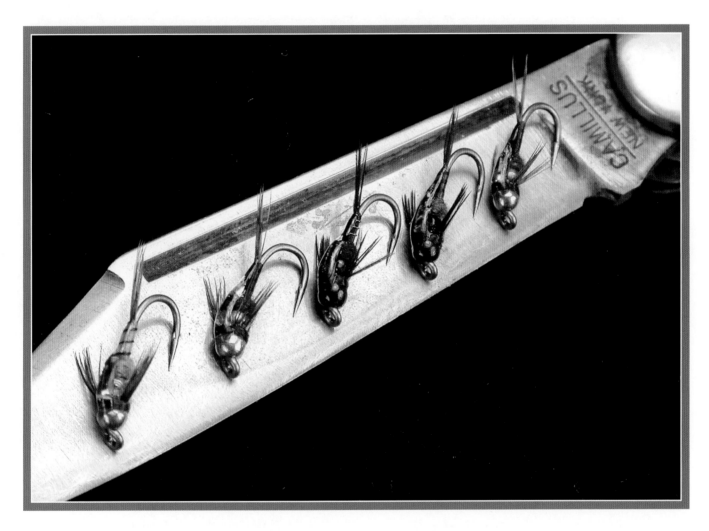

Over the years, Mike Mercer's MicroMay has proven to be a dependable addition to my fly box. I could fish the fly as a dropper under a dry, as the "copper" portion of the hopper-copper-dropper rig, or even under a yarn indicator and feel confident that it was going to take fish. I was perfectly happy with this fly for years until the day my buddy Ross Bartholomay mentioned that the bead was grossly oversized and out of proportion.

Ross and I were on the way home from a good day on the Arkansas River, and it is on late-night drives like these that we (meaning: Ross) tend to get a bit overanalytical about fly patterns. I love these drives and the time I get to spend with thinkers like Ross. In my life I have finally learned that sometimes even non–fly tiers have some great ideas, and it never hurts to hear them out.

Despite the fact that we had caught a mountain of fish that day, Ross mentioned that he thought there was

The Two Bit Hooker has become one of my favorite patterns. Its slender profile and extreme weight make it a perfect dry-dropper pattern.

some room for improvement on the MicroMay. This sounded like blasphemy to me. I have never met Mike Mercer in person, but I'm a huge fan of his flies, and hearing that there could be something on which to improve almost offended me on several levels. The MicroMay is a small, bulbous, and reasonably durable pattern, and the oversized tungsten bead not only added the necessary weight to get the fly down but also a bit of goofy charm. I always thought of this fly as a bit disproportioned, but I never really gave it a second thought until Ross mentioned it. It's like when someone calls you fat, or points out that your hairline is receding . . . and you are and it is. You are just a little too close to note things like this yourself, and it might hurt a little to know that others do. Of course, once Ross mentioned this, it stuck in my craw like an insult and made me rethink the whole MicroMay philosophy.

So rather than sit down at the bench and make the obvious adjustments like using a smaller bead that was more proportioned to the fly size, or adding a flattened lead wire underbody to slim the profile down yet keep the needed weight, I quickly stalled looking for the answer. It is rare that I don't have at least an idea about how to go about a new design or pattern, and I pride myself on being able to fix things like this. But I was stuck.

I knew that a smaller bead would certainly be more proportional to the fly, but even a tungsten bead would not be as heavy as the larger one of the original. Adding a lead wire underbody would get me the weight I needed but would ruin the slim profile. I know this because I finally broke down and tried both of these ideas and confirmed my suspicions. This wasn't going to be an easy fix. I decided to just start all over from the beginning and take stock of the attributes of the Micro-May and hope to stumble onto something to solve the weight issue along the way.

The MicroMay has a tail and legs made of sparse pheasant tail fibers and I have always noticed the tail is the first thing to go on this fly. Pheasant tail is readily available in a host of colors and does a great job of imitating the pulsing tails and legs of a natural mayfly nymph, but it is innately delicate and breaks easily.

The stripped peacock quill body was another issue altogether. It took longer to make than it really justified, but it was hard to argue with its prominent ribbing. The double turkey slip wing case was a creative way of get-

ting around the epoxy soaking through the feathers and into the dubbed thorax, but again, it seemed like a bit more work than was really necessary. There had to be a better way.

I really liked the overall profile of the fly, but I thought maybe I could come up with a few improvements and perhaps streamline the fly a bit and make it faster to tie and more durable at the same time. So I sat down and went to work with a Tiemco 921 clamped in the jaws of my vise. I put a smaller tungsten bead on the hook for lack of a better idea, resigning myself to adding split shot to the leader to keep the fly down in deeper water. I knew that a mottled hen back feather would provide a beautiful sparse tail, and its softness and flexibility would help keep it attached to the hook. I decided to use the hen fibers for the legs for the same reasons as well as the fact that I already had a special trick up my sleeve for creating the legs quickly and easily.

The body was an area of contention for me. A simple thread abdomen was the easiest, fastest, and perhaps the most realistic, particularly in small sizes, as I could readily control the diameter of the body, but it just didn't pop out at me as the right answer. It was too plain and even-toned. I tried a variety of options like twisted rod building thread, floss, goose biots, and even Super Hair a la the Jujubaetis, but found that none of these was really what I was after. I obviously liked the shine and the segmentation of the Super Hair abdomen, as evidenced by my prolific use of it on the Juju series of flies, but it was just too fat on a fly like this. It was out of place and didn't fit in with the ultra slender profile I had in mind. The goose biots had great promise when wrapped with their smooth sides out. The beautifully segmented ribbing was getting much closer to what I had in mind, but the short section of hook shank on which I had to wrap them precluded the wide overlap needed to create a slim body.

It finally occurred to me to stick with the thread abdomen but add a contrasting color thread rib. The first color variation I tried was the brown thread abdomen with black thread rib shown here in the tutorial. I was struck by the resemblance the ribbed thread body had to a smooth goose biot body, although with the thread body I was able to control the diameter and spacing of the rib much more readily. I ultimately found that using a thin thread on the smaller versions was key, as the thread work near the front of the fly would need to be

Two Bit Hookers can be tied in a plethora of sizes and colors to match any mayfly nymph. Red, brown, and black are my favorite colors in sizes 14 through 18.

as minimal as possible to keep from creating too much bulk. Now I had the answer to the body of the fly and was ready to move on to the wing case.

The MicroMay was originally tied with a strip of pearl Flashabou pulled over the turkey quill wing cases, but the bulk created by tying in the two slips of turkey and the flash was hard to control on smaller flies, and the thin strip of flash would sink down and nearly disappear into the soft wing cases. I had to find a way to get a visible flashback on there without increasing the bulk. A single strand of medium Opal Mirage Tinsel filled both of these niches exceptionally well. The Opal Mirage Tinsel is similar to the standard pearl tinsel that has been available for years, but it exudes a much more colorful flash than the pearl and is slightly more metallic. I later discovered that it also prevented the epoxy from soaking

into the underlying thorax dubbing. The medium size was just the right width to envelop the dubbed thorax and create a vibrant, glowing wing case. Almost there!

I still had but a single small bead perched at the head of the fly. The smaller bead fit the profile of the fly much better, and I had managed to really slim down the fly with the changes I had already made, but I knew that the fly would be too light to pull a dropper tippet down and stay along the bottom of faster, deeper runs. I had done all this work and still hadn't answered the original question until it hit me like a ton of bricks.

Use *two* small beads.

Using two of the smaller diameter beads turned out to be perfect for this fly. I was able to maintain the slim profile yet add even more weight to the fly than I had with the original's oversized head. With the two-bead

Mottled India hen saddles are cheap, readily available, and beautifully marked. I use them for tails and legs on many of my patterns.

idea racing through my mind I quickly found that I could easily hide one of the beads within the thorax, under the wing case where the bulk of the bead would blend in with the dubbing. I finally had it.

I finished the fly off with a bead-to-tail epoxy overcoat. The epoxy adds a bit of weight to the fly, a huge amount of durability, and even magnifies the flash and rib aspects. The best and most noticeable parts of this fly are its incredible weight and delicate profile. I immediately knew that I had a champion pinched in the jaws of my vise.

When I finally crack a brainteaser like this one, I typically sit down and crank out several more to work out any details of the tying process that may arise when tying them in quantity. I am happy to say that the overall design of this fly is so simple that there was little left to

dial in. Instead of cranking out more variations I turned instead to my boxes of thread and selected a few more bug-like hues to replicate. I tied the fly in black, light olive, a darker olive, and even red that first night and gingerly tucked the new flies into my box before mentioning my epiphany to anyone else. I guess I did mention it to my wife and kids later that night, but my revelations have become so commonplace that they hardly produce eye rolls or even yawns anymore. I would have to look elsewhere for validation. I was more excited about this new pattern than anything else I had developed since the Charlie Boy Hopper. What started out as a variation of the MicroMay turned out to be something completely different. I can't say that I planned on this being an original pattern and must admit that without Mike Mercer's little bug, this fly would never have been, but I guess I would have to credit that troublemaker Ross for the impetus to hash all this out. I now had a fly that was thinner, heavier, and more durable than its predecessors. This fly had the uber-lean profile of the Pheasant Tail Nymph, the weight of a Copper John, and durability in spades.

We fished the new fly in every way imaginable, and it produced fish like no other. I recall fishing a small black Two Bit Hooker on a short 12-inch dropper beneath a small Charlie Boy Hopper on the Colorado River one fall day. I was fishing the super-skinny riffles and edges that everyone else had waded through on their way to the deep runs. Fish were piled up in this shallow water and were feeding heavily on emerging *Baetis* nymphs. The Two Bit sank quickly on the short dropper and hung low in the water column. Brown after brown came flashing over to the fly, visibly inhaling it as it drifted subtly by. I felt like I was stealing these fish from the other fisherman, and I'm sure a few of them were kicking themselves for thrashing through such productive water. The Hooker was the perfect fly for this shallow water because an unweighted fly would not have stayed down in the fast moving riffles, and using a split shot was just asking to hang your rig up on the bottom every few minutes. The buoyant hopper suspended the heavy, but slim fly at just the right level in the water column for it to be seen by the fish, but not so low that it was grabbing onto every rock it passed.

After fishing the Two Bit for several seasons now, I have finally come to realize that while I love the profile of the Tiemco 921, this hook is just not stout enough to hold up to my aggressive fish fighting style. A recent float on the Arkansas River yielded over a hundred fish, but the downside was that Ross and I went through more than thirty of these great little flies—a few were lost on the bottom but the majority were to bent hooks. Fishing from a moving boat requires a bit more heat to be put on a fish and the lighter hooks didn't fare well. I have since been tying this fly on the 2X heavy Tiemco 3769 with much better results. The 3769 is just a bit longer than the 921 and the gap just a touch narrower, but the heavier wire has been more durable.

The name of this fly came about over the next several seasons. My oft-mentioned friend Matt Prowse and I fished this fly a lot, and he named it after his adorable wife, Bean. Now I know that this sounds contentious so let me finish the story. Matt had named the fly the

Beanie May, his nickname for his bride. I had never really put much thought into the name so Beanie May stuck, and that's what we all call it. When I submitted the fly to Umpqua Feather Merchants in late 2008, they decided that while they loved the fly and were as excited about it as I was, the name just wasn't catchy enough. These days it takes something a little more unusual to make a fly stand out from the hundreds of others in the bins, and the right name holds some importance. I came up with the Two Bit Hooker moniker based on some loose word association of the two beads and little hook. This was difficult news to break to both Matt and Bean, and I must say we had some laughs about the prospect of having to tell Bean that the fly named after her was now called something a bit, shall we say, rougher than her diminutive pet name. Thankfully, Bean was a good sport about all this.

TWO BIT HOOKER
(BROWN)

Hook:	#14-18 Tiemco 3769
Beads:	Two copper 1/16" tungsten for the #16 and 18
Thread:	Rusty brown 6/0 Danville or 74-denier Lagartun
Tail:	Mottled brown hen saddle fibers
Abdomen:	Tying thread
Rib:	Black 14/0 Gordon Griffith's
Wing Case:	Opal Mirage Tinsel (medium)
Thorax:	Rusty brown Superfine dubbing
Legs:	Mottled brown hen saddle fibers
Coating:	Five-minute epoxy
Note:	You can use either two 5/64" or two 3/32" beads for additional weight on #14 hooks.

TYING THE TWO BIT HOOKER

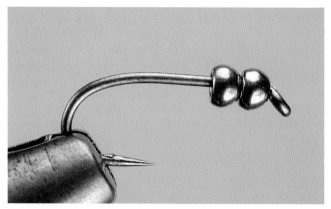

1. Pinch the hook barb flat and thread the two beads over the point. Push the beads up to the hook eye and clamp the hook in the vise.

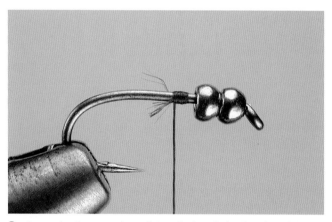

2. Start the brown thread just behind the last bead.

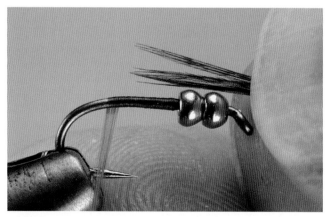

3. Wrap a thin thread base back to the hook bend. Preen about a half dozen hen saddle fibers away from the stem of the feather so their tips all line up square. Measure the tips against the hook so they are about a half shank-length long.

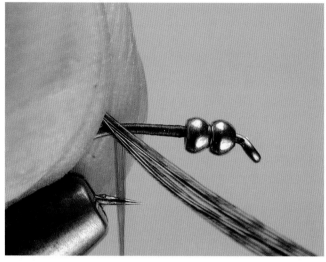

4. Grasp the tips of the fibers in your material hand and place them across the hook shank at the bend with their butt ends facing slightly down on the near side of the hook.

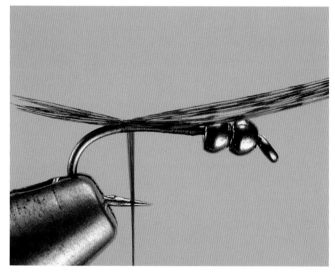

5. Bring the thread up and over the hen fibers capturing them against the hook shank. Allow the thread torque to twist the fibers to the top of the shank. If you make the wrap smoothly over the fibers they should be dragged to the top of the shank by the thread. You can put one more wrap of thread over the tails right at the bend, but no more.

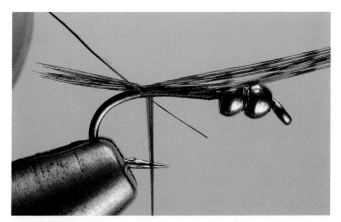

6. For the thread rib, I like to use a bobbin to keep the thread under control. Feed several inches of thread from the bobbin tube and hold the end of the ribbing thread across the hook bend as you did with the tailing fibers. The stub end of the ribbing thread should extend to just behind the rear bead.

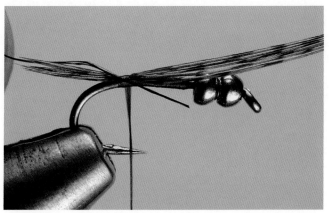

7. Make a wrap of the brown thread to capture the black thread rib right at the hook bend.

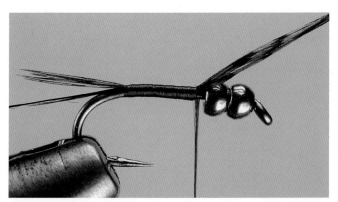

8. Wrap the brown (body) thread forward over the tag end of the ribbing thread and the butt ends of the tail fibers up to the back of the bead, securing them tightly to the shank.

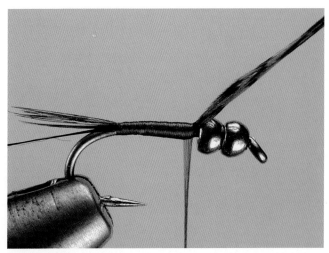

9. Work the brown thread back and forth over the rear half of the hook, building up a slight taper toward the back of the bead. This taper should remain very thin but still be apparent.

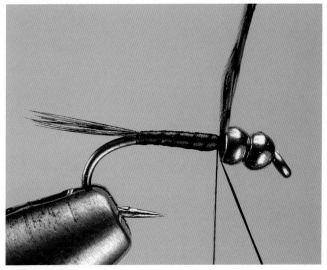

10. Spiral wrap the ribbing thread forward over the thread abdomen to the back of the bead and tie it off. You may want to twist the ribbing thread a bit before you start wrapping to cord up the ribbing. I like a flatter rib rather than a very thin, corded one, but if the ribbing thread is too flat it occupies too much of the body and makes for a fly that is more rib than body. Try to get three to five turns of ribbing up to the bead. Once you reach the bead make several wraps of the ribbing thread to tie off the brown body thread.

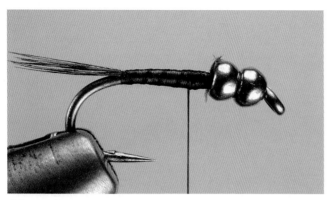

11. Clip the brown working thread flush against the shank behind the bead and trim the butt ends of the tailing fibers as well. Bring the black ribbing thread back over the front edge of the abdomen so it is just in front of the midpoint on the hook.

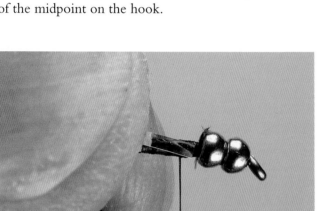

12. Lay in a single strand of the medium Opal Mirage Tinsel. I like to lean this piece in a bit toward my near side of the hook as I wrap over it so the thread will draw it up to the top dead center of the hook.

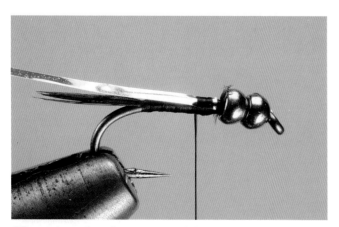

13. Make a few firm wraps of thread over the tinsel to secure it to the top of the shank. Make sure the tinsel is centered and tied back to nearly the middle of the shank.

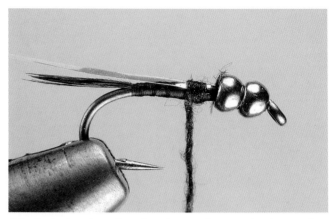

14. Dub the thread with a thin, tight strand of Superfine dubbing. Start the dubbing at the base of the tinsel wing case.

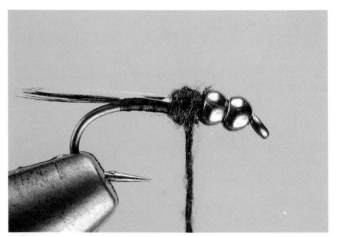

15. Build the dubbing into a ball shape behind the first bead. This ball of dubbing should be about the same diameter as the bead, but be sure that you still have a bit of dubbing left on the thread here before you go on.

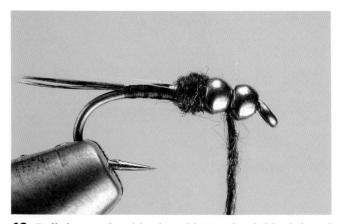

16. Pull the rear bead back and bring the dubbed thread over the rear bead and into the space between the two beads.

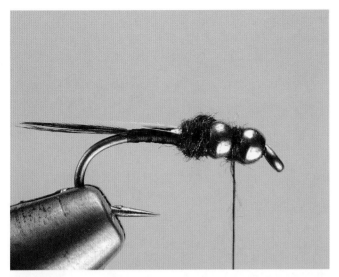

17. Make a few more turns of dubbing in between the two beads, building up the shank diameter so it is just shy of the outside diameter of the beads. This fills the void in between the beads and creates a base to tie the legs on next. If you do not dub a large enough diameter here, the legs will not sweep back along the body of the fly but rather stick out at right angles to the hook shank.

19. I use the tips of my scissors to separate the clump into two even bunches without letting go of the fibers. Lay the split clump of hen fibers in along the shank with each half on either side of the hook, but rather than laying them in perfectly square to the top of the hook shank, set them in so they are slightly rotated toward your near side. The tips of the fibers should extend to just short of the hook point.

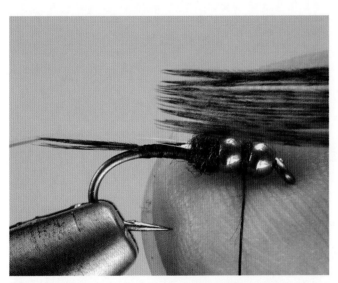

18. Even the tips of a larger clump of hen saddle fibers and measure them against the shank so they extend from just behind the first bead back to about the hook point. Carefully peel these fibers from the stem, keeping their tips aligned in the process.

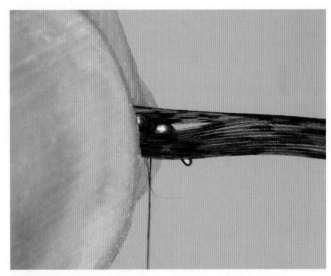

20. Reach in with your material hand and grasp the fibers tightly along the side of the shank. Hold these in place for the time being.

21. Make a loose turn of thread over the butt ends of the fibers just in front of your fingertips. Once the thread has passed all the way around the hook and is coming back toward you again on the underside of the shank, you can begin to tighten and close the wrap to anchor the fibers on either side of the hook shank. The thread torque will slide the fibers from their formerly near side offset position to square on the hook.

22. If your legs are a bit too long you can pull the butt ends gently to shorten them down if needed. Once you are happy with the length of the legs, make two more firm wraps of thread to lock them in place behind the front bead.

23. Divide the butt ends of the fibers to their respective sides.

24. Pull the butt ends of the near side clump back along the side of the fly and pin them in place with a tight turn of thread.

25. Pull the butt ends of the far side clump back on the far side of the hook and bind them in place as well. Folding the butt ends back like this will do two things: It will allow you to hide the clipped ends under the thread head behind the bead rather than having the stubble stick out near the bead, and it will make for a much more secure tie-down, preventing the legs from pulling out from under the thread wraps later.

26. Pull the butt ends out at a right angle to the shank to separate them from the tips.

27. Reach in with the tips of your finest scissors and trim the butt ends of the legs as close to the shank as you can. Do this on both sides of the hook.

28. Make a turn or two of thread over the stub ends of the legs so that you have a smooth thread band between the beads.

29. Top view of leg length and division.

30. Pull the flash forward over the top of the rear bead and the dubbed thorax, making sure it is centered.

31. Tie the flash down between the beads with two tight thread wraps. You may want to spin the tying thread a bit so it bites into the flash and dubbing here.

32. Fold the long front end of the flash back over the wing case and bind it in place again with two more tight wraps.

33. Folding the flash like this does the same thing it did for us on the legs. It anchors the material more firmly in place and prevents an unsightly stub end from sticking out over the bead, making for a much cleaner thread head.

34. Whip-finish the thread between the beads and clip.

35. Trim the excess flash as close to the thread head as you can. I try to just nick the edge of the flash with a small snip of my scissor blades, then tear the flash off across the radius of the bead. This leaves no stub end exposed.

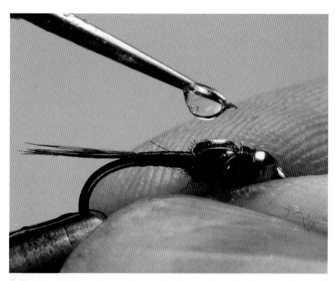

36. Hold the legs down below the hook shank and apply a small drop of epoxy to the top of the fly. I usually set the epoxy drop down on the Mirage wing case and use the tip of a fine needle to smear the epoxy all the way back to the base of the tail along the top of the fly. Bring the epoxy forward onto the back of the front bead as well.

37. Finished epoxy coat. Note there is a slight bit more epoxy across the wing case than there is at the bend.

TWO BIT HOOKER (RED)

Hook:	#14-18 Tiemco 3769
Beads:	Two copper 1/16″ tungsten beads for the #16 and 18, two 5/64″ beads or two 3/32″ for additional weight on the #14
Thread:	Red 70-denier Ultra Thread
Tail:	Mottled brown hen saddle fibers
Abdomen:	Tying thread
Rib:	Black 14/0 Gordon Griffith's
Wing Case:	Opal Mirage Tinsel (medium)
Thorax:	Rusty brown Superfine dubbing
Legs:	Mottled brown hen saddle fibers
Coating:	Five-minute epoxy

TWO BIT HOOKER (DARK OLIVE)

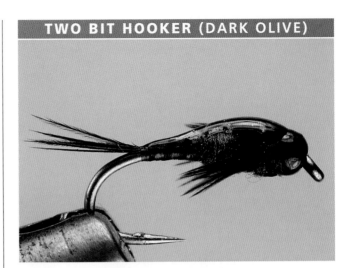

Hook:	#14-18 Tiemco 3769
Beads:	Two black 1/16″ tungsten beads for the #16 and 18, two 5/64″ or two 3/32″ beads for additional weight for the #14
Thread:	Olive 70-denier Ultra Thread
Tail:	Black hen saddle fibers
Abdomen:	Tying thread
Rib:	Black 14/0 Gordon Griffith's
Wing Case:	Opal Mirage Tinsel (medium)
Thorax:	Blue Wing Olive Superfine dubbing
Legs:	Black hen saddle fibers
Coating:	Five-minute epoxy

TWO BIT HOOKER (LIGHT OLIVE)

Hook:	#14-18 Tiemco 3769
Beads:	Two copper ¹⁄₁₆″ tungsten beads for the #16 and 18, two ⁵⁄₆₄″ or two ³⁄₃₂″ beads for additional weight for the #14
Thread:	Watery olive 70-denier Ultra Thread
Tail:	Mottled brown hen saddle fibers
Abdomen:	Tying thread
Rib:	Brown 14/0 Gordon Griffith's
Wing Case:	Opal Mirage Tinsel (medium)
Thorax:	Olive gray Superfine dubbing
Legs:	Mottled brown hen saddle fibers
Coating:	Five-minute epoxy

TWO BIT HOOKER (BLACK)

Hook:	#14-18 Tiemco 3769
Beads:	Two black ¹⁄₁₆″ tungsten beads for the #16 and 18, two ⁵⁄₆₄″ or two ³⁄₃₂″ beads for additional weight for the #14
Thread:	Black 70-denier Ultra Thread
Tail:	Black hen saddle fibers
Abdomen:	Tying thread
Rib:	Copper Lagartun wire (fine)
Wing Case:	Opal Mirage Tinsel (medium)
Thorax:	Black Superfine dubbing
Legs:	Black hen saddle fibers
Coating:	Five-minute epoxy

SIX

Caddistrophic Pupa

Across between a tomato worm and what you scrape off your windshield after a long drive, caddis pupae can be called nearly anything but pretty. Most insects have a certain streamlined appeal, but caddis pupae just look like something you pulled out of your nose. Their gangly legs, gelatinous bodies, and budding wings combine to form one of the most unpleasant-looking bugs on earth—but trout love them.

This outward appearance made it tough on me for years, as I really don't enjoy tying scraggly-looking, unkempt flies, but to really match this bug, I sort of had to look away and do what had to be done.

The Caddistrophic Pupa is built on a light wire scud hook to match the hunched-up curve characteristic of the natural. I am often asked if I think curved imitations out-fish straight ones, and to this I can confidently say

The Caddistrophic Pupa has been in development for several years now, and I am still not sure that it's completely done. Like everything else I tie, I'm always fiddling with this pattern by adding, subtracting, or substituting materials to get the look I'm after.

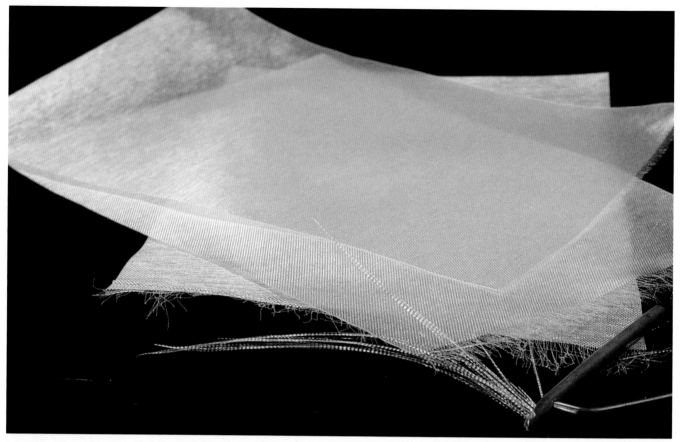

Morpho Fiber, made by Tiemco, is not yet available in the United States. It is an extremely fine pearlescent strand that adds subtle flash to the antennae of the Caddistrophic Pupa.

no. While many patterns are tied on the curved hooks to better align with the curved profile of a natural, we have to remember that most often we are looking at a picture in a book or perhaps even a live insect held in our hand. You would curl up a bit too if something plucked you out of your house and rolled you around in its palm. My point is that insects can curl up and straighten out under their own power, and at any moment in time, fish are used to seeing them in either state. That being said, I tie my caddis pupa on a curved hook because *I* like the way it looks. That's it. It's okay; we can do things like this.

The body of this fly has changed several times over the years, and I still carry several versions of it in my fly box. While I have finally settled on the dubbed body shown here, early versions were tied with two-tone wire bodies and even latex sheeting. I have used the dubbed bodies now for several years, reasoning that I can match the color of the naturals better with dubbing, and I have been happy with the results.

The shellback I use on my pattern is made from Super Floss, a stretchy spandex elastic material sold under several different brand names. I also use this same material to create the budding wings. Super Floss is durable, has great movement, and is easy to work with, making it perfect for this application. When tied in across the front of the fly as on this pattern, the Super Floss flexes and kicks in the drift, creating lifelike movement in the fly.

The rib on this fly, as subtle as it is, was a particular sticking point for me. I liked the streamlined effect created with very fine wire, but the prominent segmentation and color bands resulting from the larger Brassie-sized Ultra Wire seemed to match the color bands of the natural better, so I finally settled on using it. I think the bigger wire also adds some "hotness" to the dubbing, creating a bit more life and variegation.

Perhaps the most important and effective addition I have made to this fly is the CDC collar. When wetted down and saturated, CDC turns from an incredibly buoyant material to an incredibly lively soft hackle. Wavering strands of wet CDC immediately made me think of a caddis pupa the first time I saw them, and they complete the gangly leg effect of this bug to a T.

I finished the fly off with a loosely dubbed head of SLF Prism dubbing mixed with black rabbit fur. Mixing these two dubbings together makes for the ideal blend of flash and "bugginess." I pick the dubbing out after it is applied to further this effect and let the loose strands veil back along the body and collar.

I added the Morpho Fiber antennae one day in an attempt to add a bit of class and finish to the fly. I had originally used a few strands of well-marked lemon wood-duck flank and really liked the effect, but I soon found that these delicate fibers were short-term tenants on the fly and would break off quickly when fished. A few strands of markered Morpho Fiber fit the bill nicely and added a bit of fish-attracting sparkle to the pattern while also being much more durable. Morpho Fiber is not yet available in the United States, but a few strands of shrimp-colored Fluoro Fibre are a good substitute.

I like to think that I have managed to take this ugly little bug and make it into something that has a bit of appeal to my eye, although as I get older, I realize it really doesn't matter what I want in the fly—it's the fish who decide.

FISHING THE CADDISTROPHIC PUPA

I tie this pattern both with and without a bead, depending on where I want to fish it in the water column. Many times I have encountered fish keying on caddis just a few inches under the surface, and a pattern without a bead sinks just enough to get down and hang in the upper levels of the current. Once wet, the dubbed body provides just enough weight to get the fly through the surface film but not so much as to plummet it to the bottom. I like to fish a fly like this behind a dry and keep my eyes peeled for the small "blip" it makes when it hits the water so I can follow its drift to the fish. Most often I can see the fish rise up and eat the fly just under the surface.

Adding a black tungsten bead makes this fly more practical for everyday use. The bead pulls the fly down fast, allowing me to fish it through deeper or faster-moving water with the confidence that the fish are going to see it. I believe a weighted fly drifts more slowly than an unweighted pattern, and thus stays down where the fish can grab it longer. This may all be in my

CDC (cul de canard) is normally used for dry flies, but I have fallen in love with it on subsurface patterns because of its incredible movement when wet.

Super Floss is a spandex elastic that is not prone to dry rot like conventional rubber leg materials are. It is durable and easy to work with in a variety of applications. Spanflex, Flexi-Floss, and Super Floss are all essentially the same material and any one of them will work fine for this pattern.

head, and trust me, we all have things that are just in our heads, but I truly feel that a heavily weighted fly is more effective than one that bounces around in the currents and gets pushed up to the surface. I always fish either version of this fly all the way through the cast, letting the line pull tight at the end of the drift, and swing the fly toward the surface. Rarely do I actually get a grab when doing this, but every now and again, if the fish are really on a bite, you'll get one to chase it down and crush it. I have even had fish grab the fly as I strip in line to make the next cast. When they want it, they really want it.

The Caddistrophic Pupa under a dry fly such as the Mugly Caddis is a deadly combination, and I can remember one night where the CP stole the show. It's no secret that I love drifting rivers in a boat and drilling dry flies into bank-side targets and that was exactly the plan that Matt and I had for the day. Matt Prowse is my good friend and one of the best oarsmen anyone will ever meet. He has what seems to be an innate talent for putting me and the boat in the right place at the right time.

As we set off for our evening float, I confidently tied a #16 Mugly Caddis to the end of my leader and proceeded to cast the fly tight to the banks and under every

branch and limb I could reach. Our sense of anticipation was high, but we floated several hundred yards with caddis pelting our faces without a strike.

We eddied up and had a brief chat about perhaps hanging a dropper off the dry, as it seemed the fish were feeding mainly under the surface. Fishing an indicator is out of the question when we're in the boat. This self-imposed rule keeps both of us interested and entertained. If you think fishing an indicator is boring, try rowing the boat and watching it. You'll need a pillow. At least with a dry, the rower still gets to call out targets and see the fish rise, and in many cases, rowing and directing is just as fun as fishing, or at least that's what I tell Matt when he's in the center seat. The biggest compromise either of us will make is to concede to a dry-dropper rig, or if things get desperate, a hopper-copper-dropper.

So we elected to tie on a short dropper with a Caddistrophic Pupa under the dry. On this particular river, the dropper prevents the pinpoint bank-tight casting I prefer, and requires that I fish a bit farther out along the drop a foot or two from the bank. This drop-off leads the way from the super-skinny water along the bank out into the deeper faster currents of the river, and many fish will hang just off the drop in the safer depths and pick off bugs as they come by.

We pulled the boat out of the eddy and proceeded slowly downstream, with Matt back-rowing to keep the boat sliding along just slower than the current. I cast the dry and dropper as close to the drop as I dared, and before long we came upon a nice pod of rising fish. Now the beauty of the dry-dropper rig is that you can cover two levels of the water at once, and we had not given up on the dry fly, but simply added in the dropper to better our odds until the hatch got going. As we slid in tight to get a bit closer to the risers, I fired a cast down the seam that was feeding the fish. The boat was set up perfectly, slightly above and out from the fishes' feeding lane, allowing me a long, drag-free drift down to them. The Mugly bounced along the seam, patiently awaiting its doom, and we counted the seconds until the fish would rise up and eat it. With my eyes intently locked on the dry, I almost missed the flash underneath it. It took my mind several seconds to remember the dropper fly was still down there and the fish had just taken the easy way out and eaten the Caddistrophic Pupa instead of my dry. I finally set the hook and uneventfully either landed or broke off the fish—I don't recall which and at any given time I am prone to do either.

I do remember that we floated the rest of the river with that damn caddis pupa stealing all the takes until we finally took it off so the fish could concentrate on the dry. I'd like to say that we caught as many fish on the dry as we did on the pupa, but it would be a lie. The fish clearly preferred the pupa that evening, and it showed

me that given the choice between the adults on the surface and the pupae slightly underneath, the fish tend to lean toward the pupae. So now I am a bit more careful about letting a sunken fly steal away my summertime dry-fly fishing, but I keep this lesson close at hand when things get slow.

CADDISTROPHIC PUPA
(OLIVE)

Hook:	#12-18 Tiemco 2487 or 2457
Bead (optional):	Black tungsten (2 mm)
Thread:	Olive 74-denier Lagartun
Rib:	Chartreuse Ultra Wire (Brassie)
Shellback:	Brown Super Floss
Abdomen:	Pale olive Hare-Tron Dubbin
Wing Buds:	Brown Super Floss
Collar:	Natural dun CDC
Antennae:	Green pearl Tiemco Morpho Fiber or cream shrimp Fluoro Fibre
Head:	Black rabbit fur evenly mixed with black SLF Prism Dubbing

TYING THE CADDISTROPHIC PUPA

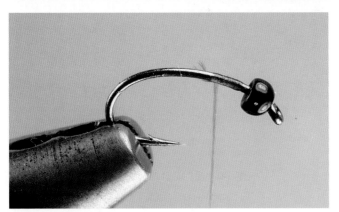

1. Place the bead on the hook, slide it up to the eye, and clamp the hook in the vise. Start the thread just behind the bead.

2. Tie in a length of the chartreuse wire at the front of the hook on the far side of the shank.

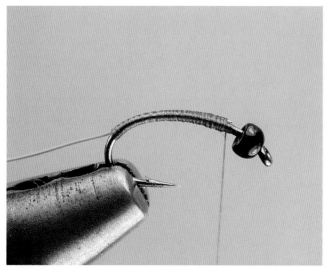

3. Wrap the thread back over the wire with tight turns to about halfway down the bend. Take care to keep the wire in line with the hook shank on the far side. Return the thread to the starting point.

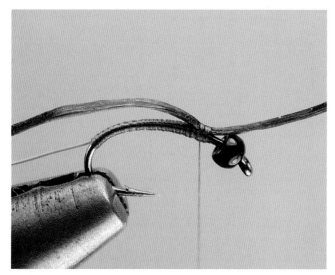

4. Tie in a piece of brown Super Floss at the starting point with two firm wraps of thread. I usually leave a short tag hanging off the front of the hook to keep the floss from pulling out in the next step.

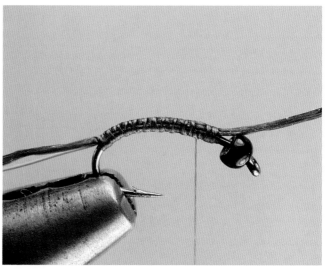

5. Pull the Super Floss taut and wrap back over it to the bend creating a smooth thread base as you go. You will need to pull the floss slightly toward you as you wrap the thread back over it to allow the thread torque to keep it centered on the top of the shank. Return the thread once again to the starting point and trim the Super Floss tag flush.

6. Dub a thin layer of the Hare-Tron onto the thread and build a slightly tapered body from the hook bend up to about an eye length behind the bead.

7. Pull the Super Floss forward over the top of the dubbed abdomen so it is somewhat taut and off-center toward the near side of the hook. Tie the Super Floss down with two firm wraps of thread, but do not clip the excess yet. If you do, the act of ribbing can actually pull it out.

8. Pick up the wire and start wrapping it forward with seven or eight evenly spaced turns to the front of the body. As you wrap, allow the wire to pull the off-center Super Floss to the top of the hook and line it up with the hook shank. Tie the wire off at the front with a few tight thread turns.

9. Helicopter the end of the wire to break it off flush and then stretch the remaining Super Floss tight and clip it close.

10. Cut a separate piece of Super Floss (or use the left-over piece you just cut off) and lay it in along the hook behind the bead. Tie it in place at the center of its length on the far side of the shank with three tight turns of thread.

11. Pull the far end of the floss back along the far side of the shank and wrap the thread back over its front edge to pin it in place along the hook.

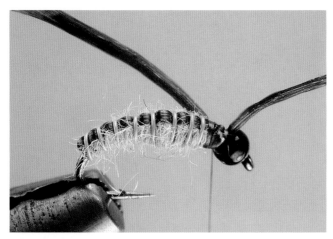

12. The floss should now be swept back along the body of the fly as shown here.

13. Pull the near-side strand of floss back along the near side of the hook and bind it in place with a few tight turns of thread as well.

14. Wrap back over the base of the Super Floss to the front edge of the body to pin the wing buds in place.

15. Trim both wing buds to about a half-shank length long. Do not stretch them when you cut as they will end up too short; instead, just lay the scissors across them at the right length and trim straight across. The wing buds should be in line with the hook shank along the sides of the abdomen.

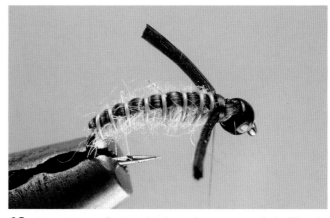

16. Top view of wing buds and segmented shellback.

17. Select two or three natural gray CDC feathers and even their tips. Preen the tip to separate the thin fibers at the top from the thicker fibers from the midpoint on the feather down toward the base.

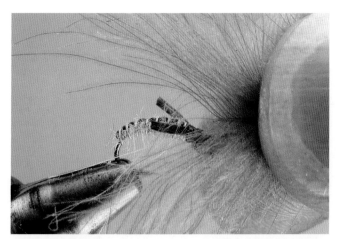

18. Clip only the center stems of all the CDC feathers leaving a V-shaped clump.

19. Lay the clump of CDC in along the shank behind the bead and at the front of the body with half of the clump on either side of the hook.

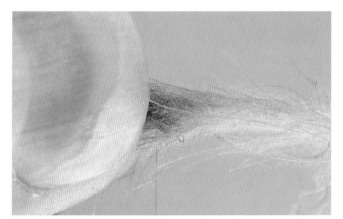

20. Reach in with your material hand and pinch the fibers in place along the sides of the fly. Let the fibers roll around the shank in your fingertips, pushing them down on both sides of the hook.

21. While still holding the tips of the feathers in your material hand, make a pair of loose wraps over their bases just behind the bead. Pull the thread toward you once you have completed two loose turns so the thread torque distributes the fibers around the shank.

22. Reach in with your thread hand and gently pull the butt ends of the fibers forward to draw the tips of the CDC forward so they extend just beyond the hook bend. Once the fibers are the right length, lock the feathers in place with several tight turns of thread.

23. Clip the butt ends of the CDC feathers as closely as you can with your fine-tipped scissors. Make a few tight turns of thread to smooth off the butts.

24. Draw about six strands of the Morpho Fiber from the sheet. Lay the fibers in with the center of their length at the back of the bead and tie them in place on top of the shank with two turns of thread. You should have half the fibers facing back over the body and the other half sticking forward over the hook eye.

25. Fold the front half of the fibers back over the rear half and bind them in place with two more turns of thread. Tied in this way, these slick fibers won't come out later. Leave the Morpho Fiber long for the time being.

26. Dub a short, ragged strand of the blended rabbit and SLF dubbing. Since you are going to rake it out later, don't worry about getting it on tightly. Dub a short head just behind the bead to cover the thread work. The dubbing should be a neat ball between the bead and the front of the abdomen and not creep up onto the body.

27. Whip-finish just behind the bead, allowing the thread wraps to slide off the back of the bead and nestle neatly into the space between the front of the dubbing and the back of the bead. Clip the thread. Use a small dubbing brush to pick out the dubbing so that it sweeps back around the fly.

28. You should now have a ragged collar that bleeds back into the body of the fly. Draw the Morpho Fiber taut to the rear of the hook and stroke across them with the very tip of a black Sharpie to create short bands.

29. Use the dubbing brush to separate the strands of Morpho Fiber. I trim some of the fibers about a shank length shorter and leave some of them as long as three shank lengths to imitate the antennae. The Morpho Fiber creates a nice glow to the fly, so I leave a bit of it on the fly in addition to the subtle antennae.

30. Finished fly, front quarter view.

31. Finished fly, top view. Note the segmented shellback and prominent ribbing.

CADDISTROPHIC PUPA (CREAM)

Hook:	#12-18 Tiemco 2487 or 2457
Bead (optional):	Black tungsten (2 mm)
Thread:	Cream 74-denier Lagartun
Rib:	Fluorescent orange Ultra Wire (Brassie)
Shellback:	Brown Super Floss
Abdomen:	Cream Hare-Tron Dubbin
Wing Buds:	Brown Super Floss
Collar:	Natural dun CDC
Antennae:	Green pearl Tiemco Morpho Fiber or cream shrimp Fluoro Fibre
Head:	Black rabbit fur evenly mixed with black SLF Prism Dubbing

CADDISTROPHIC PUPA (AMBER)

Hook:	#12-18 Tiemco 2487 or 2457
Bead (optional):	Black tungsten (2 mm)
Thread:	Olive 74-denier Lagartun
Rib:	Copper-brown Ultra Wire (Brassie)
Shellback:	Brown Super Floss
Abdomen:	Cinnamon caddis Hareline Dubbing
Wing Buds:	Brown Super Floss
Collar:	Natural dun CDC
Antennae:	Green pearl Tiemco Morpho Fiber or cream shrimp Fluoro Fibre
Head:	Black rabbit fur evenly mixed with black SLF Prism Dubbing

SEVEN

Charlie's Mysis

One of the first commercial fly orders I ever received came from Tim Heng, back in the days when he ran Roaring Fork Anglers in Glenwood Springs, Colorado. I was about 12 years old and my family and I would spend a couple weeks over there camping and fishing each summer.

I recall sitting nervously in the truck with my dad trying to work up the nerve to go in and see if I could talk these western slope guys into making a bit of a fly order with me. Up until then I had only tied flies for a small fly distributor here on the Front Range, and the prospect of getting an order from a real live fly-fishing shop was both something that I aspired to and something that scared me. This was the real deal and I wanted to make a good impression.

I went in and after I strolled around nervously for a while, Tim struck up a conversation with me that allowed me to segue nicely into my spiel. As it turned

The Charlie's Mysis is about as close to the real thing as anything you'll find with a hook, and the trout wholeheartedly agree.

out, Tim must have had a soft spot for shy kids and placed an order with me. This was the start of a great business relationship, and I continued to tie flies for Tim for the next decade or more. Tim turned into one of my best mentors, but I don't know that he ever knew that. I hope he does now. That little fly order he penned out that day gave me the confidence to move forward in this game I love, and I really do owe him a lot for that. Thanks, Tim.

One of the clearest memories I have of those trips to Glenwood and particularly from those trips into the fly shop were the faded photos pinned to the front counter. Abnormally huge, dripping rainbows and browns held by grinning fishermen seemed to be the theme here, and I was enthralled by just where and how anyone could catch fish like this. Tim patiently explained that *Mysis* shrimp would get washed through the turbines at the dam and feed down into the river, where they were eaten by these trout. He showed me a few of the patterns the shop carried to imitate these bugs, and I did my best to tie up a few of my own, albeit with all the wrong materials. I never did catch a fish on any of those patterns or anything else that was supposed to be a *Mysis* shrimp. Back in those days I was a dry-fly fisherman by necessity (I had no idea how to nymph fish) and just couldn't figure out what to do with these sunken flies. By the time I had figured out what this nymph fishing thing was all about, the *Mysis* had unexplainably stopped coming out of the reservoir and I all but forgot about them. Timing is everything, and I had missed out by several years.

Fast forward another ten years or so. I was working at a fly shop in Boulder, Colorado, and while standing behind the counter one day listening to yet another fishing story, a customer mentioned something about fishing *Mysis* on the Frying Pan River. My ears perked up, and I realized he wasn't talking about the good old days but instead was talking about yesterday! For some unknown reason, Ruedi Reservoir again began coughing out good numbers of these krill-like critters into the Frying Pan River—and the trout were waiting.

Instances like this are exactly why I never graduated from college. I cut school the next day and made the long drive over to the Pan after staying up much too late twisting up a few patterns along the lines of what Tim had shown me years back. I would like to say that I went over and put a whoopin' on those fish, but it didn't quite work out that way. I did catch some fish, and some of

them were pretty big, but I didn't really feel like the flies I had tied were what they really wanted.

Word got out on the new *Mysis* flush, and I recollect that several of us shop rats and customers all began trying to tie up a sure-fire mysis pattern. We had all observed these little bugs in the water and noted that every single live shrimp was facing upstream and about an inch or two under the surface as they drifted downstream. While most of the popular shrimp patterns were a stark white color, the real bug, while still alive, was nearly transparent and looked more like a subtle outline of a shrimp than anything more apparent. The best analogy I could come up with was that they looked like spit floating on the water. Liquid within liquid doesn't make for much of an impression, and these floating *Mysis* were far more understated than any of the reproductions I had seen.

A multitude of patterns were bounced around the shop that year involving monofilament extended bodies, hollow tubing, marabou, and the like, all of which I copied and fished, and none of which worked very well. Many of the prototypes had been tied scud-style, with the front of the shrimp at the hook bend. This arrangement would be fine if you were to cast the fly upstream to the fish so the head was facing into the current, but this made sight fishing more difficult and aligning the fly correctly was clearly a feature the fish were keying on.

Mysis shrimp are not at all like scuds and are characterized by a long, thin, wiggly abdomen and short thorax. Their profile reminded me of a damselfly nymph. I knew the right pattern would feature some sort of a body extended off the hook bend, but it remained to be seen what material could replicate the thin, nearly transparent abdomen while retaining a bit of movement.

I had to stop and observe the live shrimp a bit closer before I really had a handle on what might imitate them better. One of the most unusual traits of this little shrimp is that it had no shine to it at all. No pearlesence, no glint, no flash. It was a flat, clearish, elongated globule with little black eyes. The eyes were the easy part.

I tried several different materials like Antron, sparkle yarn, and even plastic sheeting, but all were too bright, too clear, too shiny, or too stiff to replicate the body. It was when I was tying a batch of egg flies for an order one night that it struck me that egg yarn didn't have any shine to it. I grabbed a smaller hook and went to work with a thin strand of the palest pink egg yarn I could find (I had no white egg yarn) tied off the hook bend. I dubbed a short thorax on the hook shank with some white Antron dubbing and finished the fly off with a small thread head. I ran to the porcelain fly-testing tank I kept in the other room (some folks call this a bathroom sink) and soaked the fly down to see what it would look like. The wet egg yarn had exactly the slimy look I was hoping for, with no flash or shine involved. The thorax was still too bright and the color was a bit off, but I knew that if I could just find a pack of white egg yarn I could figure this thing out finally. I hunted all over town for the white yarn, and apparently no one else was going to sneak up on me with this same idea because none of the shops around there had any. I ended up mail-ordering some from an out-of-state shop and tied up several of the prototype patterns for my next trip.

The prototypes fished better than any of the other patterns I had tried to date, but the shiny Antron thorax was still just not right. I remember driving home from the river trying to think of where I could find a dubbing material that was dull like the egg yarn, when the obvious popped into my head:

What are synthetic dubbings made from?

Yarn.

Where could I get a flat finish white dubbing?

By cutting up some egg yarn and blending it into dubbing—sometimes I feel so *dumb* . . .

I knew that I was going to be piling some miles on my car that year, making trips back and forth to the Frying Pan to test this new pattern out. I drove the rest of the way home, confident that I knew the answer to the problem. I sat down at the bench and mixed up a small batch of the egg yarn dubbing and proceeded to tie up several dozen of the "new" new mysis pattern once again. By now my fly box had several generations of the shrimp banging around it in and I could hardly find room for these.

I called my buddy Ross and told him he was going to be sick and miss work the next day. My college professors had all but forgotten about me by this time, so I was already free to go. He agreed that he was indeed feeling a little under the weather and that we should meet out along I-70 very early in the morning.

We pulled into the Bend Hole on the Frying Pan just early enough to beat most of the crowd. The secret was out on the *Mysis*, and there were lots of folks crowding the river in hopes of catching one of the giant fish that grew to grotesque proportions by feeding on the *Mysis* soup spilling from the tubes.

We hastily rigged up with the new mysis tied to the end of a 9-foot leader tapering down to 5X. We attached a tiny split shot about a foot above the fly to keep the line taut and allow better control of the drift, even though the flies were going to be fished quite near the top. My previous trips had proven to me that the flies needed to be tied with the front of the shrimp at the hook eye, not at the bend like a scud pattern. Like I mentioned, all of the shrimp in the drift were facing upstream. By tying the fly oriented to the front of the hook, we could drift the flies down to the fish with the fly facing into the current just like the naturals. The split shot merely made manipulation of the leader a bit easier once the fly touched down and afforded a bit of sink should we need it. The drill was to spot a fish and stand upstream and slightly off to one side, cast the fly beyond the fish, and draw the leader tight to line the drift up so it ran straight down to the fish. Once the fly was lined up, you simply lowered the rod tip and fed the mysis down to the fish and hoped for the best. Fish were crashing the surface all over the place around us, and it was pretty nerve-wracking to try to gather your wits long enough to put together a game plan. When we finally got sorted out and positioned, we proceeded to waylay the fish at will. I recall Ross calling out, "Man! Look at the size of that brookie!"

(Pause)

"Got him!"

CHARLIE'S MYSIS

Hook:	#18 Tiemco 9300
Thread:	White 8/0 Uni-Thread
Body:	White egg yarn
Thorax:	White egg yarn dubbing
Eyes:	Black round rubber legs (small or fine)
Guts:	Orange marker
Note:	McFly Foam will not work for this pattern.

It was that easy. Find the fish, line him up and hook him. I have never had a fly that was as effective as the new mysis was that day.

The new pattern was the spitting image of the real thing, and the combination of the realism of the fly and the position of the drift worked out to a day full of bent rods and high fives. Ross and I each caught a pile of fish, some of which were embarrassingly large. I still have a faded, slightly out-of-focus 3x5 photo of Ross clutching an enormous brown trout from that day in my journal, and every time I look at it I recall that great day when we had it all figured out. Sometimes education happens outside the classroom.

TYING THE CHARLIE'S MYSIS

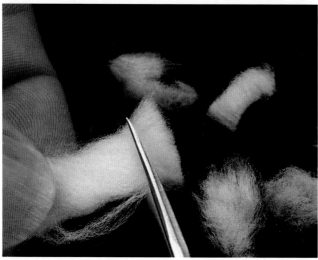

1. Wash your hands thoroughly. Even the slightest amount of dirt or oil on your fingers can discolor the materials. Once your hands are clean and dry, begin by clipping a strand of plain white egg yarn into quarter-inch lengths.

2. Put the cut-up egg yarn chunks into a Ziploc bags with a few holes punched in it. Place the nozzle of a bottle of canned air into the top of the bag and close the zipper down around it tightly.

3. Blast a long shot of air through the yarn to mix it into useable dubbing. You can now see why you needed to poke some holes in the bag.

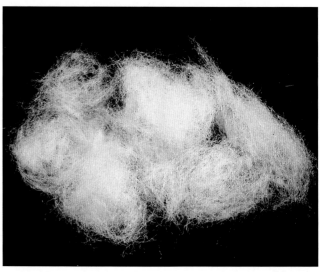

4. Now you ought to have a nice little ball of egg yarn dubbing.

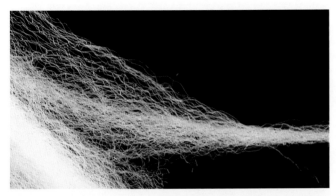

5. Grab another strand of the egg yarn and peel several fibers from the side, drawing them away from the main clump. Roll the strands in your fingertips as you draw it away from the main clump to extrude a long, thin strand.

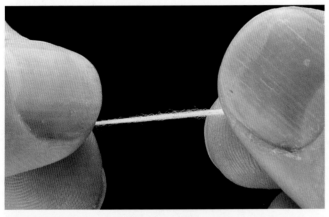

6. Grab either end of the smaller strand in each hand and roll the ends in opposite directions. This will help to cord the fibers into a single strand. Set the strand aside for the time being. I usually make several strands to have at the ready ahead of time.

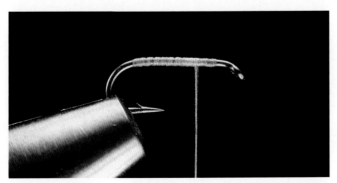

7. Clamp the hook in the vise. Start the tying thread just behind the hook eye and wrap a thread base back to the bend. Return the thread to about three eye lengths back from the eye.

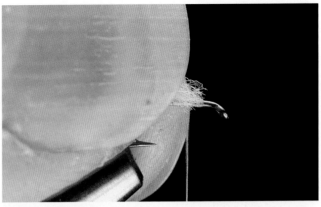

8. Clip the tapered end from the smaller strand of yarn and capture the end at the front of the hook with two firm wraps of thread.

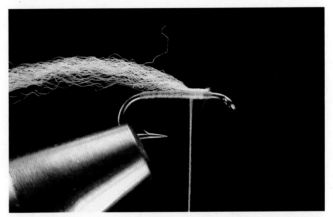

9. Form a short band of thread over the front of the yarn to anchor it in place on the top of the hook.

10. Hold the end of the yarn above the hook shank and wrap the thread back over it to the bend, taking care to keep it centered on the top of the shank. You may need to hold the yarn slightly toward your near side as you wrap back over it so the thread torque will bring it to the top of the hook.

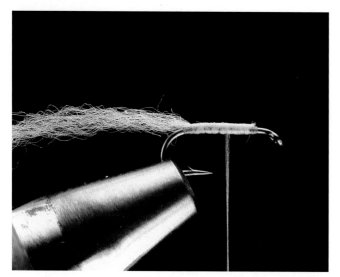

11. Return the thread to the point shown above.

12. Loosely dub the thread with a thin layer of the egg yarn dubbing you prepared earlier. Wrap the bare thread back to the hook bend so that the first turn of dubbing will be right in front of the hook bend. Use an orange marker to put a small dot of color on the thread base on the top of the middle of the hook. *Mysis* shrimp sometimes have a slight orangeish-colored smudge inside their thorax, and this little spot of marker can replicate it well. I consider this step optional, but always have a few in my box with the spot, just in case.

13. Wrap the dubbing forward from the bend to just short of the eye forming a slightly tapered, loosely dubbed thorax.

14. Make a few turns of thread just behind the eye to create a thread base and then lay a single strand of black rubber leg material across the hook at an angle in front of the dubbing. Catch the rubber leg with two diagonal wraps of thread. I use a pinch wrap here to help catch the soft rubber strand more easily.

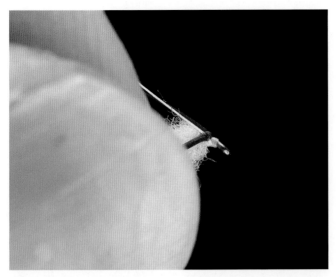

15. Pull the near side of the rubber leg back along the shank and make two more firm wraps in the opposite direction of the first wraps. You are essentially tying in the rubber legs like a set of spinner wings, using X wraps to secure them. You want the wraps to be tight and compact across the center of the strand.

16. Detail of rubber leg tie-in. Note the small thread X at the center of the rubber leg strand and that the strand is now perpendicular to the hook shank.

17. Build a small thread head in front of the rubber legs and whip-finish and clip the thread. Clip the ends of the rubber leg strand close to the shank, leaving just enough to imitate the small black eye of the natural.

18. Use a Barr Dubbing Teaser to pick out some of the dubbing along the bottom of the fly. The barbed needle of Barr's Teaser works great for selective roughening like this. Note that I have slightly bent the tip of this tool to allow better access to the underside of the shank.

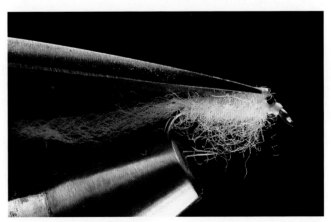

19. Trim off the fibers from the top of the fly flush with the top of the shank.

20. Trim the back end of the fly so it is about two shank-lengths long. This is longer than most naturals, but I always tie them like this and trim them to match the naturals when I am on the water. You can always make them shorter, but you can't make them any longer than they are now.

21. Charlie's Mysis after a short swim. The egg yarn presents an ultra-realistic texture when wetted and the balance of opacity and translucence work wonderfully to allow the orange marker guts to show through the overbody.

EIGHT

Wiggle Damsel

Damselfly nymphs live in ponds, lakes, and slow-moving sections of streams, and typically emerge during the summer. The delicate nymphs migrate en masse from the weed beds to the shoreline to crawl out and emerge into their adult form on dry land. This emergence can create a feeding frenzy among any fish in the area, such as bass, trout, or panfish. I have even caught small northern pike on damsel nymphs, much to my surprise. These slight nymphs range in size from about a half inch to an inch or so long and have delicate abdomens and prominent eyes protruding from hammer-shaped heads. Their legs drape back along their bodies as they swing their abdomen and tails for propulsion, creating a dramatic wiggle as they forge toward the safety of shore. Damsels are most commonly olive to green in color but can range widely within that

The Wiggle Damsel is simple to tie and wonderfully mimics the movement of the natural.

spectrum, from a pale yellowy olive all the way to a dark, nearly blackish olive. I have also encountered damsels that are more of a tan color as well, perhaps indicating their former living area was a sandy bottom rather than a green weed bed.

While many tiers would point out the prominent eyes of the damsel as their most compelling feature, I would disagree and have to name their abdomen-wiggling method of forward motion as their most important characteristic. A damsel swims like no other insect I have seen. More like a snake sliding through the water with a side-to-side swing of its tail, the damsel can move forward quickly and efficiently with little apparent effort. Its darting motion has sometimes made me mistake them for small minnows at first glance.

I have always been intrigued by damselfly nymph patterns. It seems every tier you talk to and every shop you go in has their own unique take on the pattern, and while some are similar, no two seem to be alike. There seem to be several schools of thought regarding the important parts of this bug, whether it's the conspicuous eyes or the dainty slimness that the natural possesses. Some tiers strive to replicate the bug perfectly, and at least one pattern out there is an absolute dead-on realistic ringer for the actual bug. Unfortunately, this model-building replica has about the same amount of movement as a toothpick in the water and therefore doesn't produce nearly as well as one would hope.

The other end of the spectrum ranges as far off as the ubiquitous Woolly Bugger, fished slowly and just under the surface. The bugger takes its share of fish as well, but it seems that it typically works best when the fish are so hot on the damsels that they would eat just about anything moving the right direction. Even when tied sparsely, these flies appear much more bulky than the naturals.

Somewhere in the middle, where the truth always lies, are several popular patterns from some of the best fly designers out there. Randall Kaufmann's Damsel is a simple marabou affair that plays from the impressionistic school of thought and possesses both good movement and slimness in a simple chassis. John Barr's Damsel is just a bit more advanced, with a more realistic shellback and eyes and a flowing marabou tail that adds some of the requisite wiggle to a pattern like this. All of these patterns will work at one time or another, and some of them seem to do the job nearly all the time, whether there are damsels coming off or not.

Many years ago I was asked to put together a batch of new damsel nymphs for a fishing lodge here in Colorado. Their guides had been using all the standard patterns, and it seemed the fish had become wise to them. Marty Cecil called me up and asked for something "a little different" that might turn their heads. Getting a call like this is something I've gotten used to over the years, and I am a firm believer in showing the fish something different, especially after the standard patterns have started to fade in effectiveness. I liked the look of many of the standard patterns and have always had a hard time arguing with the addition of eyes so I knew my new damsel would feature them in one form or another. One of the shortcomings common to all the other patterns I was familiar with was that they were all tied on a long-shanked, rigid hook. Real damsels bend in their middle with that side-to-side action, and this movement just couldn't be replicated with a fixed body on a stiff hook. I tried several different methods of making an extended body, some of which held promise even if they took entirely too long to produce. Knotting several individual strands of marabou together to create the abdomen and tail portion of the fly made for a body that would sway up and down on the retrieve, but the time it took to make and the huge lack of durability made me quickly abandon this idea.

The pattern that I eventually came up with actually came about pretty quickly. Joining two hooks together with monofilament (and now fluorocarbon for durability) made for an articulated chassis, and the marabou used for the body was both commonly available and easy to use. I particularly liked that I could keep the bodies slim while retaining the subtle movement from the waving herls. The addition of the bead chain eyes came after my original use of small plastic bead eyes. The metal eyes added just a tiny bit of weight and made the fly jig on the retrieve. I still tie some with the plastic eyes in the event that I'm fishing over the top of tall weeds or in very shallow water. The metal eyes are just heavy enough to jig the head of the pattern and get the fly down to the fish's level quickly when sight fishing. My Wiggle Damsel came out exactly as I had hoped. This fly has great action in the water and swims like the natural, is quick and easy to tie, and uses readily available materials. I have sort of a thing for flies that use just a few materials, and with the exception of the hooks and thread there are but three on this pattern: marabou, bead chain eyes, and tippet material. Even with the most basic tying skills, this fly is a cinch.

I most typically tie the Wiggle Damsel on size 14 hooks, although I usually have a few tied on 16s just in case. I originally used a ring-eyed 94859 Mustad hook for the rear portion of the fly because it was so cheap, but the bigger sizes have become unavailable over the years, and I have had to begrudgingly upgrade to some more premium brands to get the same configuration in the larger sizes. I currently use a #14 Tiemco 101 for the rear hook and snip the bend off with a pair of dikes. It just about kills me to use an expensive high quality hook like the Tiemco only to cut the important business end off, but I have yet to find an adequate substitute.

I use a 1X heavy 1X long Tiemco 3761 nymph hook for the front end of the fly and leave the point intact because you must have something to hook the fish with. This hook is stout enough for large fish and heavier tippets, and when it is coupled with the shank of the 101 is just about the perfect length to match most damsels.

FISHING THE WIGGLE DAMSEL

I prefer to fish my Wiggle Damsel on a floating or intermediate line over weed beds or edges where trout can pick off the strays during a damsel emergence. I most often use a slow, steady retrieve, bumping the fly along with 6- to 12-inch strips. One of the best pieces of advice I ever got on fishing damsels was, however, to vary your retrieve until you find something that works. Don't be afraid to mix it up with a few long strips, short and fast jabs, or try shaking the rod tip side to side while lifting the line. I've had good success with all of these methods, and the more I experiment, the more I'm convinced that it can't hurt to try them.

My preferred method of fishing damsels involves a high bank, perhaps a dam, and clear water that I can spot the cruising fish in. Sight fishing to cruising trout is some of the best visual fun an angler can have. I try to keep from blind fishing when I have good sight-fishing conditions so I can work the whole cast, retrieve, and bite out ahead of time. Spotting a cruiser patrolling an edge prompts a long cast to intercept the fish. The gamble in this type of fishing is that you really need to cast to where the fish is going rather than to where it is. The fly needs to enter the water softly and sink at the proper rate to get down to the trout's level without burying

itself in the weeds, so the cast and fly placement can be crucial. Of course, sometimes the fish simply changes direction and your cast ends up worthless, but sooner or later you'll get one lined up just right. I like my fly to be down to the proper level in the water column when the fish approaches it, so the trout simply encounters my fly as it glides up with a steady strip. Reading the fish's body language as its tail flicks, its fins light up, and it races toward its perceived meal is one of the best moments in fishing.

A good piece of advice, particularly when sight fishing damsels to cruising trout, is to set the hook when you see the fish rush the fly. Many anglers, myself once included, wait for the fish to grab the fly and change directions like you might with a streamer pattern. Trout can easily overrun a damsel nymph, and they often take them in midstride and just keep going. When you see the wake coming at your fly, the fish has generally already got it. File that away for your next damsel day . . . it could come in really handy.

WIGGLE DAMSEL

Hooks:	#14 or 16 Tiemco 101 for the rear hook and a #14 Tiemco 3761 for the front hook
Thread:	Pale olive 6/0 Danville
Body/Head/Wing:	Pale-olive marabou
Eyes:	Black bead chain (extra small)
Connection:	3X fluorocarbon tippet
Note:	You can change the thread color and marabou to match naturals in your favorite stillwater.

TYING THE WIGGLE DAMSEL

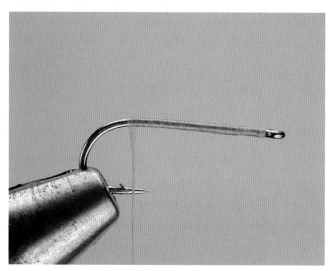

1. Place the Tiemco 101 in the vise and start the thread just behind the eye. Wrap back to the bend, forming a smooth thread base. Leave the thread hanging at the bend.

2. Select a marabou feather with nice full fibers and peel a small clump off the side of the stem.

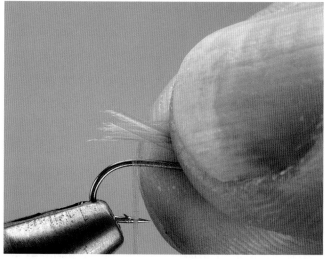

3. Break the tips off the marabou feather with your thumbnail. The natural tips of the feather are pretty delicate and quite difficult to even up. Breaking them off will leave ragged ends that are relatively square and much more durable. Measure these tips against the hook shank so they are about a half shank long.

4. Lay the marabou in at the hook bend and capture it above the hook barb with two firm wraps of thread. Make these two turns one right on top of the other with twisted thread so they don't spread out.

5. Lift the butt ends of the marabou up and back while you bring the thread in front of the strands. Wrap the thread forward up the shank to the hook eye.

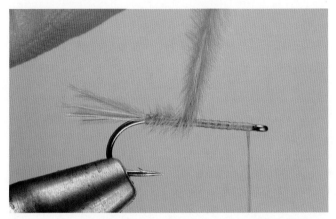

6. Begin wrapping the marabou up the hook shank. Try to keep the fibers from twisting up into a rope as you wrap. You want them to lay flat on the shank so the flues stand out from the shank. Continue wrapping the marabou all the way to the hook eye and tie it off there. There should be a very slight taper to the body resulting from the tapered flues on the marabou feather.

7. Clip the excess marabou, build a smooth thread head over the butts, and whip-finish the thread.

8. Clip the bend off the hook with a pair of wire cutters. Look away when you do this so you don't end up with the pointy part of the hook stuck in your eye or anything. Try to clip the hook bend off as close as you can to the base of the marabou tail. Set the rear portion of the fly aside for the time being and be careful not to lose it.

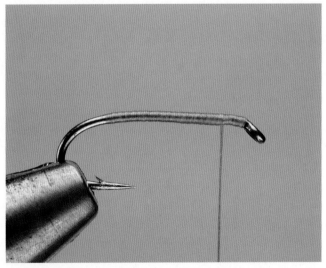

9. Place the Tiemco 3761 in the vise and start the thread just behind the eye. Wrap a thread base back to the bend and return the thread to the 85 percent point.

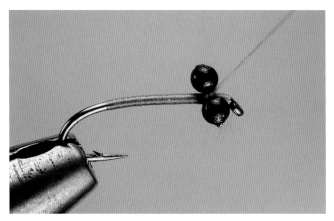

10. Clip a pair of bead chain eyes from the strand. Place the eyes on the hook at the 85 percent point and bind them in place. Start on the backside of the eyes and make three or four turns from the near back side to the front far side.

11. Now make three or four more tight wraps from the near front side to the back far side to lock the eyes in place.

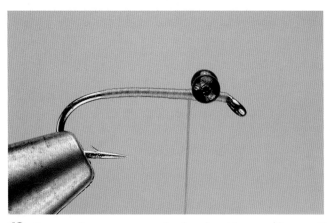

12. Square the eyes up on the hook with your fingers if needed. No glue is necessary.

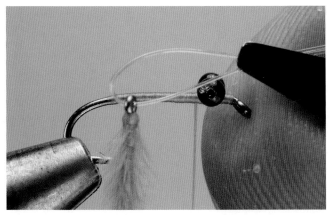

13. Pick up the rear portion of the fly that you set aside in a safe place earlier. Cut an inch-long section of tippet from the spool and thread one end through the eye of the trailer hook so you have the rear portion dangling on a loop as shown here.

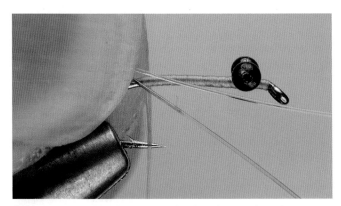

14. Return the thread to the hook bend and capture both the loose ends of the loop with a couple soft turns of thread. Pull the front ends of the mono down so the loop is just barely longer than the inside of the hook bend.

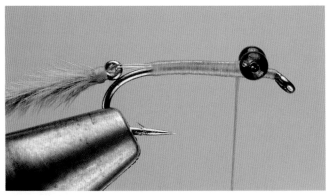

15. Clip the loose ends of the mono just short of the eyes and wrap forward over them with tight wraps. Return the thread to the hook bend.

16. Peel another small clump of marabou fibers from the stem and break their ends off like you did before. Tie the marabou in at the bend of the front hook with two stacked wraps of thread. The tips of this second clump of marabou should extend to just behind the thread head on the rear hook.

17. Lift the butt ends of the marabou and bring the thread forward on the shank.

18. Bring the thread all the way up to the hook eye.

19. Begin wrapping the marabou up the shank as you did on the rear portion of the fly. Wrap all the way up to the back of the eyes and cross between the eyes along the bottom of the hook on the near side of the shank.

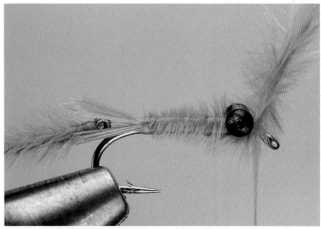

20. Bring the butt ends of the marabou up above the hook in front of the eyes . . .

21. . . . and cross back over the eyes on the top of the shank.

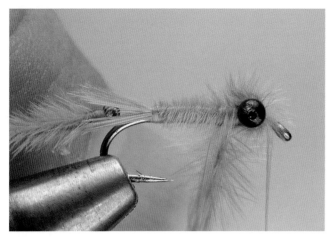

22. Bring the marabou down on the far side of the hook behind the eyes . . .

23. . . . and forward again to the front of the eyes via the underside of the shank. Tie the marabou off with two tightly stacked turns of thread.

24. Cross the thread over the top of the eyes to the point shown.

25. Make a single turn of thread around the shank over the marabou body.

26. Pull the remaining butt ends of the marabou back between the eyes on the top of the hook.

27. Bind the marabou in place with two tight turns of thread. Be sure to only use two turns here to minimize bulk.

28. Whip-finish the thread right on top of where you tied down the marabou. Clip the thread.

30. Wet the tip of your finger and sweep the fibers back along the top of the head around the eyes.

29. Pull the leftover marabou butts forward and trim them even with the front edge of the hook eye.

31. Finished fly. Note how the tail on the front hook covers the junction between the hooks. Overall profile is very thin.

NINE

Soft Hackle Emerger

nticipation is one of the best parts of any fishing trip, and today was no exception. I found myself standing waist deep in the Arkansas River holding the raft while my friends Ross and Larry parked the truck. I dragged the boat away from the ramp and hurriedly tried to gather my gear and get somewhat organized for the 14-mile float we had planned. I set about rigging my rod with an indicator and pair of caddis pupae while I waited for the guys to return. It was a warm morning, and while I was setting up, I waded out to wet down my waders before we set off. I always try to take at least a few minutes to look around and observe any fish or bug activity, and today I saw very little of either. A few random mayfly spinners here and there, a caddis or two flitting about, but nothing I could really get a read on as far as giving me a heads up for what to expect for the day.

The Fluoro Fibre wing and tail of my Soft Hackle Emerger make it an incredible fish catcher, yet it is still one of my most overlooked patterns.

We had made this trip in hopes of catching the famed Mother's Day Caddis hatch, and it looked like we might just run into some hatching bugs on the lower end of the float. We hoped to find the fish in the upper reaches feeding on caddis pupae and had a palpable excitement for what was to come.

We launched the boat around 8 A.M. and set off down the fast-moving chutes, drifting our pupae patterns along the banks and in likely pockets. I got a full half dozen casts in before my luck ran out and I hung the whole rig up on the river bottom, breaking off everything but the indicator. I reeled in and took a moment to reconsider my options. The Ark is a fast-moving, broken-water river with a huge population of medium-sized (and bigger) brown trout, with an occasional much-larger rainbow thrown in to keep your attention. The character of the broken currents and pocketwater made me decide to change up my rig to the then-new hopper-copper-dropper rig of which I had become so fond. It takes a leap of faith to bag the rig recommended by a guide with Larry's experience, and I was glad I was in the back of the boat where Larry couldn't witness my impending mutiny.

I switched my leader out to a short, 6-foot 3X version and knotted a large Charlie Boy Hopper to the end to act as the indicator. Given the lack of surface activity, I was hesitant to put on a dry of any sort, but reasoned that as long as I was going to have something floating in the water, it may as well have a hook in it, just in case. I dropped about four feet of 4X fluorocarbon tippet off the bend of the hopper and tied on a heavily weighted tungsten bead CDC Golden Stone nymph to get the flies down quickly and drifting low and slow through the seams and pockets.

When I got to the dropper fly, I perused my fly box, scanning for something to jump out at me. One of the problems with carrying as many flies as I do is the mind-bending decision that must be made every time I re-rig. We had seen very little bug activity so far and I was having a hard time coming up with a reasonable thought process to put fish on the line. Then I remembered the spinners I saw at the put-in. While I really didn't know what species of bug they were and frankly had just given them a passing glance, I recalled that they were rather large and gray in color. Scanning my fly box, my gaze settled upon a pair of #16 Soft Hackle Emergers tucked in among the rows of the same pattern in much smaller

sizes. I think I had tied these two flies specifically to photograph for the fly-tying section of my website, and the oversized flies stuck out among their brethren like a couple of watermelons in a box of apples.

Now keep in mind that the boat had continued to drift this whole time, and every moment I spent re-rigging and re-thinking my choices was time without a fly in the water. Ross had caught two fish already, and even though we are the best of friends and I love the guy, I know better than to let him get too far ahead. I grabbed one of those big Soft Hackle Emergers and tied it to a 12-inch dropper off the back of the stonefly nymph, reasoning that it could possibly pass for one of those big spinners that had drowned and washed into the current.

I confidently flipped the rig out into the water announcing "I'm back in!" as if Larry and Ross were waiting on pins and needles for me to get my act back together. I was answered with some smart aleck comment to the tune of "It's about time. We thought you fell out."

Jerks.

We all laughed at the start of the trash talking for the day, and I was now not only behind in fish but lagging woefully in the smack talk category as well. The hopper-copper-dropper rig turned out to be a good choice for this type of water, and the heavy stone dove deep quickly, pulling the emerger down along with it into each seam and pocket. I immediately started hooking fish to the point where it became a distraction for my fishing partners. Each cast put the nymphs slightly downstream of the boat with enough slack to drop straight down along the edges of every productive looking spot. The hopper landed lightly on the water and was more than buoyant enough to keep the flies drifting at the right level. The combination of the heavy stone nymph and buoyant hopper kept the tippet between them taut and poised to shudder the hopper at any indication of a take. I became Zen-like, shooting the rig out, letting the flies sink, periodically throwing a mend, and more often than not a twitching hopper gave away the presence of a brown trout that had the same idea about that Soft Hackle Emerger that I did. I continued raking fish into the boat, much to the chagrin of my previously, and mistakenly, confident boat mates.

I finally gave in and turned the other Soft Hackle Emerger over to Ross, clueing him in to the rig I had cobbled together and helping to set up his rod to match. We proceeded down the river with renewed vigor and

A Hebert medium blue dun hen cape from Whiting Farms provides long, soft hackling for my Soft Hackle Emerger.

that sense of eagerness from the morning was justly rewarded. Fish after fish chased down the emerger, although in this case I'm certain that the fish recognized the fly as a drowned spinner, a theory I had been cogitating on for several years.

The flat folded wing and slender body of this fly were originally designed as an emerging mayfly pattern as the name suggests. I had developed it back in my guiding days as an alternative to the South Platte River favorite, the RS2. My reasoning back then was that I wanted something that presented a similar silhouette but was just different enough to stand out from what all the other guide's clients were throwing. The Platte could be a somewhat crowded piece of water back then, given that it is a world class fishery within an hour or so of a major metropolitan area. Having a little ace up your sleeve always seems to pay off, and so I always try to mix things up a bit for pressured fish. The initial versions of this fly were tied in the ever-present small South Platte River size range of 18-22 and had proven to be just what I had hoped for: just enough of a difference from the RS2 to turn a jaded fish's head, but still similar enough to make it recognizable. Given that the RS2 is an emerger pattern, and coupled with my exemplary fly naming skills, I took the fact that I had added a soft hen neck hackle collar and longer wing and came up with the extraordinarily creative name of Soft Hackle Emerger.

I fished this fly for several years with the impression in my head that it was imitating an emerging *Baetis* nymph or cripple. Typically tied to a length of 5X tippet under an indicator, the SHE produced fish often enough to become a staple in my box. In the years since the fly's origination, it has bounced around the back of my head that I may have stumbled on to something that is entirely different from what I had originally planned.

I have since learned that female *Baetis* spinners don't fall upon the water's surface and die like most other mayfly spinners; they instead crawl down into the water to lay their eggs. I recall fishing a section of the South Platte one day with two of my favorite clients. Each time they would back out of the water to land a fish, their wader legs were covered with spinners migrating down toward their feet and into the water. Literally hundreds of small, grayish-colored spinners would be lined up in formation on the wader legs. I found it interesting that the spinners preferred the dark-green-colored waders that my clients wore to the tan waders that I did. Perhaps it was simply that I was in and out of the water much more than the clients were—or perhaps they really do prefer green?

It was much later that I finally put the pieces together. It was while I was working with John Barr on *Barr Flies* that he related to me the phenomenon of the drowned spinner. His research had indicated this unusual fact about *Baetis* spinners and when he related this to me the lights went on. Generally speaking, when I hear about something like this my mind immediately sets about trying to design a pattern to imitate it, but in this case, it occurred to me that I already had! Flashing back to the formations of spinners crawling down my clients, I remembered the neatly folded wings sloped back over the bodies, and the glistening aura produced by the air bubble they capture for the trip down. Shazam! My little Soft Hackle "Emerger" had most likely been imitating these drowned spinners all along. The longer Fluoro Fibre wing I had employed created just the right bit of shine as well as the profile of the naturals' folded wings. The sparse soft hackle collar must have been imitating the insects' legs, all askew as they fell into the drift once dropping their eggs. I have never felt so smart and so dumb at the same time.

I later changed the tail on my pattern from split Microfibetts to a few strands of white Fluoro Fibre with the reasoning that the crumpled soft appearance would go further toward the goal of matching a real spinner.

I still fish the SHE as an emerger pattern from time to time, simply because I have developed so much confidence in it, but most often I knot it to my leader whenever I see any amount of spinner activity, particularly in the early mornings. And while I most often include this pattern in a hopper-copper-dropper rig, I have more recently taken to fishing it dry, or at least damp, behind a more visible pattern like a Parachute Adams. The SHE sits flush in the surface film, sometimes on its side, which can replicate the position of the naturals quite well. I do not apply floatant to the fly, as I prefer to let it hang just ever so slightly below the surface. This technique works particularly well when fish are rising randomly because I believe they get used to seeing these drowned spinners in the drift and know what they are. An added bonus to fishing the fly near the surface is that you still can see the rise and take in many cases.

The SHE is really a simple little pattern that found greatness well after its misdirected inception. It requires little in the way of sophisticated tying skills, and perhaps its most important feature is its slimness. Real spinners are slight and lean, generally as skinny as the hook shank alone, so be sure to keep your patterns thin to better match this bony profile.

I have since added additional color variations to the Soft Hackle Emerger to better replicate other mayfly spinners and emergers. Pale Morning Duns are known to hatch out under the water's surface and swim, in their adult form, to the surface. A pale yellow-bodied Soft Hackle Emerger has proven deadly for me during PMD hatches, and the pattern matches the bedraggled look of the naturals like a mirror. I also tie the SHE in a rusty brown color as well to match the prolific "rusty spinners" we have out here. I know there are several species of mayflies that turn various shades of brown when they molt into spinners, and the darker version seems to fit this bill precisely. I even have some friends who have tied this pattern in all black to use as a small caddis emerger on rivers like Montana's Bighorn with good success. The old-school, wet-fly profile this fly presents seems to bring a bit of the past into the present.

SOFT HACKLE EMERGER

Hook:	#16-24 Tiemco 101 or 100SP-BL
Thread:	Gray 8/0 Uni-Thread
Tail:	White Fluoro Fibre
Abdomen:	Gray muskrat or beaver dubbing
Wing:	White Fluoro Fibre
Hackle:	Blue-dun hen neck
Thorax:	Gray muskrat or beaver dubbing

TYING THE SOFT HACKLE EMERGER

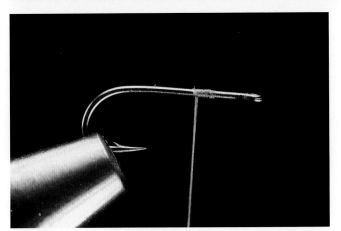

1. Clamp the hook in the vise, and start the thread at the point shown above, but don't wrap back very far. We're about to tie the tail in and we want to keep the thread base to a minimum, so I will show you a little trick to help with that.

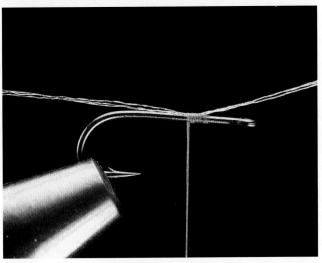

2. Tie in three strands of white Fluoro Fibre at the starting point. Be sure to leave the butt ends long at the front of the hook.

3. Fold the butt ends back and wrap over them to anchor the Fluoro Fibre in a loop.

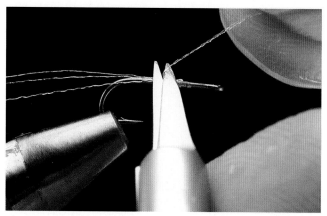

4. Clip off the butt ends of the Fluoro strands just behind where you tied them down. Folding the strands like this will prevent the slick fibers from pulling out later. Leave the thread hanging just forward of midshank.

5. Dub the thread with a very thin strand of dubbing. Leave a bit of bare thread between the hook and the start of the dubbing. Use the bare thread to wrap back over the remaining three strands of Fluoro Fibre to the hook bend.

6. Make sure the Fluoro Fibre stays on the top of the shank as you wrap back, and the first turn of dubbing should occur right at the hook bend. I try to keep this fly very thin and this two-for-one tie-in technique works to that end. Make that first turn of dubbing at the bend and work forward again to the starting point, making a thin, smooth, level body.

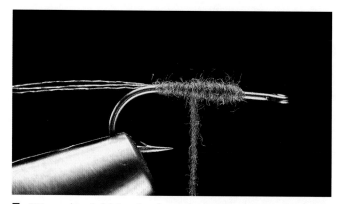

7. Wrap the dubbing back to the midpoint on the body for a second layer on the front half of the abdomen.

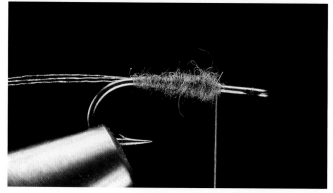

8. Work the dubbing forward again to the starting point, finishing off the taper at the front edge of the abdomen. You want a nice thin taper from the base of the tail up to the 80 percent point.

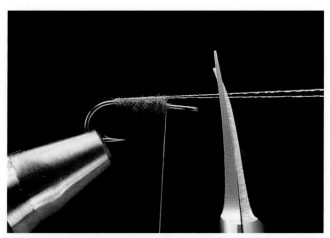

9. Pull the Fluoro Fibre tails forward over the shank and trim them just beyond the hook eye.

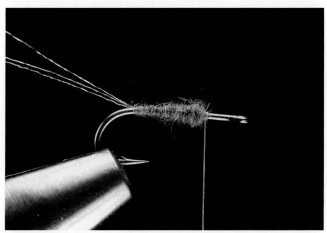

10. You should now have a relatively long tail splayed out across the back of the hook. I don't worry about splitting or otherwise adjusting the tails on this fly, as the Fluoro is so soft that this would be pointless.

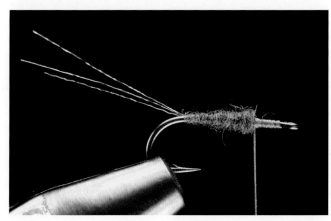

11. Wrap the thread from the front edge of the abdomen up to the hook eye and back again, creating a thread base for the wing that is to come.

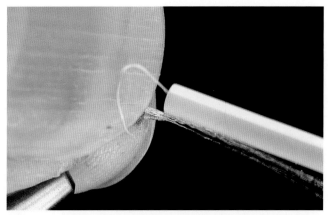

12. Clip 12 to 15 fibers from the Fluoro clump and tie them in at the center of their length at the front of the abdomen. Using a pinch or loose wrap here will help keep the material centered on top of the hook shank. Make a few turns moving forward over the Fluoro to anchor things down.

13. It should look like this when tied in.

14. Pull the long front end of the Fluoro Fibre back over the top of the fly and grasp it along with the backward facing half. If you just tie in a heavier clump and clip the butts, the wing *will* pull out later. With the loop, the wing is anchored securely.

15. Wrap back over the looped portion of the Fluoro Fibre at the base of the body, stacking the front and back halves of the wing into one unit. Don't worry about the length of the wing just yet.

16. Clip the fibers from the base of a hen neck feather that has fibers equal to about 1½ hook gaps, leaving the short bristles to help secure the feather to the hook.

17. Tie in the hen feather by the trimmed butt end at the front edge of the body with the outside of the feather facing you or forward and the inside facing away or toward the shank.

18. Grab the tip of the feather in your hackle pliers and hold the tip taut above the hook with your thread hand. Wet the tips of your thumb and index finger on your material hand. Close your fingers in a circle around the feather (with the tips of your fingers meeting in front of, not on, the feathers) and draw the feather forward with the pliers while you draw your fingers back, stroking the hackle to the backside of the stem. Pull down slightly on the feather fibers to crease them to the backside of the stem.

19. The nicely folded hen feather has fibers swept back to the rear of the feather stem. You don't need to fold much feather here, just enough to make two or three turns around the hook.

20. Make the first turn with the feather at the front edge of the abdomen. I prefer to use hackle pliers to wrap hen neck feathers because they are typically too short to wrap comfortably by hand and the pliers allow better placement of the hackle turns.

21. Make one or two more turns of hackle in front of the first turn for a total of no more than three. Tie the feather off at the front of the wraps with two tight turns of thread.

22. Clip the excess feather tip.

23. Reach in with your thread hand and push the hackle fibers back along the hook shank, taking care to keep them evenly distributed around the hook shank. Pinch the fibers down tightly against the shank to sweep them back.

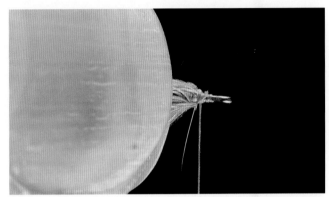

24. Hold the fibers back along the shank with your thread hand while you reach in with your material hand and transfer them. Keep the fibers distributed around the shank while you hold them in place. Squeeze the base of the hackle tightly to help crimp the fibers back.

25. Without letting go of the fibers, make several turns of thread back slightly over the base of the hackle to hold the fibers in place.

26. You just want the fibers to sweep back, not to be pinned flat against the body.

27. Dub another thin strand of dubbing and start wrapping it with the first turn right behind the hook eye. Work the dubbing back to the base of the wing.

28. Return the dubbing to the hook eye, forming the thorax. The back of the thorax should be a bit thicker than the front edge of the abdomen and taper back down to the eye.

29. Make a few tight turns of thread behind the eye and whip-finish the thread. Trim the thread. Trim the back of the wing even with the outside of the hook bend.

SOFT HACKLE EMERGER (BLACK)

Hook:	#16-24 Tiemco 101 or 100SP-BL
Thread:	Black 8/0 Uni-Thread
Tail:	White Fluoro Fibre
Abdomen:	Black muskrat or beaver dubbing
Wing:	White Fluoro Fibre
Hackle:	Blue-dun hen neck
Thorax:	Black muskrat or beaver dubbing

SOFT HACKLE EMERGER (PMD)

Hook:	#16-24 Tiemco 101 or 100SP-BL
Thread:	Light cahill 8/0 Uni-Thread
Tail:	White Fluoro Fibre
Abdomen:	Pale yellow muskrat or beaver dubbing
Wing:	White Fluoro Fibre
Hackle:	Blue-dun hen neck
Thorax:	Pale yellow muskrat or beaver dubbing

SOFT HACKLE EMERGER (RUSTY)

Hook:	#16-24 Tiemco 101 or 100SP-BL
Thread:	Rusty brown 8/0 Uni-Thread
Tail:	White Fluoro Fibre
Abdomen:	Rusty brown muskrat or beaver dubbing
Wing:	White Fluoro Fibre
Hackle:	Blue-dun hen neck
Thorax:	Rusty brown muskrat or beaver dubbing

TEN

Mole Fly

Some friends of mine aren't going to be very happy seeing the Mole Fly in this book. Several of my fishing buddies have called me up or come to the shop to plead their cases about why I shouldn't include this fly in this book. Their reasonings are entirely selfish, but when I really sit down and think about it, I have to agree with them. I mean, if I were to let it get out that this simple little two-step fly is perhaps the most effective *Baetis* emerger pattern that any of us has ever fished, the world may become a different place. Who knows what could happen by releasing a pattern like this to the general population?

So with this in mind, I won't mention anything about how effective this fly can be during *Baetis* and even midge hatches. I won't say anything about how quick, easy, and cheap this fly is to tie, nor will I bring up the fact that this little fly has sometimes been referred to as "The Answer." No, none of that will come up here. I might mention a few stories and examples here and there, and maybe a few details on tying and fishing it,

If I had to pick only one fly to use on fish rising to *Baetis* or midges, the Mole Fly would be my hands-down choice.

but this will be just between us friends, and I'm sure you'll keep this close to your vest just like my buddies and I have over the last several years. We wouldn't want a secret weapon like this to fall into the wrong hands.

Seriously, I have kept this pattern a closely guarded secret over the many years since its inception. The effectiveness of this pattern astounds me to this day, and I have always feared it would become so popular that it would stop working its magic. I truly hope this doesn't become the case, and I include the pattern here because I have learned that it's not what you keep to yourself in life that counts, but what you share with others. Please reserve my spot in heaven now and forgive me for what I am about to do.

Here in Colorado we are blessed with a year-round fishing season. Several bottom-release reservoirs trailing cold, clear tailwater rivers are sprinkled throughout the state, and even in the depths of winter a die-hard angler has, at the very least, the opportunity to get out and fish dry flies at any time. From the end of summer through late spring, Blue-Winged Olives (aka BWO or *Baetis*) are one of the most common hatches. These little olive-gray mayflies range in size from about an 18 through a 24, and even a 26 can be pretty prolific here in Colorado. Given the right time of year and reasonable conditions, they can be a great source of food for the trout and entertainment for us fishermen.

Fall brings the best hatches of the year, and I look forward to the cooler, overcast days with a bit of rain spitting down, and sometimes even snow. The bugs seem to stay on the water trying to dry their wings during inclement weather, which leaves them exposed to feeding trout for longer periods. Of course, by autumn, most of our nearby rivers have been gone over a fair bit, and while the fish still need to put on the feedbag before winter, they have a summer's worth of learning under their belts too. These pressured fish are much harder to fool at the end of the year than at the beginning, and this trait coupled with the smaller size of the fall *Baetis* makes for some of the most technical fishing to be had.

I love challenging dry-fly fishing, and there is little I enjoy more than walking up to a river and seeing noses poking out along the subtle seams and edges. My BWO fly box is stuffed with hundreds of patterns and sizes, all tied to imitate the adult and emerger stages of this bug. Fishing hatches like this requires a variety of patterns in your box, as each fish may be feeding on a slightly different stage of the hatch, and it is wise and sometimes nec-essary to change the profile or shape of your fly if a fish has either inspected and rejected your fly or eaten your fly without getting hooked. Long leaders and casts are the norm for this type of fishing, and you must present the fly with a drag-free drift.

The small size and darker colors of these flies make them harder to see on the water, so misses are not all that uncommon. It's particularly frustrating to have picked out a fish, timed its rises, nailed down the right cast and fly pattern, and finally gotten everything lined up just right only to miss the fish as it rises up and eats the fly. The requisite slack in the leader, the angles of the casts, and the small size of the fly all work against you in situations like this. When it finally all comes together and you set the hook, only to have the leader float through the air back at your face, it can be some of the most frustrating fishing to be had. But I love it.

The saving grace of this type of hatch is that it tends to be repeatable. Once they start, the bugs hatch at nearly the same time every day for quite a while and can be counted on to pull the fisherman back to the water as much as he can get away with. Everyone wants a second chance. Each day that I fish this type of hatch, I lie in bed at night trying to fit one more piece into the puzzle. Whether it's playing with a new leader design, cleaning up my fly line, or sitting at the bench trying to spawn the next great fly, I become consumed for weeks at a time with this fishing.

I have fished the *Baetis* hatches in Cheesman Canyon on the South Platte River every fall since I was in high school. There has always been sort of an informal group of *Baetis* "junkies" collected at the bottom end of the canyon each year, and each of us is always trying to come up with the pattern that will work every time. Some of the patterns get pretty complicated, while others border on too simple. Cut wings, parachutes, and CDC patterns in a plethora of configurations have all been cast upon these waters with varying degrees of success. Sometimes a fly is tied with a particular tough fish in mind. You know, like that big rainbow that sits at the slot at the top of the run near the triangle-shaped rock picking off the cripples with one wing flapping—that kind of thing. Other flies are more general, and we anglers hope to throw the fly at enough fish to find the few that are looking for that exact profile.

It is this combination of cerebral activity, fly design, leader length, tippet size, and casting ability that brings me back to these fish every year. I may go out and only catch three fish on any given day, maybe ten if things go really well. The draw is not in the number of fish landed but the amount you can learn by observing and tweaking your tactics and patterns.

I recall fishing these hatches back in the day with a #20 Parachute Adams and having a fair share of success. Then the next year the fish would be a bit more selective and you'd have to change up to something smaller, darker, and more realistic. Patterns like the Comparadun and Sparkle Dun were always good choices. Flies like the No Hackle and various cripples became popular and effective. Some guys resorted to fishing a small nymph on a short dropper behind a dry, and that caught plenty of fish too, but in my opinion it wasn't what any of us hiked into the canyon to do. To be done right, these fish needed to be fooled with a fly on or in the surface, not under it. I want to beat them at their own game, and if they are eating the naturals from the surface, I want to catch them on a fly that is floating.

Then CDC feathers came around and changed everything. CDC is short for cul de canard—the soft, buoyant feathers surrounding the preen gland on a duck. These feathers float well but low in the water, move subtly in the current, and allow flies to be tied much more sparsely than conventionally hackled dry flies. Everyone began experimenting with these new feathers, and I was no exception. The quality of the CDC feathers available in those days was pretty low, but they allowed me to tie sparse little patterns that would still float well in the gentle currents, and they fooled fish better than any of the previous patterns. The cycle started all over again, with everyone tying and trying different little variations on the theme using CDC feathers in place of hackle and hair. Some of the most exciting advancements I had ever seen occurred within the progression of flies in the early 1990s. We finally figured out that the inherent buoyancy of the CDC feathers meant we could use less material than we would have on a hairwing or hackled fly. The flies became much more slender, easier to keep floating, and even a bit easier to find and follow on the water. The evolution of the patterns changed much over the years since then, and I always looked forward to fishing over selective fish with this new generation of flies in my vest.

One of the most compelling traits of a CDC feather is its versatility. It doesn't need to be wrapped like a hackle to be buoyant, nor does it need to be tied like a clump of hair to do the job. As long as the fibers are on the fly in some form, the fly can float reasonably well. It became sort of an all-purpose feather, taking the place of conventionally applied hair and hackle, and even branched off into its own standalone patterns.

The Loop Wing Emerger was developed during this same time period, using a loosely folded CDC feather as a "wing case" to replicate the bursting wing case of an emerging nymph. The material and placement set this fly low in the film but still visible on top, and it fooled selective fish consistently. I recall fishing my first versions on DePuy Spring Creek in Montana one summer and absolutely cleaning house with them. The picky spring creek trout became pushovers for this never-before-seen pattern, and my buddies and I enjoyed tremendous success with these new flies.

Over the years I realized that CDC flies could remain pretty simple affairs and didn't need to be dressed up with a lot of unnecessary details. The feather fibers themselves created a bit of soft movement to the fly while still providing great flotation. I continued tying and using various CDC flies for many years and was glad to have found such a great new material to work with.

A few years later, I was twisting up a batch of flies late at night for the next day. The *Baetis* were hatching heavily and the fish were well into the swing of things. I had been guiding a long string of trips and needed to refill my boxes with a fresh supply of emergers and cripples, so I was cranking out variations and stuffing them in my fly box. One of the catches with guiding the same water for several days and even weeks was that the fish could become wise to your fly patterns over time. I was always making small adjustments and tweaks to the patterns to keep them fresh, and was still chasing that perfect fly idea, so anything and everything that fell from the vise was fair game on the water the next day. In this quest I constantly changed the materials and hooks I used to tie the flies, hoping to simply alter the profile of the flies enough to make them seem a bit different. Many of these flies were simple, quick, and easy cripple and emerger patterns—some were on straight shanks, some on curved shanks, some with the looped wing, some with spent wings, and some tied Comparadun style. It was that night that I tied the first Mole Fly by accident and with no apparent fanfare. It was just another variation that I tied and stashed away in my fly box.

Now, fishing these hatches generally meant that I went through several patterns in the course of the day, and it was sometime later in the day that I finally pulled the new variation out and tied it on my tippet. I had already had a pretty good day, but there is always that one fish that just seems to outsmart you every time. This fish was a nice rainbow lying up tight against the far bank. He was sipping emergers with great regularity and had inspected each of the patterns I threw over him but was having none of it. I rummaged through my fly box and pulled out the new fly and knotted it to the long tippet. I cast the fly a foot ahead and a foot beyond his feeding lane and tugged the fly perfectly into position to drift right down his alley. The fly bobbed along smoothly with no hint of drag and the rainbow moved smugly up and confidently ate the fly. This was a great victory after having been snubbed by this fish on so many previous casts. To have the fish move so deliberately to the fly and eat it so confidently meant that there was something that looked alogether right to him. I win.

This fly became an integral part of my fly box for many years before I ever gave it a name. Since I really never intended to let this cat out of the bag, I figured a fly with no name would just make it that much easier. I discreetly tied and fished it for many years, thinking I had covertly come up with a new pattern that no one else would ever know about. A few years later I recall perusing an article written by John Betts on Advanced Wing Duns, a category of archaic patterns from old-time England. Right there in the article was the picture of a fly that so closely resembled my secret weapon that I just had to dig deeper. While the pictured fly was not exactly the same as my fly and had predated it by about a hundred years, the resemblance and design was uncanny. This fly was called the Mole Fly, after the River Mole in England. It was tied with a scruffy body and forward-facing duck quill wings. I was a bit deflated to find that I had somehow, unknowingly reinvented a hundred-year-old pattern, and so I dubbed the new fly with the same moniker in honor of its predecessor. The Mole Fly finally has a name, but that doesn't mean I'm gonna tell anyone about it.

FISHING THE MOLE FLY

In the years since, I have developed the theory that the Mole Fly works as well as it does because of the way the fly sits in the water. Tied on the curved-shank Tiemco 2487, the dark body sinks below the surface while the wing protrudes to the top, imitating the bug's emergent wings and showing up well to the fisherman. I prefer the down eye of the 2487 hook because it lets the fly sit correctly on the water, where a ring-eyed hook like the 2488 makes it sit more horizontally. I have tied this same fly on a straight-shanked hook, and it doesn't work as well, I believe, because the body doesn't sit in the surface the same way. I find that if I wet down the body of the fly with river water or saliva before casting it, I can count on it to sit on the water correctly right from the first cast. Once the fly has caught a few fish, the body gets slimed up and sinks readily. For this reason, I tie all my Mole Flies with natural fur dubbing like beaver or muskrat. These dubbings can be brushed out to create a loose shell of a body that will soak up a bit of water and sink just through the surface film. Using good quality CDC from TroutHunter in Idaho has also proven to be a key element in keeping this fly afloat. I always use natural-dun-colored CDC feathers on this fly now, as I have yet to find a need for anything else. I have also tied the Mole Fly with various other colors of dubbing and even a thread body but have always returned to the original version with brown beaver dubbing and a natural CDC wing.

The #20 has become my go-to pattern for any fish rising to adult *Baetis*, but I have tied this as big as a #10 and as small as a #24, all with good results. The bigger versions work well for Pale Morning Duns and even Green Drakes while the tiniest of the flies cross over well from *Baetis* to midges. I still find that I can usually get away with a #20 no matter what the actual size of the real bug is—even for Green Drakes, oddly enough. I think this is because of the telescopic nature of an emerging mayfly. As the nymph reaches the surface and splits its wing case, the adult starts to creep out, effectively increasing the size of the nymph. Think of overlapping half an adult mayfly over the front half of a nymph and you'll get the idea of the telescope theory. How far out of the shuck the adult has gotten will determine the overall length of the two attached bug stages. The nymphal husk is replicated by the loosely dubbed body hanging below the surface film, and the forward-facing CDC wing imitates the wings and thorax of the adult as it emerges from that shuck. I have always believed that trout only see what is right about a fly pattern and are never concerned with what might be wrong with it. Evidently, the CDC wing and dubbed body of the Mole Fly, coupled with the position of the fly on the water's surface, matches what the fish are hoping for perfectly.

People always ask me if I can actually see the Mole Fly on the water and I must admit that I am blessed with pretty good eyesight. I prefer to fish the Mole all alone on the end of a long, light tippet. A lot of my friends fish it behind a more visible fly like a Parachute Adams to make it a little easier to find.

CDC is an incredibly buoyant material but once wetted and matted down sinks like a wet sock. The trick to keeping your fly dry even after catching a few fish is to be sure to rinse and dry the fly after each one. I remove the fly from the fish, hold it in my forceps, and violently swish the fly back and forth in the water to rinse the fish slime from it. I then use a microfiber towel called a Wonder Cloth to buff the wing until it dries out and puffs

back up again. Then, I treat the wing with Tiemco Dry Magic, which is compatible with CDC, unlike some other treatments. I place a small drop on my fingertips and rub them together to liquefy the floatant before lightly applying it to just the wing of the fly. The Dry Magic keeps the CDC from becoming saturated far longer than the plain CDC would stay dry by itself. I can catch a half dozen fish before I have to start really working to dry the fly out. In a "worst"—case scenario, where I'm catching fish so fast that I can hardly keep up with maintaining the fly, I just cut off the wet one and tie on a fresh fly. Mole Flies are so simple to tie that there is no excuse not to have at least a couple dozen in your box at all times.

TYING THE MOLE FLY

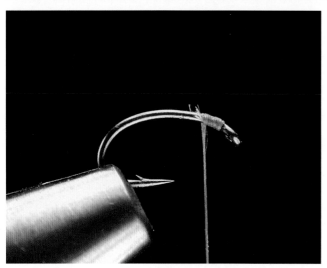

1. Clamp the hook in the vise. Start the thread immediately behind the hook eye and wrap a thread base back to the point shown above.

MOLE FLY

Hook:	#16-24 Tiemco 2487
Thread:	Gray 8/0 Uni-Thread
Wing:	Natural dun CDC
Body:	Brown beaver dubbing

2. Select a thick CDC feather with a thin stem.

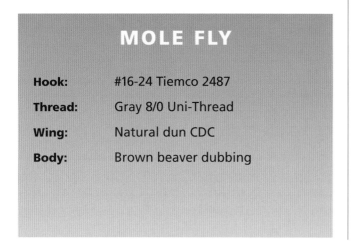

3. Pinch the tip of the feather down into a clump and tie it to the shank just behind the eye with two taut wraps of thread.

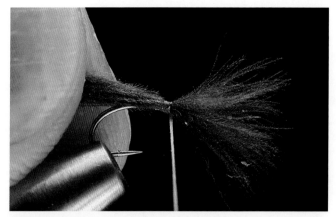

4. Hold the thread taut while you pull the butt ends of the feather back to shorten the wing down to about a shank-length long.

5. Anchor the measured wing with a few more tight wraps of thread. I try to make a narrow band of thread here to keep everything locked down.

6. Reach in from the back of the hook with the tips of your scissors and trim the butt of the feather off at a long angle.

7. Wrap down over the tapered butts of the wing all the way back to about halfway down the hook bend. Return the thread to the midpoint on the shank.

8. Dub a thin strand of beaver fur onto the thread leaving a bit of bare thread between the top of the dubbing strand and the hook. Use the bare thread to work back to the end of the thread base, making the first turn of dubbing about halfway down the hook bend.

9. Wrap the dubbed thread forward to the base of the wing, forming a slight taper as you work toward the front. The tapered butt ends of the wing will help build the taper up here, so you don't really need to overlap much of the dubbing.

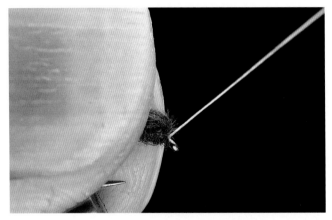

10. Preen the wing back along the hook shank and bring the thread to the front of the wing just behind the hook eye.

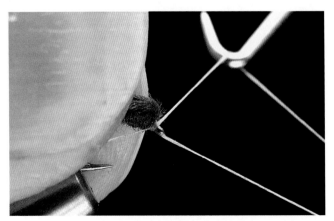

11. Hold the wing out of the way while you whip-finish the thread at the eye. Clip the thread.

12. Use a dubbing brush to roughen up the beaver fur body a bit. I like the dubbing to shag out so that it wets down more easily and sinks the back of the fly adequately.

13. Finished fly, side view.

14. Now, before you toss the butt end of the feather into the trash can, be aware that it can be used to tie at least one, and maybe two, more Mole Flies.

15. Clip the center stem of the feather only, leaving the V-shaped notch in the tip of the feather as shown here. This eliminates the thick stem so you just have the soft CDC fibers to work with. Clip the stem just a touch more than a shank length down from the tip of the feather.

17. The nature of CDC feather fibers allows you to use a feather for more than one fly with no ill effects.

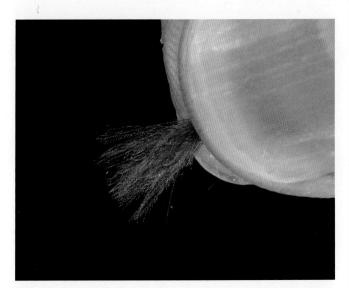

16. Bundle the tips and proceed to tie this secondary clump onto the shank for a second fly. Depending on the length and quality of the feather, you may be able to do this even one more time, yielding three flies from one feather.

ELEVEN

Mugly Caddis

As a fly tier, I pride myself on tying cleanly constructed patterns. Loose bits of dubbing, ragged wings, or disproportioned parts are not something you will find in my fly box or my bag of tricks. As a matter of fact, I have been known to spend an inordinate amount of time stacking and re-stacking hair wings or trimming individual hairs out of spun deer hair bugs to perfect their shapes. I am a bit of a Type A kind of guy and patterns like this Mugly Caddis are, I assure you, not the norm for me. The Mugly Caddis came about after an evening fishing the Last Chance section of the Henry's Fork of the Snake. I had fished most of the afternoon and into the early evening with little success. There were sporadically hatching caddis popping here and there, and more than enough rises to get the impression that the fish were about to get on them. Buying in to the lore of the Henry's Fork, I dug through my caddis box for my tightest, most realistic caddis patterns and cast them fruitlessly to every rising fish within my range. There were several other anglers within sight, as the Fork is a broad flat river

It's ugly, disheveled, and ragged, but the Mugly Caddis gets the job done on picky fish.

104

with a refreshingly positive sense of camaraderie among nearby anglers. You could hear muffled swearing from most of the other guys, and I was just as frustrated with my inability to hook any of the many rising fish. But there was this one guy downstream to my left and closer to the middle of the river. I first noticed him when I heard a splash and looked to see him hooked up to a leaping rainbow. My first thought was, "Whew, it's about time someone caught one," with a sense of expectation that I would be playing the same role very soon. I went back to timing the rises of a good fish just a bit upstream. I worked my technical little low-floating caddis patterns over this fish without generating any interest at all. Recalling the mantra I recite to my kids when I take them fishing, I took a deep breath and straightened my back while I repeated, "A good fisherman is *patient*," several times over and over in my head.

I heard another splash behind me and turned to see that same guy with yet another fish on, this one bigger than the first. He laughed audibly, not at the rest of us unoccupied fisherman in the peanut gallery, but rather, I like to think, at his own success.

I knew that being surrounded by rising fish tends to make an angler sloppy, and it is far better to pick a single fish and watch it closely for any clues to exactly which stage of the insect it is eating than to flock shoot the whole bunch and put them down. I redoubled my efforts and watched closely as my fish rose again. I had a good view of my target as it rose and could see nothing on the water where it came up, giving me reason to believe it was either eating spent caddis lying flat in the surface film or perhaps a caddis emerger rising from the bottom and trapped in the meniscus. I thought I had it all figured out and tied on a flat floating spent pattern that I was sure would solve the puzzle. I started my backcast and was interrupted by a hoot from downstream. Glancing back over my shoulder, I hoped to see that someone had fallen in, but instead I saw that *same guy* hooked up to another good fish. I could hear the other anglers harrumphing and see them go quickly back to rummaging through their fly boxes for their own answer.

I finally cast my new pattern over my timed riser with much the same result as before: zero reaction. Not even an inspection rise could be drawn from these hypertechnical fish. I even stooped so low as tying on a foam beetle and passing it over him a time or ten. While a beetle is a perfectly legitimate trout pattern, it is sort of frowned upon by the Idaho locals as being a given. I was not too proud to give it a try, although in this instance it had the same result as if I had tied on a marshmallow. I began to frantically dig through all of my fly boxes hoping that something would jump out at me, all the while doing my best to ignore that guy downstream, who was hooked up yet *again*. I could sense the crowd growing angry and even heard a few guys blurt out breathless things like, "Seriously?" and "Really?" They were as exasperated as I was. Here everyone on the river had rising fish in front of them feeding readily on something, and only one of them was catching anything. I had yet to even have a fish *look* at any of the several patterns I had thrown. I decided to take a break and headed to the bank to sit and watch for a while. This is a tactic I use commonly to make it look like I am one of those uberpatient old-school guys who can simply take up a good vantage point on the bank, watch closely, and plan an attack. In reality this is my way of keeping myself from angrily breaking my rod over my knee, swearing out loud, and throwing my vest into the water, but it looks good from the other side and sometimes it even works.

I walked up to the observation platform extending out over the river and watched the other anglers, the successful one in particular. He wasn't a very good caster, and to make matters worse he seemed to be a beginner. His leader was heavy and only about six feet long. He didn't leave his fly on the water long enough, and his drifts dragged after only a foot or two. He'd rip his line and leader off the water and plow it back in after about a dozen false casts, breaking every rule I could think of.

But this guy was catching fish.

Lots of them.

Big ones.

I hated him.

I think everyone else on the river was on my side on this too, because he was not only catching fish pretty regularly, but he was the only guy actively casting; everyone else had either retired to the bank or was madly digging through their boxes. Some guys were even digging their flasks from their waders to help ease their frazzled nerves. But this one guy was just busy catching fish. A beginner. On some of the most technical trout water in the world. With a 6-foot leader and a splashy cast. Lots of fish.

Eventually this guy either decided he had caught enough or perhaps figured out that should this display

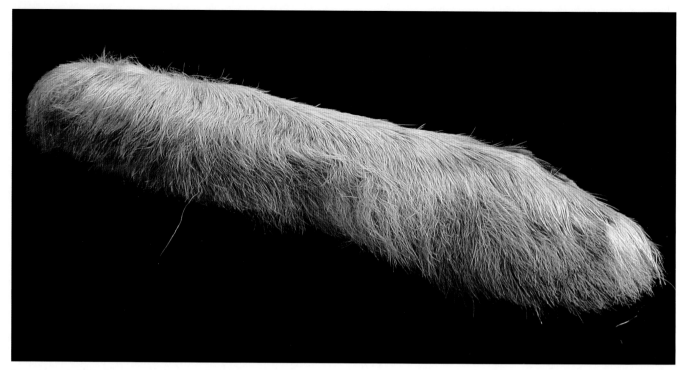

Snowshoe rabbit foot underfur is a crinkled, buoyant fur that adds surface area and flotation to my Mugly Caddis. One foot will tie hundreds of flies.

go on he could be in serious jeopardy on his way back to the parking lot once night fell, but he waded to the bank and worked up near me. Several options ran through my mind, from knocking him down and breaking his rod to going the polite route and striking up a conversation. As it turns out, I'm really glad that I went with the latter as this guy turned out to be very friendly and was as surprised by his success as anyone. I asked sheepishly if I could see the fly that he caught all these fish on, and he gladly turned his rod over, showing me the pattern tethered to his hook keeper. I excitedly looked closely at the fly, hoping to be clued in to some super techy new caddis pattern that I could add to my repertoire but was instead immediately disappointed with the ragged bit of dubbing and hair I encountered.

The fly on which he had been crushing some of the most educated trout in the world was a chewed No-Hackle Elk Hair Caddis that had lost most of the hair in its wing; its dubbed body had come nearly completely unwound and was trailing off the back of the hook in a long ragged strand. The fly was barely holding together, and I knew it couldn't have been floating very well. I was disappointed and more than a little offended by the success of this pattern, especially considering that I had several boxes full of beautifully tied, anatomically correct imitations that had been completely ignored.

I went back to my room that night and tried to come up with an "on purpose" version of this guy's chewed-up fly, and the result came to be known as the Mugly Caddis. A long-fibered dubbing, generously picked out, formed the body and shuck, and a sparse CDC overwing topped with a few random strands of well-marked deer hair completed the fly, which bore a striking resemblance to the fly that was about to explode on that guy's hook keeper. I went back to the river the next night and fished the new pattern to those same fish and found that perhaps it was the combination of the long-trailing body dubbing and sparse wing that matched the naturals so well. My friend from the previous evening wasn't back that night, but I like to think I took his place as I stepped in and proceeded to frustrate everyone else with the amount of fish I was fooling. Having remembered my feelings from the night before, I was careful to pass out a few of the flies to the other anglers and even left the river before it got dark to help insure my safety. It'd be silly to risk churning everyone up for two nights in a row.

I later fine-tuned the pattern and replaced the underwing with snowshoe rabbit foot hair that held up better to repeated maulings by the fish, but other than this small change, the Mugly Caddis has remained true to the original pattern from that fateful, frustrating night. The more I fished the Mugly, the more I came to understand its ugly-duckling charm. The loose dubbing becomes translucent in the water and hangs well below the surface, even dragging the front of the fly down low into the surface film. The sparse wing provides just the right profile to match an emerging caddis wing and just enough flotation to keep the fly propped in the surface film like a trapped emerger. I usually fish the Mug behind another higher-floating pattern on rougher water but use it all alone on flat water, letting the fly slide unobtrusively into the trout's feeding lane. I will often let the fly sink a bit and mend aggressively to gently tug the fly toward the surface once it comes into the trout's field of view. This rising motion has become a

great trigger to fish keyed on emerging caddis and has fooled some pretty tough fish along the way.

I have even fished the Mugly as a nymph with a heavier fly to pull it down through the water column. The rough dubbed body and sparse wing make it a great underwater emerger as well as a dry fly, and the versatility of this pattern makes it one of my favorites when I recognize a true hatch of emerging caddis.

The Mugly Caddis is not my style of pattern and I still find its bedraggled nature a little offensive, but I have learned to overlook the shortcomings in its looks for its hard-working get-it-done attitude and misleading profile. Sort of like that guy on the Henry's Fork.

TYING THE MUGLY CADDIS

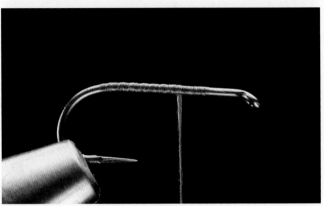

1. Clamp the hook in the vise. Start the thread at the 75 percent point and wrap a thread base back to the bend. Return the thread to just behind the starting point.

MUGLY CADDIS

Hook:	#12-20 Tiemco 100SP-BL
Thread:	Camel 8/0 Uni-Thread
Abdomen:	Brown Stone Nymph Whitlock SLF Dubbing
Underwing:	Natural cream/tan snowshoe rabbit foot hair
Overwing:	Fine natural deer hair
Thorax:	Same as abdomen

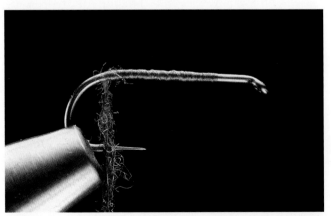

2. Dub the thread with the SLF dubbing, leaving a bit of bare thread between the top of the dubbing strand and the hook shank. Use the bare thread to work back to the hook bend so the first turn of dubbing comes around the shank at the hook bend.

3. Build a dubbed body with a reverse taper, fatter at the back than the front, ending with the front of the abdomen at the 75 percent point.

4. Wrap the thread from the front of the body up to the hook eye and back again, forming a thread base for the underwing.

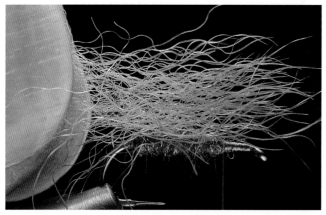

5. Clip a clump of snowshoe rabbit foot hair from the foot. Clean most of the loose underfur from the clump. You don't need a particularly heavy bunch of hair. Clip the butt ends of the hair so the bunch is about twice as long as the hook shank.

6. Lay the hair in on top of the hook at the front edge of the body and bind it in place at the center with two tight turns of thread.

7. You should have the tips of the hair facing out over the hook eye and the butt ends extending just past the hook bend.

8. Fold the tips of the hair back over the top of the fly and bind them down with a few firm wraps of thread. Folding this material for the wing makes for a denser wing with less bulk and adds durability to the pattern.

9. Cut, clean, and stack a small clump of well-marked deer hair. Measure the deer hair against the underwing so that it's about the same length.

10. Put two loose turns of thread around the hair at the front edge of the body, right over the base of the underwing.

11. Tighten the thread toward you while you hold the tips in place, flaring the butt ends tightly down to the shank.

12. Work the thread forward through the flared butt ends of the hair. Make tight, close turns over the butt ends to anchor the hair in place.

13. Clip the butt ends of the deer hair as close to the shank as you can.

14. Dub another short strand of dubbing onto the thread and build the thorax from the index point back up to the base of the wing. Return the dubbed thread back to the index point and whip-finish. If you try to dub from the base of the wing forward to the eye over the tapered butts of the hair wing, the dubbing will slide down the hill and pile up at the hook eye. That's not good for anyone.

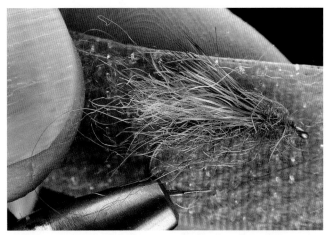

15. Use a strip of Velcro to rough out the dubbing on the fly, working from the eye to the bend. You really want this fly to be shaggy, so get after it with the Velcro.

16. Fold the Velcro in your fingers and use it to pick out the sides of the thorax dubbing as well. Sweep all the loose fibers back toward the hook bend.

17. Finished fly, side view.

18. Finished fly, bottom view.

19. Finished fly, top view.

MUGLY CADDIS (OLIVE)

Hook:	#12-20 Tiemco 100SP-BL
Thread:	Camel 8/0 Uni-Thread
Abdomen:	Golden Stone Nymph Whitlock SLF Dubbing
Underwing:	Natural cream/tan snowshoe rabbit foot hair
Overwing:	Fine natural deer hair
Thorax:	Same as abdomen

TWELVE

Charlie Boy Hopper

I had been working a long stretch of days in late summer on Tarryall Creek, a tributary of the South Platte in Colorado's South Park. Tarryall is a medium-sized meadow creek with plenty of oxbows and meandering cut banks, and it is perfect hopper water. My clients had been enjoying some good fishing with flies like Dave's Hopper and Schroeder's Parachute Hopper, although I can't say I was thrilled to stay up until midnight each night to replenish my supply of these complicated and somewhat fragile patterns. I

needed a pattern that was durable and didn't take forever to tie.

Developing the Charlie Boy Hopper took an embarrassingly long time, especially given the simplicity of the finished pattern. The early versions of this fly, and several other failed attempts, were all tied with various foam bodies ranging from foam sheeting wrapped on the hook to hard foam blocks whittled and lathed to shape with a Dremel tool. I even experimented with old-school elk-hair bodies. Wrapping a foam strip looked good but

Natural hoppers come in many colors and sizes. Tie your imitations to match the hoppers in your local waters.

Easy to tie, durable, visible, and extremely buoyant, Charlie Boys fish well alone or with droppers.

crushed all the air out of the foam and made for a poor floater. The Dremeled bodies looked great too, and they floated well, but the time and labor that went in to each fly was just too much. It was also hard to make the bodies small enough to match most of the hoppers I had been seeing. The elk-hair body, borrowed from Mike Lawson's Henry's Fork Hopper, looked right, but the combination of its time-consuming construction, the lack of long-term floatability, and the poor durability made me look elsewhere for that perfect material.

While none of these options produced the fly I was looking for, I knew foam held promise. I went to work with 2 mm foam sheets and tied a variety of Chernobyl Ant–style flies. Chernobyls float well and can be highly visible, but I couldn't get over the fact that they looked like Muppets cobbled together from scraps of fly-tying material. I wanted something with a bit more class.

After several weeks of tinkering, I stumbled upon the perfect hopper body late one night. I had folded, glued, and tied foam strips to the hook shank, but while the final pattern was supposed to feature the fold at the front of the hook, I had first tried folding the foam at the back in an effort to make a foam version of the Henry's Fork Hopper's extended body. Though my weary mind made me do it backward, the course of my hopper changed right then and there.

With the body dialed in, I moved next to the legs. I had been trying several different materials for legs on the prototypes over the previous few weeks and had settled upon round rubber legs given their inherent wiggle, widespread availability, and ease of use. While the knotted pheasant-tail-fiber legs you see on so many hoppers are attractive to the angler, I find that they lack any movement and take far too long to produce. The angled and tapered effect of the pheasant tail remained appealing to me, although I believed in the movement of the straight rubber legs. I would later find a happy compromise between the two.

Once I had the foam body and rubber legs, I thought I had just what I was after, and I rushed to tie up a dozen or so for the next day's trip. And while the new Charlie Boy with its foam body and rubber legs pulled stagnant late-summer fish up from the bottom of the river, it was with a bit of disappointment that my clients and I discovered that the fly floated so low in the water that it was hard to see.

To fix this problem, I flared a thick deer hair wing to the top and left the butt ends of the hair long enough to form a semicircle of hair on the top of the fly. The surface area of the tips combined with the flared butt ends drastically improved the buoyancy of the fly, and the little bit of upright profile the wing provided was more than enough to make the fly stand up and be seen. Finally, the Charlie Boy Hopper was done . . . or so I thought.

Shortly before Umpqua Feather Merchants selected the pattern for national distribution, John Barr suggested I add an underwing to the fly to cover the threadwork on the top of the foam body. The Thin Skin I tried just rolled and coiled up, and the Web Wing, which was both attractive and durable, absorbed water. Then one day I really sat down and thought it all out and decided that the fly didn't need an underwing at all. I mean, a hopper's wings can be spread out like the deer hair suggests, or they can be neatly folded over their back, as the underwing would suggest, but they can't be both. Working on the theory that the hoppers fish see in the water don't land there on purpose, I decided to stick with the deer hair and eliminate the underwing.

Knotted legs are the newest addition to my hopper. While designing the BC (Barr/Craven) Hopper with John Barr, I came up with the idea of knotting three strands of rubber legs together and trimming the bottom two strands below the knot. This arrangement creates a silhouette similar to the pheasant tail fibers, but the legs have a built-in wiggle and a bow-legged profile that acts as an outrigger to keep the fly floating upright.

FISHING THE CHARLIE BOY

I tie up about a hundred or so Charlie Boy Hoppers for my box each winter, and it seems I need more every year. I fish them a lot. I rely most heavily on the #8 tied on a Tiemco 100SP-BL, but I make sure to have sizes 6 through 10 in tan (my favorite), olive, black, chartreuse, yellow, and even red. I use this fly as a general terrestrial pattern to match a variety of different aquatic and terres-

I precut all my foam for both the Charlie Boy and Baby Boy Hoppers with a metal T-square and a razor blade. Precutting saves tying time and makes for a more consistent fly.

trial insects, from grasshoppers to cicadas to adult stoneflies and even crickets and large beetles.

I most often fish the Charlie Boy as the indicator fly in a dry-dropper or hopper-copper-dropper rig. When tied with a sufficiently thick wing, it actually floats better than many heavier dressed patterns and certainly floats longer than hair wing and hackle flies like Stimulators. At times, especially in late summer, I also love fishing the Charlie Boy as a single dry on the end of a 9- to 10-foot leader while wading up the edge of a broken riffle or cut bank.

When float fishing, I often fish a Charlie Boy on a 7½-foot 3X leader with a smaller Parachute Adams, Humpy, or GTH Variant off the back. Fishing the double-dry rig with the hopper in front allows me to do several things that I couldn't with one fly alone. Mending the line sometimes skates a single fly out away from the bank, but with the hopper out front even an aggressive mend only twitches the hopper a bit, prodding some movement into the rubber legs while cushioning the mend against the back fly so it remains drag free. In addition to helping me keep track of the smaller pattern behind it, the hopper draws plenty of attention itself.

TYING THE CHARLIE BOY HOPPER

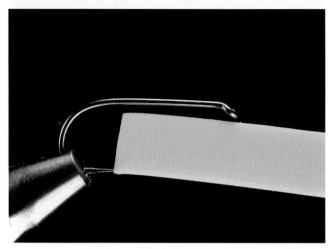

1. Begin by cutting a strip of 2 mm foam as wide as the hook gap and at least 3 inches long. Use a cutting board, metal straight edge, and razor blade—scissors make it much harder to get a clean straight cut.

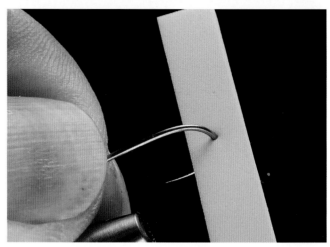

2. Poke the hook point through the foam about three-quarters of an inch from the end of the strip. Make sure the hook point is centered in the foam.

CHARLIE BOY HOPPER
(YELLOW)

Hook:	#8-10 Tiemco 100 or 100SP-BL
Thread:	Yellow 3/0 Danville Monocord
Body:	Yellow Thin Fly Foam (2 mm)
Legs:	Yellow round rubber (medium) marked with a red Sharpie
Wing:	Natural deer hair
Note:	Use Tiemco 5212 for #6 and Tiemco 5262 for #4 (the weight of the heavier hook helps to keel the bigger fly and assure it lands upright). The gap on the 5212 is too narrow for smaller flies, which is why I prefer the Tiemco 100 with the larger gap.

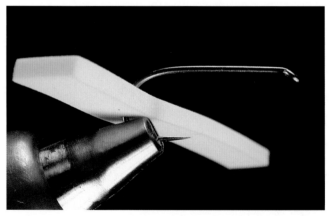

3. Place the hook in the vise with the foam on the hook bend.

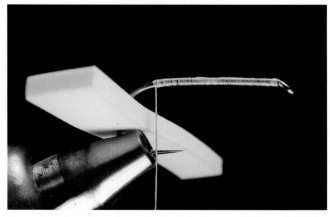

4. Start the thread at the hook eye and wrap a tight thread base back to the bend.

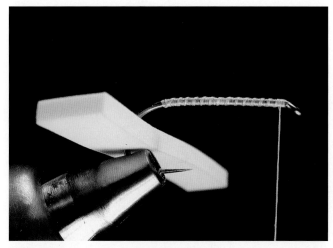

5. Return the thread to the hook eye.

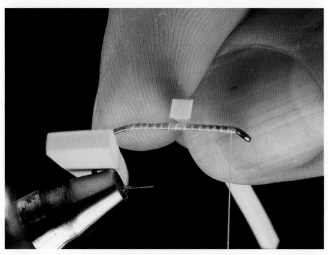

6. Cut another strip of foam from the sheet that is about 2 mm by 2 mm.

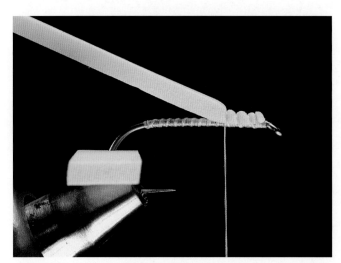

7. Tie this thinner "binder" strip of foam to the hook shank right behind the hook eye.

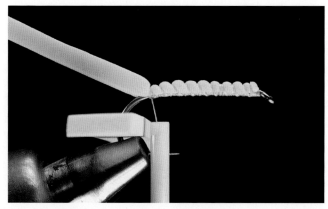

8. Spiral wrap tightly back over the foam strip to the hook bend and then break off the excess.

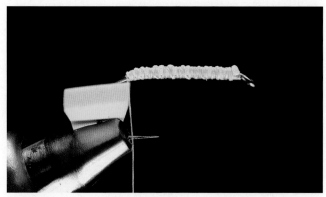

9. Run the thread up the hook shank over the binder strip and back again to the bend, compressing the foam to the shank and leaving a cross-hatched thread pattern on the shank. This binder strip is going to give us some shank diameter and texture, which will allow glue to adhere to it better, so it need not be pretty. Leave the tying thread hanging at the hook bend.

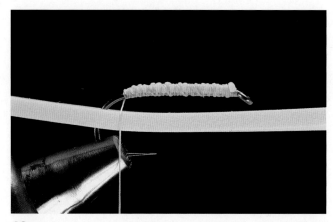

10. Pull the long end of the wider foam strip forward so the strip is in line with the hook shank on the underside.

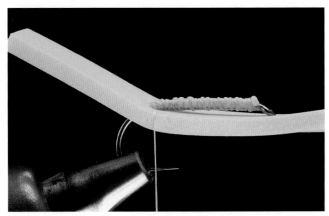

11. Lift the wide strip of foam up under the hook and pull it up to the peak of the hook bend so it touches the back of the binder strip. Note that the foam will tilt slightly upward. If yours doesn't do this, your binder strip is not bound far enough back. Pull the foam strip taut under the hook shank and measure where the hook eye lines up with the foam.

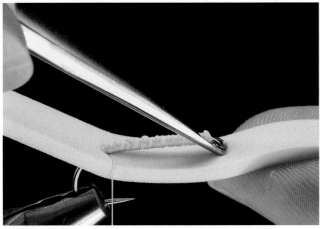

12. Use the tips of your scissors to poke a hole through the foam from the top where the hook eye lines up.

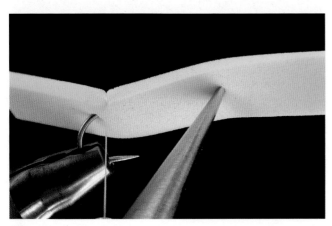

13. Poke a hole in the bottom at this point as well.

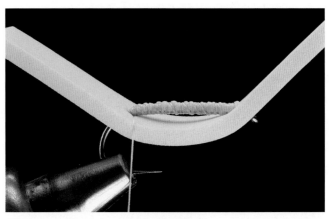

14. Push the foam over the hook eye so the eye protrudes through the front side of the foam.

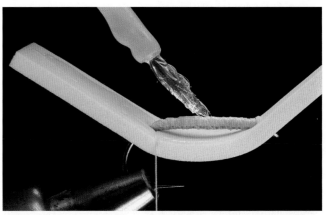

15. Put a thin coat of Zap-A-Gap on the entire upper surface of the foam, including the binder strip. I find this much easier to do with the newer brush applicator bottles of Zap-A-Gap. I trim the brush to keep it from picking up too much glue. Brush a bit more glue along the foam that extends out past the hook bend as well. Too little is better than too much.

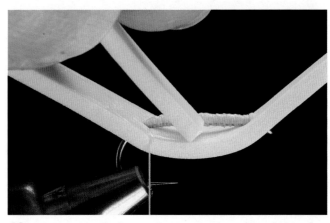

16. To ensure a light, even coat, I often spread the glue with a scrap of foam.

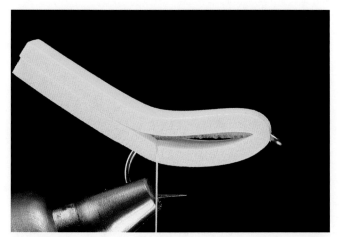

17. Quickly, before the glue starts to dry, fold the front end of the foam back over the top of the shank, pinching it together from the front of the hook all the way back off the hook bend. Try to get the edges of the foam to line up together along the sides of the shank. The foam should be slightly elevated at the rear of the hook, not coming straight out from the bend. A common mistake on this fly is to glue the foam too flat off the bend, which will cause problems with the body later. If the glue doesn't grab the foam portion along the shank yet, no problem. You just want to get the extended portion of the foam body to stick together off the rear of the hook. The rest of the body will be held together by thread wraps.

18. To create the first segment at the hook bend, make two complete turns of thread around the foam at the hook bend. Pull the thread toward you to compress the foam all the way to the hook shank. Make one more tight wrap over the first two to anchor everything. Make sure these wraps are all on top of each other and as upright as possible.

19. The body ought to look like this now.

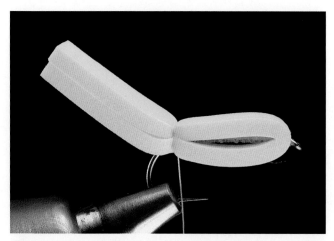

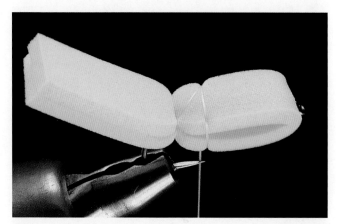

20. Cross the thread lightly across the top of the foam body about one fourth of the way forward. You will be making three more distinct bands of thread as you move forward on the body, each one about a fourth of a hook shank apart. So while there are indeed three bands of thread, don't make even thirds, make fourths.

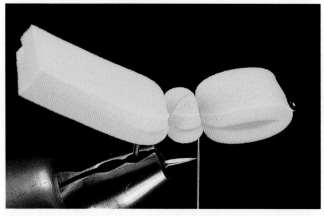

21. Cinch the thread down by making two complete turns and tightening the thread toward you to compress the foam.

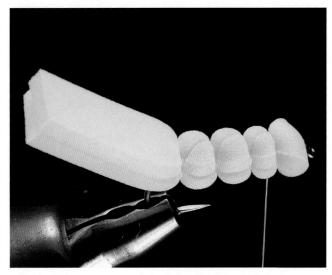

22. Make another upright segment one fourth of the way forward on the hook shank with two more tight turns of thread. Continue forward by crossing on the top of the shank and make one more evenly spaced segment for a total of four bands of thread and three crosses.

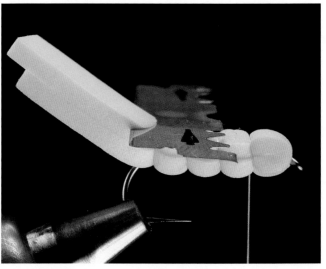

24. Carefully break a double-edged razor blade in half lengthwise. Use one half of the blade to cut through the extended foam. This cut, once finished, appears to be made at an angle, but it is a straight cut following along the top of the body. Make one straight cut through the foam without sawing back and forth. The double-edged blades are very sharp and will slice right through the foam with only light pressure.

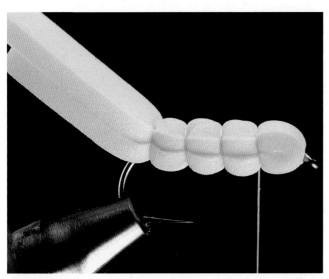

23. Note the angle of the foam extending back from the hook bend. This angle is essential to ensure the fly looks right.

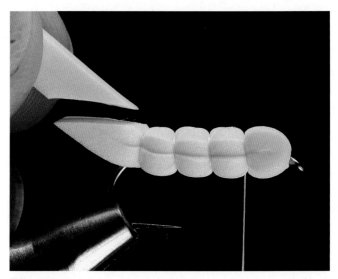

25. The finished cut should be in a straight line along the top of the foam body.

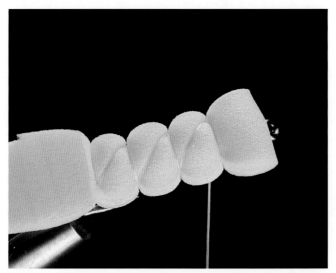

26. Rotate your vise so you can see the top of the fly clearly. The head of the fly (the last segment nearest to the hook eye) is now wider than the rest of the fly. Real grasshoppers have heads that are actually smaller than their body—unlike most of the conventional deer hair head flies—so I trim the foam a bit.

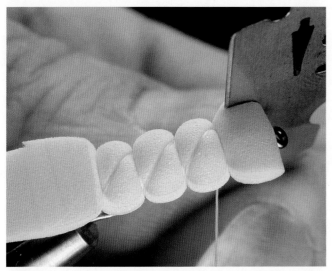

27. Cut a sliver of foam from each side of the head, squaring the head off so that it is the same width as the rest of the fly.

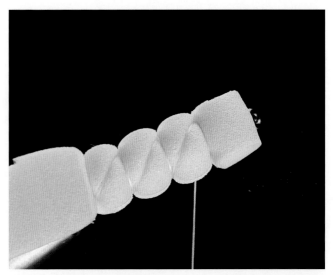

28. Both sides trimmed.

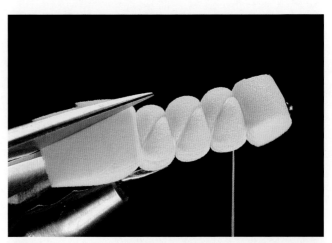

29. Now clean up the extended portion of the body. The back end is a bit wider than the fly body as well. Use your scissors to trim a tapered slice from each edge of the body.

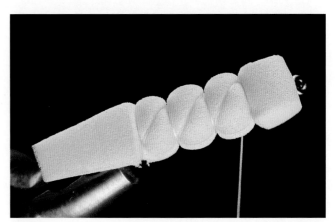

30. The finished body should look like this. The rear of the body is tapered but not cut to a point.

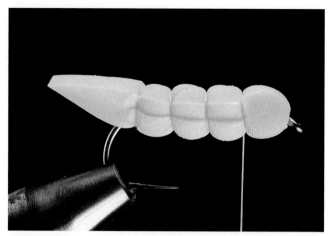

31. Now, your thread should be hanging in the last segment behind the head of the fly in preparation for tying in the legs.

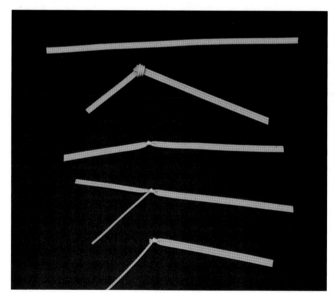

32. Take three strands of rubber legs about three inches long, and without separating them, tie them in an overhand knot to form the kicker legs. Keep the strands flat throughout the knot so they lie flat without twisting. Tighten the knot firmly by pulling steadily on either end. Trim off two of the three strands on one side of the knot for the lower leg section.

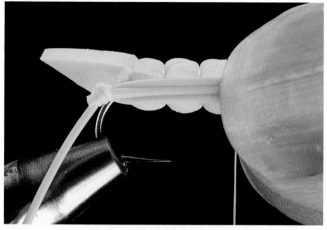

33. Place the prepared leg up against the side of the fly with the knotted knee at the hook bend.

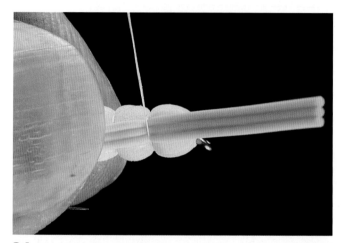

34. Lash the leg tightly into the first segment behind the head with two tight turns of thread. Be cautious about building up too many wraps of thread here. Use no more than two as all of the thread wraps from this point on will be added to in the leg tying process.

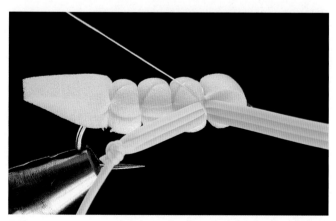

35. After tying the leg in, cross the thread back again across the top of the body to the second segment back.

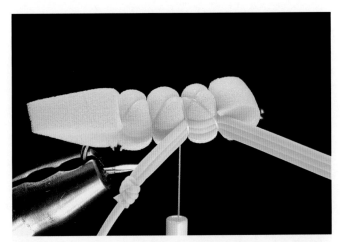

36. Trap the leg again against the side of the foam body with two more tight turns of thread.

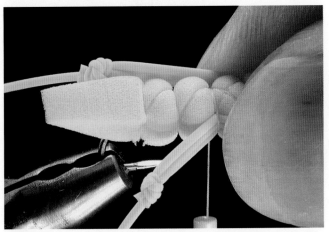

37. Prepare a second leg in the same way and lay it against the far side of the foam body, making sure that the knee is even with the knee on the near-side leg.

38. Catch the far leg with two tight turns of thread in the second segment back. Cross the thread back to the front segment by coming across the top of the body.

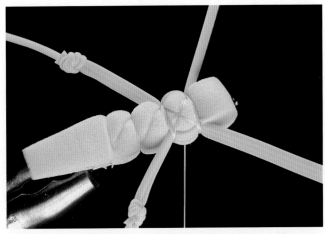

39. Bind the front end of the far leg in place in the first segment with two more tight wraps of thread.

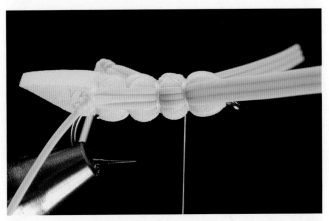

40. I try to keep the upper portion of the legs parallel with the body of the fly instead of elevated above it. This lowers the center of gravity on the fly and helps it to land and float upright.

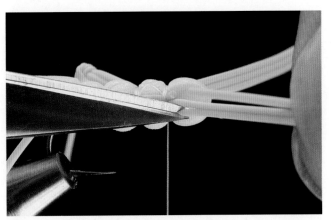

41. Carefully reach in with the tips of your scissors and trim off the top and bottom strands of rubber from the front end of the legs so that only the center strand remains.

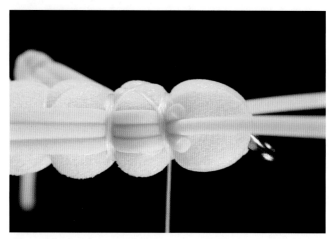

42. Detail of front leg. Trim the top and bottom strands from the far leg as well.

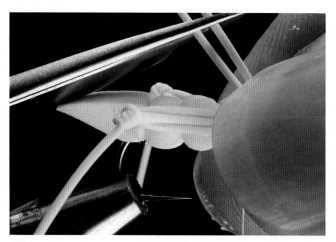

43. Pull the remaining single center strand of rubber up above the hook and trim them both so they are just slightly shorter than the distance from the body to the knotted knee on the lower portion of the leg.

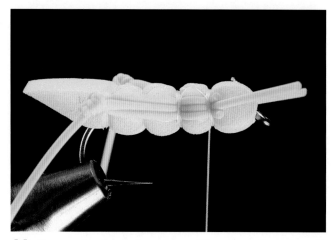

44. Leave the back legs long. The extra length will come in handy later.

45. Cut and clean a generous bunch of deer hair. If you intend to fish these flies as indicator flies or in heavier water, bulk the wing up a bit. For flat water, tie them a bit more sparsely. The amount of hair shown here is for a more buoyant fly.

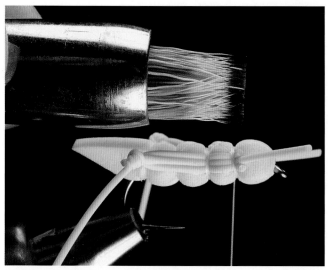

46. Place the hair in your stacker and even out the tips. The two thicker hairs in the above photo are broken tips and need to be removed.

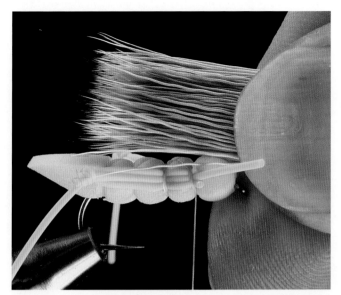

47. Measure the stacked clump of hair against the hook so it is a shank length long. I visually mark the intersection of the butt of the hairs and the hook eye with the edge of my thumbnail so I know where to trim the hair in the next step.

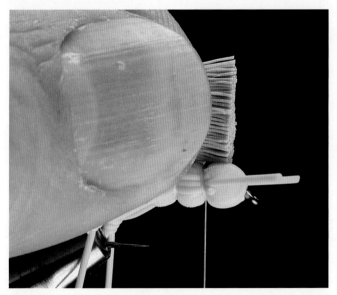

48. Trim the butt ends of the hair as cleanly and as straight as you can at the pre-measured one-shank-length-long point. Lay the hair on top of the hook with the bottom of the bunch actually touching the foam body. You want this hair flat against and parallel to the top of the foam body when you tie it down.

49. Wrap two taut turns of thread around the hair. You do not want to flare the hair yet, just capture it with two loops of thread. About a quarter of a hook shank worth of hair butts should be in front of this thread wrap.

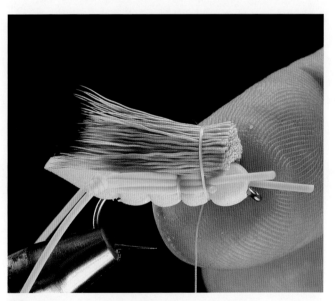

50. Place your index finger against the hair and the foam body on the far side of the hook. Holding the hair in place like this will keep it from rolling around when you tighten the thread to flare the hair.

51. With your index finger still planted along the far side of the fly, pull firmly and steadily down on the thread to flare the hair. The butt ends of the hair will flare down into the crease between the segments and distribute across the top half of the fly.

53. Grasp the single strand of rubber on the lower leg in your thumb and forefinger and roll the leg a bit to twist the strand several times. Hold the twist in the leg and pull the leg a bit to stretch it slightly.

52. Whip-finish the thread right through the butt ends of the hair. I try to work three tight turns of thread right through the butts over the top of the thread wraps that flared the hair. Clip the thread.

54. While the leg is stretched and twisted, use a marker to run a single clean stripe of color down the leg from the knee to as close to your fingertips as you can get.

55. Release the stretch and twist and you should have a very cool stripe (looks like a barber pole) around the lower leg. For even legs, repeat the process on the far leg with the same amount of twist and stretch. Fish will not eat a fly that has three stripes on one side and four on the other, so don't say you haven't been warned.

56. Trim the lower back legs so they are about the same length as the upper portion of the leg.

57. With a Sharpie, draw elongated ovals on the sides of the head for the eyes. I find that flies with eyes cast much more accurately because they can see where they are going.

58. Finished fly, side view.

59. Finished fly, bottom view.

CHARLIE BOY HOPPER (OLIVE)

Hook:	#8-10 Tiemco 100 or 100SP-BL
Thread:	Olive 3/0 Danville Monocord
Body:	Olive Thin Fly Foam (2 mm)
Legs:	Chartreuse round rubber (medium), marked with a blue Sharpie
Wing:	Natural deer hair
Note:	Use Tiemco 5212 for #6 and Tiemco 5262 for #4.

CHARLIE BOY HOPPER (CHARTREUSE)

Hook:	#8-10 Tiemco 100 or 100SP-BL
Thread:	Chartreuse 3/0 Danville Monocord
Body:	Chartreuse Thin Fly Foam (2 mm)
Legs:	Chartreuse round rubber (medium)
Wing:	Natural deer hair
Note:	Use Tiemco 5212 for #6 and Tiemco 5262 for #4.

CHARLIE BOY HOPPER (TAN)

Hook:	#8-10 Tiemco 100 or 100SP-BL
Thread:	Tan 3/0 Danville Monocord
Body:	Tan Thin Fly Foam (2 mm)
Legs:	Brown round rubber (medium)
Wing:	Natural deer hair
Note:	Use Tiemco 5212 for #6 and Tiemco 5262 for #4.

THIRTEEN

Baby Boy Hopper

To me, fly tying is in many ways like a big puzzle that you never get all the pieces to. Sometimes you are given a batch of parts and a framework to fit them in, but you usually end up having to make up a piece of your own to really fill everything in. It turns out that the Baby Boy Hopper needed more than its fair share of additional pieces, but nothing feels better than putting them all together.

Given the huge numbers of small hoppers I see bouncing around my favorite rivers in the spring and early summer, I figured a tiny little hopper might be handy to have. I began by tying the standard Charlie Boy in smaller sizes on the same hook style but quickly found that while I could certainly downsize the hook and cut the foam narrower, 2 mm foam filled in the gap making the fly utterly useless. Nothing like having a fish crash your hopper and coming up empty every time! I tried tying the fly with 1 mm foam, but there wasn't enough foam to float the fly or form a body that I liked. So I was back to the drawing board.

Baby Boy Hoppers are the perfect size to imitate early summer hoppers and can be a stealthier option than a more over-sized pattern as the season progresses.

I often have trouble shutting down for the evening, and some of my best fly-tying ideas come to me when I'm lying in bed just before I go to sleep at night. So one night, as I lay there awake, I tried to solve the riddle of making a tiny Charlie Boy work. I knew I needed to use the 2 mm foam to get the body shape and buoyancy I wanted, but that hook gap issue kept jumping back at me. Finally, after mulling it over for quite some time, a light came on.

I would love to say that I came up with the idea of using a short-shank, wide-gap hook for the fly, but in reality what popped into my head that night was a photo that a young friend of mine had posted on an internet bulletin board about a year earlier. Weston Reynolds, a gifted fly tier and member of the United States Junior Fly Fishing Team, had tied what turned out to be exactly what I was after . . . the Charlie Boy Hopper on a short-shank, wide gap Tiemco 2499. Weston's version of the Charlie Boy was the answer to my puzzle.

The next morning I sat down at the bench and dug out the materials to tie up a few Charlie Boys, but instead of the Tiemco 100SP-BL hooks I had been using, I selected the Tiemco 2499SP-BL per Weston's "advice." With its spade-shaped barbless and slightly upturned business end, the 2499SP-BL had become one of my favorites for many smaller nymph and midge larva patterns. My only gripe with this hook is the sizes stop at 18, about a size or two too big to really be useful for many Colorado patterns.

I cut a strip of foam just slightly narrower than the hook gap and proceeded to follow the original Charlie Boy pattern, complete with three body segments. I ran into several issues as I worked, and I recalled that these issues were what made me pass over the idea of recreating the fly in Weston's photo so quickly. The three body segments created with the thread bands along the body creased the foam too much and too often. I still ended up with a fly that was mostly compressed foam, and I know all too well that compressed foam doesn't float well.

I decided that I needed a much smaller thread to keep the segments proportioned to the shorter shank. I eventually figured out that I could also eliminate one body segment to leave more of the foam uncompressed and buoyant. Applying these changes made the pattern a viable option in my mind, and I set about polishing up the tying details. I ended up using Gordon Griffith's 14/0 thread to create the body on the fly, because this thread is thin and flat enough not to generate too much bulk.

I had tied this fly quite a few times with the straight rubber legs like I had originally used in the Charlie Boy, but when Brian Schmidt and Riley Cotter asked me about a smaller version of a hopper for the Umpqua Feather Merchants catalog I began tinkering again. I sent Brian and Riley a few of the smaller hoppers tied on the 2499, with straight legs and a simple flared deer hair wing. Brian somehow took one of the strands of rubber leg on the fly and tied it in an overhand knot, creating a jointed leg like I had used years back on the BC Hopper that John Barr and I came up with. This was an impressive feat, given that the back end of the leg that Brian knotted was about a quarter-inch long, but I had to admit that the knotted leg was undeniably sexy and added both realism and "bin appeal" to the fly. We all agreed that the production patterns should have the knotted legs, and I set out to tie the samples. Some things are much easier said than done, and it wasn't until I actually sat down to tie the several dozen samples that I encountered a whole new issue.

The most efficient way to tie a quantity of any pattern is to cut and prepare your materials ahead of time, and with this in mind I set to work on cutting the foam to the appropriate widths; cutting, separating, and knotting the rubber legs; and counting out the hooks. When I actually started tying, I immediately ran in to what seemed to be an impossible snag. While I could set the leg in neatly along the side of the fly with the knot aligned correctly to represent the leg joint, I found that the thread torque would grab that grippy little rubber strand and twist it all about on the hook, making my little hoppers look as if they were dancing a jig, spread eagled and bent in every direction, which was not what I was hoping for.

It occurred to me that I could just tie the legs in straight and make good old Brian recreate his magic knot 247 times, or I could simply leave them straight and bag the knotted leg idea. The catch was I had already tied a few dozen of the flies trying to work out a technique to get the legs on straight, and I really didn't like the idea of starting over again. I picked up a few of the flies and began tugging and twisting the misshapen legs to see if I could get them lined up properly. I found that I could roll the strand of rubber leg in my fingertips, and if I pulled on the leg at the same time I could manipulate the twist down the strand and under the

Sometimes it takes a smaller hopper to hook small- to medium-size fish. The smaller profile of the Baby Boy allows fish to get their mouths around it better. JAY NICHOLS PHOTO

thread wraps holding the leg in place. With a bit of tweaking, I finally came upon the trick I show here, and I remember heaving a great sigh of relief when I finally solved this puzzle.

FISHING THE BABY BOY HOPPER

The first hoppers in the spring in Colorado are small, wingless, and typically bright green, though I believe their coloration has more to do with their environment than anything else, as I have also seen them in drab olives and tans. These small hoppers are abundant in most years, and I am confident that trout know what they are when they accidentally make their way into the water.

I have fished many small streams with these tiny hoppers and fish not only crush them, but they can really get their mouths wrapped around the small pattern, increasing the number of fish I hook. I can always tell when I'm fishing a hopper that's too big when I get fish to make a grab only to come up empty on the hook set.

Smaller hoppers are also the ticket for fooling late-season fish jaded by too many rubber-legged attractors. I think of the Baby Boy as my "stealth" version of the hopper and use it when I encounter fish that look at but shy away from larger patterns. Oftentimes, late-season pressured fish will become extra cautious around larger hoppers, to the point of nosing and even rejecting naturals. Downsizing the fly to something less alarming and seemingly more "safe" can sometimes be just what is needed to convince these fish to commit.

I tie the Baby Boy in sizes 12, 14, and 16 on the 2499, which gives me flies that range from one inch all the way down to about a half-inch long. In many cases, the smallest of the Baby Boys can cross over to fill in for caddis, small stones, and crickets. Yet, the diminutive size of the Baby Boy does not preclude it from being used in a dry-dropper rig, or even as the indicator in a scaled down version of the hopper-copper-dropper system. I have really come to enjoy fishing super shallow riffles late in the fall with a Baby Boy in a size 12 tethered to the end of a 6-foot 4X leader followed by a small, weighted *Baetis*–type nymph like my Two Bit Hooker and finally a Jujubaetis or even Jujubee dangling beneath everything else. I often find the fish are less prone to become aware of their impending fate with this stealthier system and have had some great fishing in water that is typically considered too shallow to produce. Scaling down both the fly and tippet sizes allows for a stealthier cast, and shortening both of the droppers allows better contact between the indicator fly and the droppers.

The smaller hopper can really pull fish up in skinny water, and there has been more than one day where I end up clipping off both droppers and simply fishing the single dry. With just a single hopper at the end of the leader, I find I can make my cast tight to the bank, landing the fly softly and controlling the drift better than I often can with the droppers attached. The single fly allows manipulation of the cast that is not as easily done with a multi-fly rig. I also find it strangely refreshing to go back to my old ways of one fly at a time.

TYING THE BABY BOY HOPPER

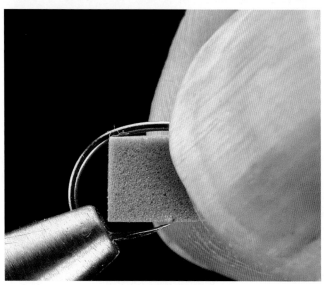

1. Begin by cutting a strip of the 2 mm foam just slightly narrower than the hook gap. The strip should be about three inches long.

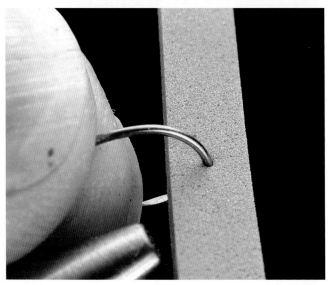

2. Poke the hook point through the foam about an inch from the end and make sure the point is centered on the foam.

BABY BOY HOPPER
(OLIVE)

Hook:	#12-16 Tiemco 2499SP-BL
Thread:	Olive 14/0 Gordon Griffith's
Body:	Olive Thin Fly Foam (2 mm)
Legs:	Lime-green round rubber (medium)
Wing:	Fine deer hair (hock)

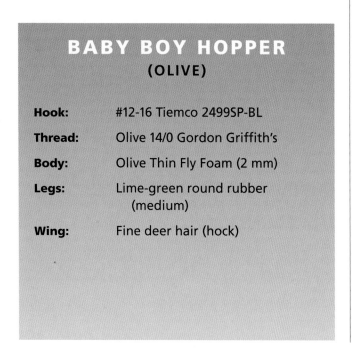

3. Place the hook in the vise with the foam attached as shown here. It helps to point the long end of the foam away from you so it is not in the way during the tying process.

4. Start the tying thread behind the hook eye and wrap a smooth thread base back to the bend. Return the thread to the hook eye.

5. Use a 2 mm by 2 mm strip of foam as a binder strip. This strip of foam will add some surface area and a gluing surface to the hook shank to assure a good bond when you glue the body to the shank.

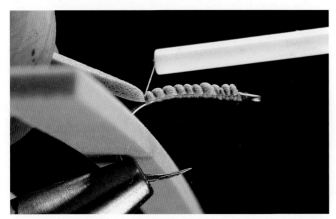

6. Start by tying the binder strip down right behind the eye. Now continue wrapping back over the binder strip, securing it to the top of the hook shank all the way back to the bend.

7. Snap the butt end of the binder strip off the hook with a sharp tug. Wrap the thread back to the hook eye, cross-hatching the binder strip with the thread wraps as you go. Wrap the thread back to the back edge of the binder strip.

8. Pull the foam up under the hook so it sits tight against the back of the binder strip at the bend. Poke a hole through the foam from the top at the point at which the eye intersects the foam.

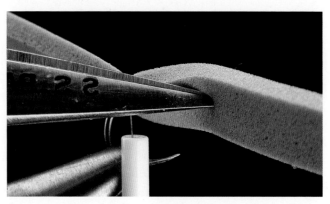

9. Push the tips of your scissors through the foam from the bottom of the foam as well to make sure the foam doesn't tear in the next step.

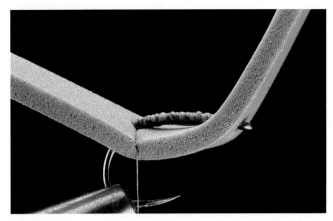

10. Pull the foam up so the hook eye passes through the hole. You should now have the foam threaded onto the hook at the bend and the eye as shown here.

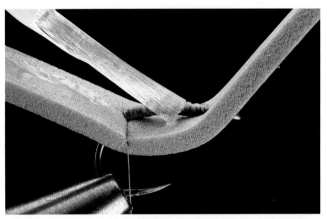

11. Put a thin layer of Zap-A-Gap on the upper surface of the foam. Make sure to go all the way from the eye and continue well up onto the extended portion of the foam. A thin layer is all you need.

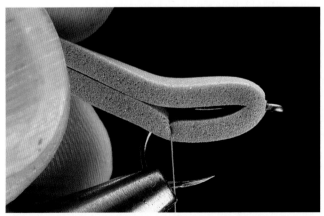

12. Fold the front end of the foam over the top of the lower section and press the two pieces together at the bend. Be sure that the extended portion of the foam beyond the bend is slightly elevated.

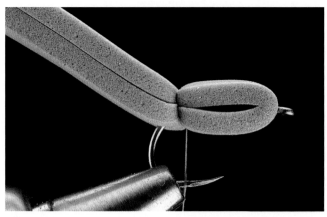

13. Make three tight turns of thread at the hook bend to create the first segment. Make the first half turn a little loose, and then tighten it as you come around for the second turn.

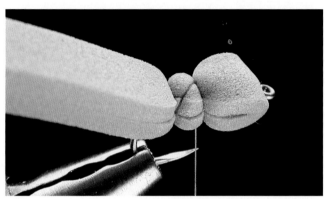

14. Cross the thread lightly across the top of the foam body about one-third of the way forward and make two more turns of thread to create the front of the first segment.

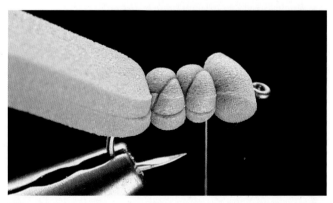

15. Make another upright segment one-third of the way forward on the hook shank with two more tight turns of thread. Continue forward by crossing on the top of the shank and make one more evenly spaced segment for a total of three bands of thread and two crosses.

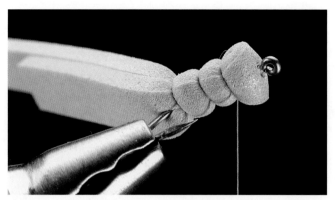

16. You should now have a fly that looks a little something like this. All the crosses are on top of the fly, and the bottom of the fly will only show a nicely segmented body.

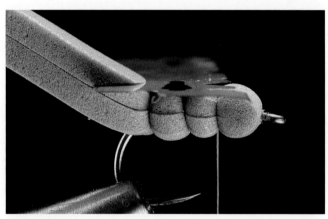

17. The foam should extend from the hook bend at the angle shown. Use a double-edged razor blade to make a straight cut through the extended foam. This cut, once finished, appears to be made at an angle but is truly a straight cut following along the top of the body. Make one straight cut through the foam without sawing back and forth.

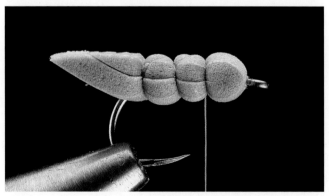

18. The finished cut looks like this. See how the cut is in a straight line right along the top of the foam body?

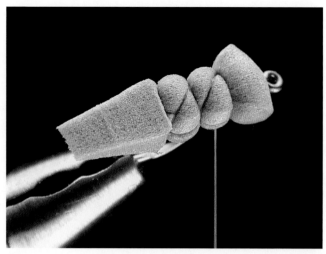

19. Now, clean up the extended portion of the body. Since the back end of the fly is a bit wider than the rest of the fly, cut some foam from each side to form a tapered end. I don't try to cut the body to a point, but merely taper it a bit toward the back end. Trim the other side. Note that the head of the fly (the last segment near the hook eye) is also a bit wider than the rest of the fly.

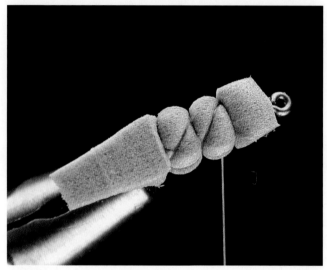

20. Trim a sliver of foam from each side of the head to square it up.

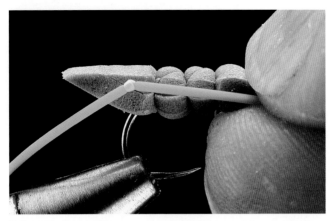

21. Take a single strand of medium rubber and tie a tight overhand knot in it. Lay the leg up against the side of the hook shank with the knot even with the hook bend. Don't worry if the leg doesn't line up perfectly as you will be able to adjust this later.

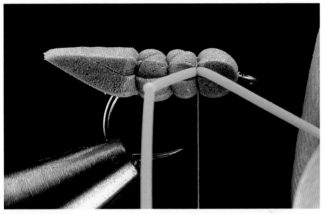

22. Catch the front end of the leg with a wrap of thread in the first segment behind the head. Make two firm wraps of thread over the leg.

23. Cross the thread back into the second segment as shown here.

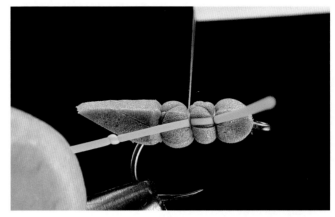

24. Catch the back end of the leg in the second segment with two more firm wraps of thread. It is likely that the leg will twist under the thread torque and kick the lower leg out to the side.

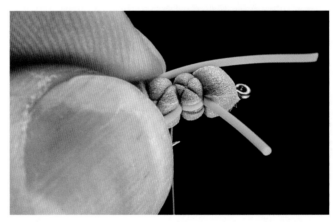

25. Knot another piece of rubber leg as you did with the first and lay it along the far side of the hook with the knot even with the bend. Catch the leg in the second segment with two firm wraps of thread.

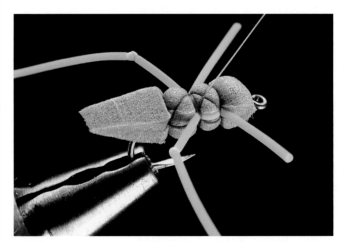

26. Once the leg is caught in the second segment, cross the thread back to the front segment.

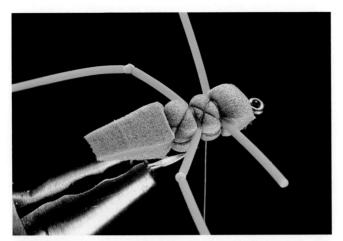

27. Catch the front of the leg in the first segment with two more tight turns of thread. You can see here that the legs are all askew and flailing about in all directions.

28. Grab the front end of the leg and twist it in your fingertips. Pull the leg forward a bit, and the twist will work its way down the leg and start to influence the back end. Twist and pull some more to set the leg in place with the lower section from the knot (knee) down is pointing straight down.

29. The near leg ought to look like this now.

30. Twist the far leg in the same manner to position it like the first leg. The twist here is exaggerated to be clear. You need to twist the leg and shorten it down slightly at the same time to allow the twist to work back down the leg and move the other end into position.

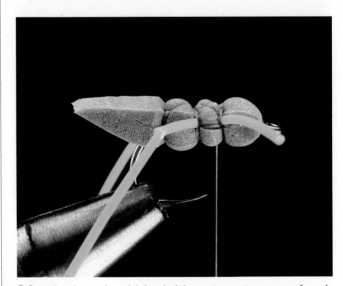

31. The legs should look like mirror images of each other as shown here. Note that the knots are now just slightly in front of the bend.

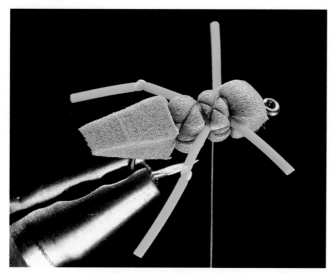

32. Clip the legs so the thigh and shin are about the same length. The ends of the back legs should extend just past the end of the body, and the front legs should be about half as long as the back ones.

34. Place the hair, measured to length, in your material hand and clip the butt ends as straight across as you can. Lay the hair on the top of the fly with the butt ends just behind the front of the fly body. Make two taut, but not tight, wraps of thread over the hair, taking care to keep them one on top of the other.

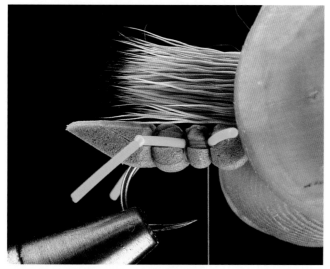

33. Clip, clean, and stack a clump of deer hock hair. Measure this clump against the hook so it is about as long as the hook shank. Deer hock is a fine short-tipped hair that comes from the lower leg of the deer. This hair is perfectly suited to smaller patterns as both the length and the smaller diameter is well proportioned to smaller flies. Deer body hair can sometimes have more solid tips that lend little buoyancy to the fly while deer hock maintains its inside diameter nearly all the way to the tips.

35. Place your index finger against the far side of the fly as you draw straight down on the thread. This keeps the hair from sliding over the shank when you flare it.

36. Whip-finish the thread right through the butt ends of the hair. Clip the thread.

37. Use a Sharpie marker to draw an elongated oval-shaped eye on each side of the head.

38. Bottom view. Note the bow-legged appearance of the rubber legs.

39. Top view. The flexed deer hair wing adds buoyancy and visibility to this tiny hopper.

40. Front view. The deer hair wing should be directly on top of the foam body.

BABY BOY HOPPER (TAN)

BABY BOY HOPPER (CHARTREUSE)

Hook:	#12-16 Tiemco 2499SP-BL
Thread:	Cinnamon 14/0 Gordon Griffith's
Body:	Tan Thin Fly Foam (2 mm)
Legs:	Tan round rubber (medium)
Wing:	Fine natural deer (hock)

Hook:	#12-16 Tiemco 2499SP-BL
Thread:	Olive 14/0 Gordon Griffith's
Body:	Chartreuse Thin Fly Foam (2 mm)
Legs:	Lime green round rubber (medium)
Wing:	Fine natural deer hair (hock)

BABY BOY HOPPER (CRICKET)

Hook:	#12-16 Tiemco 2499SP-BL
Thread:	Black 14/0 Gordon Griffith's
Body:	Black Thin Fly Foam (2 mm)
Legs:	Black round rubber (medium)
Wing:	Fine natural deer hair (hock)

FOURTEEN

GTH Variant

It was inching toward dark and the fish were really eating well, but finding my Lime Humpy in the fading light was becoming harder and harder. I knotted on an H&L Variant per Matt's advice, and sure enough, the bright white wings and tail showed up wonderfully. Unfortunately, the fish just didn't want to eat it. Apparently it was a bit too dark. I rummaged through my fly box and came up with an appropriately sized Royal Wulff, and we managed to scratch a few more fish up before the takeout, but I was left with the taste of defeat as well as a new challenge.

On the drive home that night, I considered combining these flies into one highly visible, variable color attractor pattern. As I drove I tried to decide which parts of each fly I would use, the wings from this one, the body color and shape of that one, the tail of the other . . . I couldn't wait to get home to hit the vise and dial this "new" pattern in. Well, it was about 11:00 P.M. when I

My GTH Variant combines attributes from several of my favorite patterns and is a powerful attractor pattern.

Opal Mirage Flash has taken the place of traditional pearl tinsel on my bench. Mirage has more vibrant color and luminescence than standard pearl tinsel.

finally pulled in the drive, and it took at least a few more minutes to convince my angelic wife that I would really be to bed in "just a little bit" while I ran downstairs to piece together my new Franken-Fly.

I had decided during the drive that I was going to use the white calf hair wings from the Wulff and H&L for my new pattern, and use white calf for the tail like in the H&L. These flies are super popular because they show up really well on the water, are durable, and float well, so the basic core of the fly was an easy decision.

I thought of using a dubbed body for the fly, but it occurred to me that if I did, I would just be tying yet another version of the Wulff. So I decided instead to make the profile of the H&L Variant body but substitute a few materials to give me a bit more durability as well as the option to alter the colors. I ended up using 70-denier Ultra Thread for the abdomen and a thorax of black peacock Ice Dub. The H&L, with its stripped-peacock-quill body and peacock thorax, has been time-tested and proven, but frankly it doesn't hold together all that well. Peacock is inherently delicate and no amount of glue, coating, or wire ribbing really seems to help. The thread body of my new fly would be coated with Gloss Coat for shine and durability. The dubbed thorax was not only much easier to form consistently, but it was more durable as well.

When I finally got to the point to hackle the fly I was at a bit of a standstill. I could go with the traditional heavy brown hackle collar, maybe branch off into a darker furnace or black, or even go lighter in an effort to make the fly more visible. The mixed brown and grizzly hackle collar is a mainstay in my fly boxes, and the Parachute Adams really is one of my favorite flies. It made sense to add these parts to the new fly, both from the aesthetic standpoint as well as what the fish have already told me. Brown and grizzly was the answer! I wrapped a heavy hackle collar on the fly in the vise and was really quite happy with this very first version. Typically, I'll hatch some great idea in my head and when I finally sit down to tie, it fails miserably. I was pleasantly surprised that this one went so well, and I headed off to bed just a few minutes after my angel began to snore.

The Mirage Tinsel tag was added later, in an effort to include a bit of flash in the pattern. I tried wrapping it over the thread abdomen at first, but it made the fly look like it was dressed up for an all-night rave. Seeing as how I was ripping off all the other patterns anyway, I decided to lift the tag idea from some of the old wet-fly patterns and used the Mirage as a small band at the rear of the fly under the tail. I later discovered that two post wraps around the tail elevated it so that the bright little tag sat nearer to or even into the water's surface where the fish could become entranced by its old timey magic. The new fly came around pretty quick given how long it typically takes me to be happy with a new pattern. I had just combined parts from the Royal Wulff, H&L Variant, Lime Humpy, the Adams, and even some old wet flies. Old parts, new fly?

I fished this new combination often for the rest of the summer whenever I would normally fish the Humpy or some other attractor dry, particularly when fishing late in the evening or in low light conditions. This fly falls into my "slim" attractor category; flies like hoppers or Stimulators fall into the "chunky" category. I like using this kind of fly when the fish are just a little shy of the typical bigger attractors as its somewhat smaller profile seems to fit the fishes' feeding pattern a bit better than a chunky fly, which needs more of a commitment. With its flashy tag, bright colors, and bushy wings, I hesitate to call this fly subtle, but it is certainly a bit more reserved than the larger attractor dry flies common on our western waters.

Of course, a hair-wing fly like this is right at home in broken pocketwater and on small streams. Its incredible buoyancy and visibility make it a natural for picking pockets, and the brighter colors can make high-country brookies and cutts get suicidal. I have also had great success fishing GTH Variant as an indicator dry over shallow holding fish. The bright wings make the fly easy to follow while the bushy hackle creates just enough flotation to keep a small dropper suspended at the right level.

I have since found that a small GTH Variant fished tight to the bank from the boat or even prospecting through a wide riffle can pull fish up. I had great fishing late this summer throwing a small wine-colored version to fish sipping Tricos on the Colorado River, which came as a surprise to me. Apparently the fish seem to think this fly fits well enough into the Trico genre to move for it, and the hair wings and tails make for a much more visible fly for the angler. I love revelations like this, as they prove to me the more I think I know, the less I really do.

I have added several color variations to the GTH Variant in the past few years such as a darker wine-colored version, a hot pink, and even a bright blue in addition to the original lime color to round out the spectrum. The dark version works well for darker insects like Tricos and small *Baetis*, and in larger sizes, even Green Drakes. The bright pink version is sort of my take on the attractor style of the Royal Wulff with a twist that makes it just different enough from the patterns that everyone else is throwing. The blue version was developed to test the same theory that brought about my deep blue Poison Tung, and it seems that theory works out similarly for a dry fly as it has for the nymph: that blue color pulls fish in from long distances, particularly on overcast days and in the evenings. Of course the lime version was developed to feed off the effectiveness and popularity of flies like the Lime Humpy and Lime Trude. I won't say that I even have the most basic understanding of why these odd colors work as well as they do, but I can only speculate that these colors show up to fish differently. The distances moved by fish to eat these flies and the consistent effectiveness of these patterns has proven to me that sometimes getting a little wild is just where we want to be.

TYING THE GTH VARIANT

GTH VARIANT
(LIME)

Hook:	#10-18 Tiemco 100SP-BL
Thread:	White 74-denier Lagartun
Wing:	White calf body hair
Tag:	Opal Mirage Tinsel (medium)
Tail:	White calf body hair
Abdomen:	Fluorescent green 70-denier Ultra Thread
Thorax:	Black peacock Ice Dub
Hackle:	Brown and grizzly
Note:	Finish the fly with black 70-denier Ultra Thread.

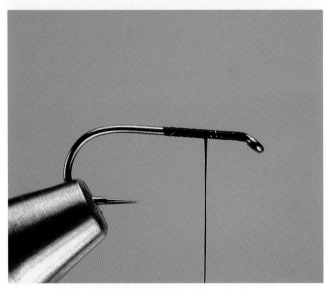

1. Typically I tie this fly using white thread throughout because it blends right into the wings on the finished fly. But for the sake of photographic clarity I will be using black to show some of the thread work in the next several steps.

Attach the thread just behind the hook eye and make a smooth thread base back to the midpoint on the shank. Return the thread to the 75 percent point on the shank, or the middle of the front half of the shank.

2. Cut, clean, and stack a clump of calf body hair. You really want to make sure that you have cleaned all the short hairs from the clump before putting the hair in the stacker. The amount of hair will vary with the size of the fly you are tying, so try to visualize how much hair you will need to create two wings. Remove the hair from the stacker and measure the clump against the hook so it is a shank-length long.

3. Tie the butt ends of the hair down to the shank with a firm band of thread. Make the first turn of thread over the hair at the 75 percent point shown above and then wrap back toward the bend to create the band. You want to make sure you have a quarter of the shank left exposed in front of the wing. The tips of the hair should extend beyond the tie down about a shank length, so check the measurement using the shank of another hook of the same size and style as you are tying on.

4. Continue wrapping a smooth band of thread back to just short of the midpoint on the shank. Try to keep the butt ends of the hair on top of the hook as you wrap over them.

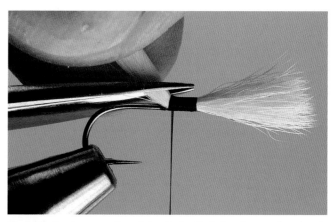

5. Lift the butt ends of the hair slightly above the shank and trim them at a slight angle. I try to make this cut as parallel to the shank as I can to help taper the butt ends cleanly back down to the shank.

6. You want a cleanly tapered butt end on the wing. Trim any straggling hairs so that they don't get in the way later.

7. Wrap the thread back over the tapered butt ends of the hair to the bend. Don't worry about completely covering the butt ends with thread, as you can achieve that in the next several steps. Try to keep the wraps to a minimum.

8. Tie in a short length of pearl Mirage Tinsel on top of the shank at the hook bend with just two turns of thread.

9. Begin wrapping the Mirage Tinsel around the hook traveling back and down around the hook bend.

10. Make about three or four turns of tinsel around the apex of the hook bend.

11. Reverse the direction of travel with the tinsel and overwrap the previous turns of tinsel back to the starting point. You have essentially made a double layer tag of tinsel down around the hook bend. Unwind one turn of the thread that you used to tie the tinsel in and then trap the long end of the tinsel under it. This move allows you to tie the tinsel both in and off with only two turns of thread to keep a slim profile. Clip the remaining tinsel as close to the shank as you can.

12. Cut, clean, and stack another clump of calf body hair that is one-half to one-third the size of the bunch for the wings. Measure this clump against the wing, being confident that the wing is a shank-length long. (If you're not confident the wing is the right length, why are you tying in the tail? We've already talked about this!)

13. Lay the smaller clump of calf hair against the hook bend and tie it in on top of the shank with a band of thread wraps moving forward from the hook bend. Stop just short of the middle of the hook, making sure the hair stays on top of the shank.

14. Lift the butt ends of the tail clump up above the shank. Note the distance between the butt ends of the wing and where you stopped the thread band securing the tail. They are close together but definitely not overlapped.

15. Bring the tips of your scissors in from the rear of the hook and lift the butt ends of the hair up and away from the hook shank. Make a clean cut as parallel to the shank as you can.

16. The trimmed ends should provide a smooth transition to the butt ends of the wing, eliminating any gaps between the two.

17. Wrap forward over the butt ends of the tail right up to the base of the wing, creating a smooth and slightly tapered thread underbody.

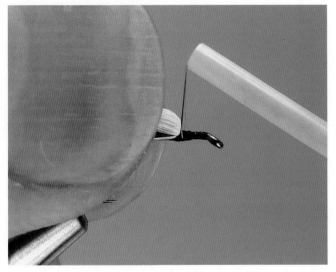

18. Close the tips of your thumb and index fingers of your material hand under and around the hook shank and draw them up from the bottom of the hook to sweep the calf hair wing up and back along the shank. This ensures you get all the hairs in one swipe. Make several tight turns of thread right at the base of the wing. I try to keep the length between my bobbin and the hook short here for precise placement of these thread wraps. Build a thread dam against the base of the wing to prop it at a right angle to the hook shank. I try to push the end of the bobbin behind the wing on the bottom side of the hook to assure that the wraps butt as tightly as possible against the base of the wing.

19. The wing should now be close to perpendicular to the hook shank. If the wing is still angled sharply forward you'll need to go back and build a better thread dam. Note that there are a few hairs splayed out on the sides of this wing and that it is fanned out a bit. You'll fix that in the next step.

20. Grasp the entire wing in your thread hand and pass the thread from the front of the wing to the back edge of the wing two times.

21. These thread wraps gather the hair into a single clean clump.

22. Eyeball measure about half the wing clump. You want two wings that are as even as possible. Grasp the far half of the wing clump in your material hand and bring the thread diagonally between the two bunches of hair from the backside of the near clump to the front side of the far clump. Do this about four to six times. The trick to evenly splitting a bunch of hair into two wings is to make these wraps very tight and directly on top of each other. Vertically stacked thread wraps will help to separate the hair into two even bunches whereas wraps that are spread out will push the wings down and forward.

24. Bring the thread to the immediate base of the wings at the front. Grasp the near wing in your material hand and make another half dozen stacked turns of thread going from the front of the near wing to the back of the far wing. Be sure those thread wraps stay on top of one another.

23. Before you make another set of diagonal wraps in the opposite direction, make an anchor wrap of thread all the way around the hook shank behind the wings. This wrap will prevent the previous thread wraps from influencing the wraps on the other side.

25. Now make another anchor wrap of thread all the way around the shank behind the wings. You have just divided the hair clump into two even bunches of hair. The hair clumps need to be equal because a fly tied with uneven wings will spin when you cast it and turn your tippet into a tangled, furled mess.

26. Here is a close-up of the base of the wing. Note that the thread wraps are all nicely stacked on top of one another and there is little bulk between the wings.

27. When I post the wings, I turn the bobbin upside down and with slightly overlapping turns of thread, I work the thread up the base of the wing to pull the fibers together into a neat bunch. The direction that you post each wing is important. If you wrap the base of the far wing counterclockwise for a right-hander and clockwise for lefties, thread tension tends to pull the wing back and more upright than if you go in the opposite direction.

28. Wrap the thread post on the base of the far wing first and pull the wing upright on the last wrap with rearward thread tension. Bring the thread smoothly under the shank without relaxing the tension on it and finish with a tight anchor wrap around the shank behind the wings.

29. You will post the near wing just like the far wing only this post will need to be made in the opposite direction of the far wing. So if you are tying right-handed and have posted the far wing by wrapping counterclockwise, you'll want to post the near wing by going clockwise to keep the thread tension going back toward the tail on the last turn.

Finishing the posts in the correct direction will help to maneuver the wings even more upright. As you pull back on the thread at the top of the post draw the thread tightly to the rear of the hook to stand the wing up a bit more than it was before.

30. To anchor the thread again, wrap from the top of the wing post around the hook shank.

31. Now you have two perfectly divided and upright hair wings. I apologize for the complicated explanation, but you probably didn't buy this book to get the short answer.

32. If your wings aren't close to a 45-degree angle to each other as shown here, position them with your fingers so that they are. Don't be shy about pulling and prodding them into position. Tight thread wraps on the posts will allow you to position the wings in any configuration you like. If the wings won't stay where you put them, your post wraps probably weren't tight enough.

33. Wrap the thread smoothly back to the base of the tail with as few turns as possible.

34. Grasp the tail and make two turns of thread around its base as you did when you posted the wings. These wraps will compress the hair in the tail into a cleaner bunch and help to elevate it as well.

35. Make an anchor wrap around the shank immediately in front of the tail to lock everything in place.

36. Bring the thread back up to the front of the wings and whip-finish and clip the thread.

37. Here I have switched to a fly tied with white thread, which blends into the wings better than black thread and makes for a cleaner looking fly in the end.

38. Start the fluorescent green thread at the point shown (60 percent point). I use a separate bobbin to work this thread as it is much easier to quickly wrap and form the body.

39. Build a smooth and slightly tapered thread body all the way back to the base of the tail. Work forward again, overlapping layers of thread as needed to create a slight taper toward the front of the hook. You may need to stop and unwind the thread every now and again so it lies flat.

40. Whip-finish the green thread behind the wings and clip.

41. Put a drop of Gloss Coat on the thread body, being sure to coat it all the way around the hook shank. I also like to add some cement to the bases of the wings to lock everything down. Typically I will tie several body blanks like this at a time and cement them as I go. By the time I get a half dozen or so done, the Gloss Coat has dried to a shiny smooth finish on the first fly, and I can continue on with the tying process from there.

42. Now use some black thread to better blend into the dubbing and hackle yet to come. Start the black thread right on top of the front edge of the green thread body.

43. Twist on a small amount of the black peacock Ice Dub and wrap it to form a ball of dubbing. Make sure you have some space between this ball of dubbing and the wings for the hackle.

44. Select and prepare a brown and a grizzly hackle feather. The feathers should have fibers equal to 1 to 1½ hook gaps. Strip the butt ends of the feathers, and lay them with the inside of the grizzly feather facing the outside of the brown feather, or vice versa, it doesn't really matter which one is where. Tie the feathers in at the same time at the front edge of the thorax dubbing with the inside of both feathers toward the shank of the hook. Notice that the stripped portions of the quills extend to just behind the hook eye and that there is a bit of bare stem beyond the tie-in point at the base of the feathers.

45. Wrap forward over the stripped quills up to the eye of the hook and back again to the front edge of the thorax. Return the thread to the hook eye once more, forming a smooth thread base for the hackle and tightly securing it as you go.

47. Make at least two more turns of hackle in front of the wings and end with the feathers at the back edge of the index point. The tips of the feathers should be upright.

46. Grasp both hackles in your fingertips and wrap them at the same time. The first turn of hackle should be right at the front edge of the dubbing ball. Make three turns of hackle behind the wings, keeping the wraps as upright as possible.

48. Hold the tips of the hackles above the hook and again, as upright as possible while you take the thread straight up and over their bases two times to tie them off. Holding the feathers at a steep upright angle eliminates any chance of catching loose hackle fibers in the thread wraps.

49. Grasp the base of the tips of the feathers immediately above the hook eye as shown here. The trick to this is to grab the feathers closer than a hackle fiber length from the hook eye. By grabbing the feathers right down at the hook eye, you can be sure to bundle all the fibers, and the center stem, in your fingers. Hold everything tightly together and reach in and make a single clean snip with the tips of your finest scissors. No mess, no stubs, no loose hackle fibers left over.

50. Build a few wraps of thread to cover the stub ends of the hackles, but don't go crazy with the thread turns. Your whip-finish wraps will help to build and smooth the thread head as well.

51. Build a smooth thread head with three to five turns on the whip-finisher, cinch the thread down tightly, and clip it.

52. Rotate the fly in your vise so that the fly is upside down with the eye at the top. Place a thin drop of Gloss Coat on the thread head, letting a bit of the excess run back into the hackle wraps. By turning the hook to this eye-up orientation, you make the hook eye the high point and eliminate any chance of the cement running into and clogging the hook eye.

53. Finished fly. The tail should angle slightly up, and the hackle collar should be thick and dense.

GTH VARIANT (WINE)

Hook:	#10-18 Tiemco 100SP-BL
Thread:	White 74-denier Lagartun
Wing:	White calf body hair
Tag:	Opal Mirage Tinsel (medium)
Tail:	White calf body hair
Abdomen:	Wine 70-denier Ultra Thread
Thorax:	Black peacock Ice Dub
Hackle:	Brown and grizzly

GTH VARIANT (BLUE)

Hook:	#10-18 Tiemco 100SP-BL
Thread:	White 74-denier Lagartun
Wing:	White calf body hair
Tag:	Opal Mirage Tinsel (medium)
Tail:	White calf body hair
Abdomen:	Peacock blue 70-denier Ultra Thread
Thorax:	Black peacock Ice Dub
Hackle:	Brown and grizzly

GTH VARIANT (PINK)

Hook:	#10-18 Tiemco 100SP-BL
Thread:	White 74-denier Lagartun
Wing:	White calf body hair
Tag:	Opal Mirage Tinsel (medium)
Tail:	White calf body hair
Abdomen:	Fluorescent pink 70-denier Ultra Thread
Thorax:	Black peacock Ice Dub
Hackle:	Brown and grizzly

FIFTEEN

Lead Eyed Gonga

Few things are as fun as throwing streamers from a moving boat. The repetition of cast, strip, strip, cast, strip, strip, as you ply each likely hole creates a heightened sense of anticipation for the inevitable strikes that are to follow. Watching a big brown trout flash on and chase your fly is reward enough, but the grab is what keeps you casting. Seeing a big predator close in, open his mouth, and hit your fly like it owes him money is spectacular, and I simply love throwing streamers.

I have worked on the Lead Eyed Gonga for many years to get it right at the bench and on the water. The original version had a complicated three-color marabou wing, tied in and lashed over the body of the fly like a Matuka. I added a short marabou collar to the pattern to imitate a natural sculpin's large pectoral fins, and completed the fly with the spun craft fur head and lead eyes. This beta version worked well enough, but the tying process became much more complicated than it really needed to be, so I began to tinker with the design.

I like my streamers to have some volume and bulk as well as weight. The Lead Eyed Gonga has all of these characteristics.

The ubiquitous Woolly Bugger is, to this day, one of the best streamers ever devised, but its inherent lack of detail leaves a bit of room for improvement. Coupling the best attributes of the bugger with the highlights of the original Gonga has produced a realistic fly that is simple to tie.

Working from the bugger perspective, I used a heavy marabou tail. Marabou should be included in just about every streamer as this lively feather gives a lifelike illusion when stripped through the water. Marabou can also create volume in a fly, presenting a large profile without a lot of bulk. While I do believe there are situations that call for a sparse, delicate streamer pattern like Chris Schrantz's Platte River Spider, I still firmly believe in the power of "The Meat," and to that end, I like flies with some weight and profile to them.

In place of the typically sparse saddle hackle of the bugger, and to stay in my volume-based theme, I use a thick, oversized schlappen feather to palmer the body of the fly. Schlappen feathers come from the base of a rooster saddle and are nearly all web. These soft feathers create a breathing body on the Gonga and allow me to vary the colors at will. I wrap the schlappen with several evenly spaced turns over the body, creating a solid profile without too much inherent weight. I finish the body of the fly with a couple more turns of schlappen at the front to create a shoulder on the fly that replicates the taper of a natural baitfish. I really think of the schlappen as the body of the fly rather than the dubbed portion underneath it. I use Ice Dub along the shank in a thickly dubbed rope to create a soft bed for the hackle wraps to bite into as well as to add a slight bit of flash on the finished product. Brushing out the dubbing and hackle once the fly is completed leaves some straggling fibers of flash peeking out along the body, rather than an obvious, and sometimes overwhelming, chunk of Krystal Flash or Flashabou. Even a fly like the Gonga needs some subtlety.

The latest addition to the Gonga has been the chrome Sili Legs tied in at the front of the body. Many streamers incorporate rubber legs to provide life and movement to the fly, and these new metallic silicone-based legs enhance the fly with a mottled glimmer. I like the action of the Sili Legs, particularly in slower pockets where I can finesse the fly a bit by pumping the rod tip. The legs will open up and collapse along the sides of the fly, contributing even more life to the profile and perhaps replicating the fluttering pectoral fins of the real thing.

The head of this fly is perhaps its most unique attribute. Conventionally, streamers like this have been tied with a heavy spun deer hair head to push water, creating micro sound waves in the water that can help the fish find the fly. Unfortunately, deer hair heads present several liabilities, not the least of which is the propensity to float. I needed a material that could create the same type of profile without the buoyancy or time requirements of the deer hair. I turned to the same materials I use on my Ragin' Craven pattern. Using the soft craft fur or Polar Fibre for the head of this fly turned out to be just the solution I was after. By placing the butt ends of these fibers into a dubbing loop, I found I could create a thick, flowing chenille that could easily be shaped with scissors and wrapped in and around the lead eyes and that would sink like a rock, yet shed water on the back cast. Applying the material with the dubbing loop has also proven to make the fly incredibly durable, a feature I enjoy when faced with the prospect of tying more of them. I hate having a productive fly get chewed beyond recognition after only a few casts.

A pair of medium-sized lead eyes, painted with both an iris and a pupil, creates a lifelike head as well as a target area for the fish to home in on. I tie the eyes in on the bottom of the hook shank to keep the fly riding hook point down. Tying the eyes on the top of the shank

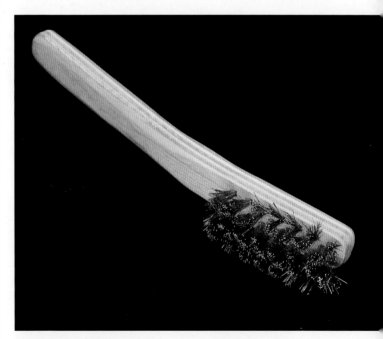

The Collier Dubbing Brush is an invaluable fly-tying tool. I use it for everything from combing out dubbing to cleaning deer hair, and it is particularly valuable for flies made with Craft Fur and Polar Fibre.

results in the fly swimming with the hook point up, and while this seems like a good idea based on the idea of reduced snagging, I find that flies that ride hook up tend to hook poorly, and they can also damage the fish. The large gap hooks I prefer for flies like this dig too deep into the roof of a fish's mouth when tied upside down, and the hooking mortality can be more than I am comfortable with. For the fishing I do—pounding the banks—snagging the bottom is less of an issue, so the prospect of a snag-free fly is less important than a solid, less-damaging hook up.

For color variations, olive was the first choice, based on the coloration of the real sculpins in our part of the country. It occurred to me at some point that many of the fish that were dining on the Gonga had perhaps never even seen a real sculpin and that I should try some other colors. One of my favorite streamer colors over the years has been a pale creamy yellow, which I believe imitates the buttery belly of a small brown trout. When you think about it, a predatory trout looking up at a streamer or real baitfish sees the fly from the bottom.

This light-colored variation is easy to see, and being able to see the fly well and track it throughout the retrieve has proven indispensable to me. With a solid visual lock on the fly I find that I'm better able to

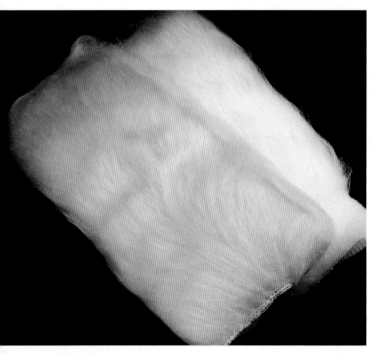

Polar Fibre is a fine, dense synthetic fur useful for tails and wings on a variety of patterns. I use Polar Fibre in both my Gonga and Bonefish Junk patterns.

manipulate it, especially when it's being run down by an angry brown. I added a hot spot of bright yellow marabou on the top of the tail to make the fly even more visible to the angler and create a streaking flash of color.

The third color variation I have developed is the rusty version. Based on the effectiveness of flies like Tim Heng's Autumn Splendor, the rusty brown-orange translation seemed to be an obvious hit. While not an exact match for anything I have ever seen, color variations like this add some attractor value and can, at times, present just the change-up fish are looking for. I have since found that many of our western rivers are inhabited by good populations of crayfish, and the Rusty Gonga can imitate these quite well when stripped and hopped across the riverbed, particularly if fished under an indicator.

I also tie this fly in black. Black is the first, and sometimes only, color choice of many anglers, and I am no exception to this. The stark profile of a very dark fly, particularly on a dark, overcast day, is hard to argue with.

FISHING THE GONGA

When I fish the Gonga, or any other large streamer pattern, I start with a 9-foot 0X leader attached to the end of my floating fly line on a 9-foot 6-weight rod. In most cases, I prefer the combination of the floating line and a long leader when fishing a heavily weighted fly. The longer leader allows the fly to sink to adequate river depths, yet not be pulled back up so quickly by the floating fly line. Typically, the retrieve length from the boat is relatively short, so using a sinking line is not necessary. I always cut the level tippet section from the mono leader and replace it with a high-quality fluorocarbon tippet. Occasionally I like to throw a cast up into the bushes just to check for any overly aggressive squirrels or other rodents lying in wait for a tasty morsel, and the abrasion resistance of the fluorocarbon tippet holds up much better than monofilament.

Though I don't believe I catch more fish because of the fluorocarbon, I do spend more time fishing and less time replacing tippet when I use it instead of monofilament. I tie the fly on using a no-slip mono loop, which allows the fly more freedom of movement at the end of the leader and lets it swing from side to side a bit more than a clinch knot or other tightly bound version.

I will often fish streamers in tandem, with a larger, more bulky and heavily weighted fly like a Gonga on the end of the leader, and a sparser, more delicate and unweighted pattern tied on a dropper behind. I tie the dropper section to the eye of the larger fly with a five-turn clinch knot and pull the knot off center on the right side of the hook eye so the tippet trails down one side of the fly. I pull the knot to the right side because the hook eye is smooth and solid on this side and there is no chance of the tippet abrading where the wire closes back to the shank on the left.

Streamers are the only flies I rig in tandem with an eye-to-eye connection, as I find that retrieving these heavier and more bulky flies keeps the dropper tippets taut, and having it tied to the hook bend can sometimes inhibit strikes. This is perhaps entirely in my head, but I feel better about fishing them this way so that's what I go with. Your mileage may vary.

The actual retrieve of flies like the Gonga can vary greatly depending on the water type, species of fish, and speed of current. I generally start by casting the fly as close as possible to the bank, and I immediately start stripping the fly out from the bank at a right angle to the current. I try to keep my rod tip low, usually in the water, to keep a direct line of contact between me and the fly.

Oftentimes, a fish will be sitting in a quiet little pocket waiting to ambush some poor baitfish or smaller trout, and this retrieve makes the fly appear to have spotted the predator and is making a hasty retreat. Just like grizzly bears, brown trout can hardly resist something that runs from them, so we want our fly to run away just fast enough to illicit this chase response. You must be careful to strip the fly just fast enough that the fish has to commit to running it down, yet not so fast that he can't catch it. There is a delicate game of cat and mouse in a situation like this, and many times the fish will follow the fly far out into the river. This is where reading the fish comes into play. A fish that is hot on the trail and totally committed will generally crush the fly no matter how fast you strip, but sometimes you get a fish that is interested but just won't make that mistake. In these cases I try to slow the fly a bit, pausing my retrieve to allow the fish to close in, perhaps even pumping the rod tip to make the fly jig a bit and give the impression that this innocent little fish is somehow injured or tired and will be an easy meal. Varying the retrieve and reading the fish's body language goes a long way toward converting

A Dyna-King Dubbing Whirl creates tight dubbing loops quickly and easily. It is simple to use and produces great results.

follows into takes, but it's something that is learned from time on the water observing the fish in action. Some days the fish just want to play chase, and frankly, that can be great fun in and of itself, but getting them to close the deal and blast the fly is the ultimate satisfaction. I think this says something interesting about my own perceptions, as I get great satisfaction out of fooling these pea-brained little critters.

When I finally do get the fish to grab the fly, I just keep on stripping long and hard to drive the hook into its mouth. Lifting the rod pulls the fly up at an angle and almost guarantees a missed strike. It is imperative to strip-strike, keeping the rod tip pointed at the fly and the line drawing tight with each strip. Strip striking also keeps the fly in front of the fish, giving it a chance at a follow-up strike in the event that it, or you, missed the first time. I have had lots of great streamer-fishing days where I have not landed a fish. The exhilarating flashes and follows of a large fish chasing down a streamer is great fun by itself, and I find that while I enjoy the strike as much as anyone else, actually hooking and landing the fish is somewhat anticlimactic. The heavy tippets employed in this type of fishing negate the need to "play" a fish, and in most cases I can just strip the fish in, giving it little headway to pull line. Every now and again you'll get a fish that needs to do a bit of headshaking, and perhaps even make a little run, but I will usually just lower the rod tip as the fish pulls, giving it a bit of headway before dropping the hammer again and putting the heat on it. I try to get the fish's head up to the surface as quickly as possible and skate it toward the net. When done right, the fish is landed quickly and efficiently without any excessive lactic acid build-up and can be safely returned to the water just a bit wiser, but none the worse for wear. Fish that are overplayed can generate excessive amounts of lactic acid, which can lead to death if they are not revived properly. I always try to land my fish as quickly as possible to eliminate or at least reduce any harm done.

TYING THE LEAD EYED GONGA

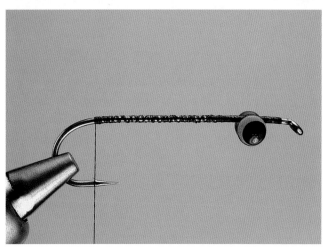

1. Attach lead eyes about three eye-lengths back from the hook eye on the underside of the hook shank with several firm X wraps. Apply a small drop of Zap-A-Gap to the thread wraps to lock everything into place. Continue wrapping the thread back to the hook bend, forming a smooth thread base.

2. Measure a marabou feather against the shank so it is equal to about half a shank length.

LEAD EYED GONGA

Hook:	#2-4 Tiemco 5263
Thread:	3/0 Danville Monocord
Eyes:	Lead, painted yellow
Tail:	Sculpin olive marabou
Hackle:	Olive grizzly-variant schlappen
Body:	Olive Ice Dub
Legs:	Green/black Chrome Sili Legs
Head:	Olive Polar Fibre

3. Tie the first marabou feather in at the bend with several tight turns of thread. It should extend just slightly more than half a shank-length beyond the bend. Measure another marabou feather so it is equal in length to the first and tie it in on top of the first. The tail is full on this fly.

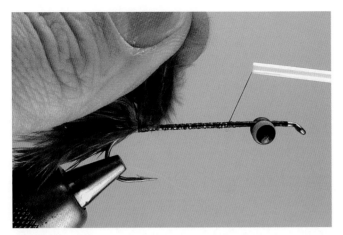

4. Lift the butt ends of the marabou feathers up and wrap the thread along the shank to just behind the lead eyes.

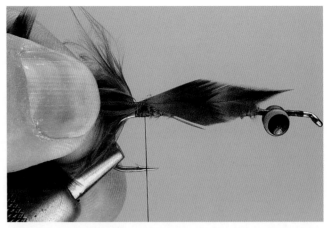

7. Select a soft, wide schlappen feather and preen the fibers back along the tip as shown above. Tie the tip of the feather in with the outside facing you along the near side of the hook.

5. Lay the marabou butts along the shank and bind them in place with a few tight turns of thread.

8. Dub the thread with a heavy loose layer of Ice Dub and begin the body at the hook bend.

6. Clip the remaining stub ends of the marabou as close as you can and wrap back over the marabou along the shank to the hook bend.

9. Wrap the dubbing forward loosely, creating a full, shaggy body. Dub all the way up to just behind the lead eyes. The body should have just a slight taper.

10. Hold the schlappen feather above the hook so it is taut and fold the hackle fibers back to the rear side of the quill as you would for a wet fly collar. You want all the fibers creased back to the backside of the stem. (See the Soft Hackle Emerger for more details on folding hackle.)

12. Stroke the fibers back along the body and, at the same time, brush out some of the body dubbing with a wire brush. Pinch the hackle down tight against the body with your fingers so that it slopes back.

11. Palmer the schlappen feather forward with evenly spaced turns to the front of the body. Stroke the hackle fibers back as you wrap, and tie the feather off at the front of the body with several tight turns of thread.

13. Lay three long strands of Sili Legs in at the front edge of the body and bind them down at the center of their length with half of the strands lying parallel to the shank along the near side of the hook.

14. Pull the other end of the Sili Legs back along the far side of the hook and bind them in place with two tight turns of thread so that they lie along either side of the hook. Do not trim them to length just yet as their length will make it easier to keep them out of the way in the interim.

15. Pull the Sili Legs back along the sides of the hook and push them into your material spring to hold them out of the way in the next few steps.

16. Cut a long, slim clump of Polar Fibre or Craft Fur from the "hide." Try to keep the fibers aligned in a sheet as shown here. You are going to cut the top half of these fibers away and use them to make the collar in the next step.

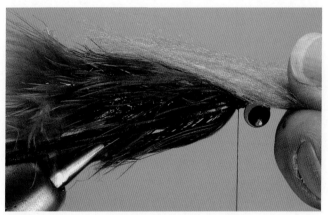

17. Lay the tips of the Polar Fibre clump in along the top of the hook so that the tips extend to the base (front end) of the tail.

18. Tie the tips in place with several tight turns of thread. You want these fibers to form a collar around the top 180 degrees of the hook. Clip any remaining butt ends as close as you can.

19. Form a dubbing loop with the thread and insert the Dyna-King Dubbing Whirl into the bottom of the loop.

20. Lay the butt ends of that clump of Polar Fibre into the dubbing loop and trim the edges as square as you can, using sharp scissors. I find it easier to trim the fibers square after I have placed them in the loop. Make sure that the fibers are spread out evenly and there are no heavy clumps in the loop. You may need to add an additional clump of butt ends to the loop to fill out the head.

21. Spin the dubbing whirl to create a fur rope as shown here. You only need a few inches so don't get carried away. Use that wire brush (Collier's Dubbing Brush) to stroke the fibers in the rope downward. This will make them lie back, similarly to the hackle we folded earlier.

22. Make two turns of the Polar Fibre rope behind the eyes and at the front edge of the body. Use the brush to stroke the fibers back out of the way as you wrap.

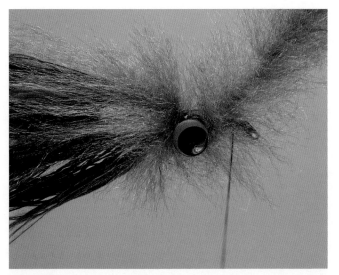

23. Make a figure eight around the eyes with the rope. That is, come from behind the eyes and under the hook around the base of the near eye, and then continue around to the back of the far eye.

24. Now come up again on the back side of the near eye and finish by crossing that wrap to the front of the eyes over the top of the near eye. You want to fill the head out a bit as you wrap, so make sure to make a complete figure eight.

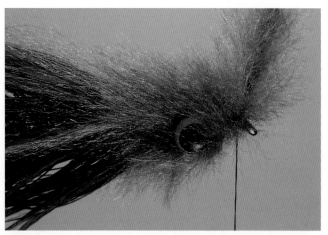

25. Make two more wraps of the rope in front of the eyes to finish out the head shape. Keep using that brush as you wrap to stroke the fibers back along the way.

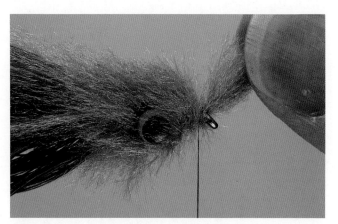

26. If there is still extra rope left over, let the dubbing whirl hang so it will untwist a bit and loosen up on the Polar Fibre strands. Once it has untwisted a bit, you can go in and tie off the loop with far less bulk than if you had skipped this step. Make sure to tie the loop off tightly.

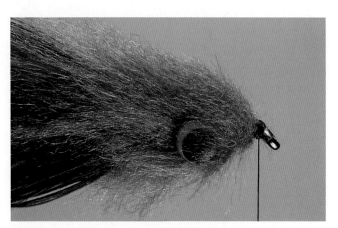

27. Form a smooth thread head and whip-finish.

28. Now, get back to work with that brush and stroke all the head fibers back along the body. You want to brush out any trapped fibers here as well.

29. Trim the head into an elongated, tapered shape as shown here. There is really not much trimming needed. I just go in and trim along the outsides of the eyes to expose them a bit and smooth off the overall shape of the head. If you do this right, it only takes a few snips.

30. Use a Sharpie marker to make bands along the top of the head and the collar. Keep these bands pretty narrow and don't try to work them too far down into the head.

31. Guess what? More brushing! Use the brush to smear the ink throughout the top of the head and the collar. Your goal is to darken the top of the fly but still leave some variegation.

32. Now you can trim the legs. You want them to extend back to just short of the end of the tail. Once trimmed, they'll dangle down along the underside of the hook. Make sure to separate them if they try to stick together.

33. This is a better view of the leg length in relation to the tail.

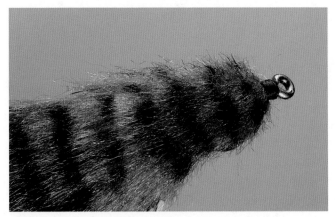

34. Top view of head. Note the tapered shape and width.

35. Finished fly. Pay attention to the overall shape of the fly and make sure the collar covers the entire top of the body. The Gonga should have a streamlined shape and wide head.

TALLOW GONGA

Hook:	#2 Tiemco 5263
Thread:	Tan 3/0 Monocord
Eyes:	Lead (medium), painted yellow
Tail:	Yellow over tan marabou
Hackle:	Tan Metz Magnum saddle or tan schlappen
Body:	Pale yellow Ice Dub
Legs:	Gold/black Chrome Sili Legs
Head:	Shrimp Polar Fibre, colored with yellow and sepia marker on top

RUSTY GONGA

Hook:	#2 Tiemco 5263
Thread:	Brown 3/0 Monocord
Eyes:	Lead (medium), painted red
Tail:	Brown over rusty marabou
Hackle:	Grizzly dyed orange Metz Magnum saddle or orange dyed grizzly variant schlappen
Body:	Rusty brown Ice Dub
Legs:	Copper/black Chrome Sili Legs
Head:	Root beer Craft Fur

BLACK GONGA

Hook:	#2 Tiemco 5263
Thread:	Black 3/0 Monocord
Eyes:	Lead (medium), painted green
Tail:	Black marabou
Hackle:	Black schlappen
Body:	Peacock black Ice Dub
Legs:	Green/black Chrome Sili Legs
Head:	Black Polar Fibre

SIXTEEN

Bonefish Junk

I went on my first saltwater fishing trip nearly twenty years ago now and have since become thoroughly addicted to the warm salt air and turbocharged fish found in these tropical destinations. I don't get the chance to spend as much time in the salt as I would like these days, and I'm not sure that this would even be possible given my current level of addiction, but I love to spend a day wading or standing in the bow of a flats boat hunting fish.

It was January 3, deep in the midst of a long and snowy winter back home when I found myself wander-ing an enormous white sand flat off of South Andros. I found it hard to keep myself focused on the water, scan-ning to and fro for signs of feeding bonefish, instead peering into the distance and enjoying the warm sun on my face and shoulders. I felt like I was getting away with something as I chuckled to myself over the date and my present location.

Now anyone who has done any bonefishing knows that the fish very rarely come at you at the proper angle. You generally wade with the tide and wind, hoping that a fish will present itself for a direct shot, but reality sets

The waving Super Floss legs and mottled carapace of the Bonefish Junk combine to create an accurate representation of a fleeing or hiding shrimp.

Kurt Olesek with an Ascension Bay permit taken on the Bonefish Junk.

in when they either sneak up from behind you or just magically appear off to your right, creating the dreaded right-hand wind presentation that usually ends with the fly stuck in some part of your anatomy. Sure enough, on this day they came from the right, my distraction costing me the chance to reposition before they got in range. A school of modest-sized bones swept in and swirled around me like a pack of fighter jets. I stood stock still and hoped that I might become part of the scenery until I could get my act together and make a cast. The bones curled around me in a tight group, when I saw one fish peel off quickly to chase down some unseen morsel. I learned more about bonefishing in the next five seconds than I have in all my time in the ocean. The bonefish zipped over about five feet, stopped, and then made a circle or two like a dog about to lie down. He pushed his bony snout into the bottom stirring up a cloud of aquatic dust, and I saw the shrimp blast out of the sand and quickly dart several feet away. The shrimp settled to the bottom and I lost sight of him, but Mr. Bonefish knew his plan. The fish closed in on the hapless shrimp and piled onto him like a high-speed car accident.

I was always under the impression that bonefish prey moved slowly and that your fly ought to move in short darts, providing the fish ample opportunity to close in and catch it. This visual display of a shrimp moving relatively long distances and the bonefish's easy adjustment and even aggressiveness over this behavior changed the way I fish and tie flies for these lightning bolts with fins. I never did manage to get a cast to that fish or any of the other fish in the school, as I had become enraptured with the Discovery Channel–like display of predator and prey while my line had wrapped all around my wading boots. I just stood there and laughed like a goofball, as I am prone to do after blowing a shot. Now that I think about it, I laugh a lot in the ocean.

Most bonefish flies have never struck me as particularly imitative. Sure, the Crazy Charlie can look a bit like a shrimp if you squint your eyes and tilt your head just right, and there's no arguing with the fact that many of these flat out catch fish, but there's always been a thought in the back of my mind that we, as fly tiers, could do better. Saltwater fly tying seems to attract a different breed of angler and fly tier than trout tying does. Many of the most successful salt guys are guides or hardcore anglers who view fly tying as a necessary evil rather

Making the Eyes

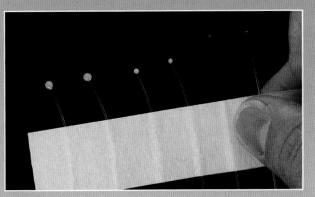

To make the eyes for this fly or any other mono stalk-style fly, I begin by straightening a piece of heavy mono by stretching it tightly between my hands. In this case I'm using 25-pound-test Mason hard monofilament so it takes a bit of pulling to straighten it out. Clip off several three- to four-inch-long sections and place them across the sticky side of a piece of masking tape. Once you have the desired number of strands set perpendicularly to the tape, place another strip of tape over the center of the mono strands and directly across the top of the first piece of tape, essentially sandwiching the mono between the layers of tape. Clip the ends of the mono so they all extend out from the tape about the same distance on both sides. In the upper right photo you can see the plain mono on the right. Once you have all the mono lined up, melt a small ball on the end of each strand with a candle or cigarette lighter, as seen in the center of the photo. Finally, mix up a small batch of five-minute epoxy and add a drop or two of fluorescent green paint while you mix. The paint does change the consistency of the epoxy a bit, but for our purposes here this change will not affect the outcome.

Now, hold the eye blank by the tape strand and dip each melted mono ball into the epoxy so it picks up an appropriately sized glob. You can do this with two to a hundred eyes on the same blank. Once they have hung to dry for 15 minutes or so, you are all set to use them.

than something that can be fun on its own. The creative process is passed over many times in favor of just plain getting it over with and this, I think, is where the proliferation of super-simple, yet not quite finished, patterns has come from. Creative saltwater tiers like Tim Borski changed the way we all look at saltwater patterns over the last decade with more realistic patterns designed to fish properly and imitate real food sources.

It seems the favored patterns of yore are quickly being replaced by modern versions that attract fish with subtle movement, accurate colors, and proper design, and not only look like actual food sources, but act like them as well. The popularity that saltwater flats fishing has attained over the past several decades has also bred fish that have become more selective to even the best-presented patterns. Now, I know that bonefish aren't the pickiest eaters, and the general trick to this whole game is to get the fly to them without spooking them, but a

fly tier like me always has to have some sort of advantage, even if only perceived, and this is what led me to start tinkering.

My Bonefish Junk pattern started off as a simple variation on the ubiquitous Gotcha. This all began with the addition of a pair of hot-tipped Sili Legs to the standard pattern. A conventional Gotcha is a relatively hard-bodied fly with no moving parts save for its Craft Fur wing. The addition of a set of white legs tipped in hot orange added both a bit of wiggle and some color to an otherwise subtle fly, and both the Bahamian bonefish and guides loved it. But it was the down time in between these yearly pilgrimages that made this landlocked Colorado boy start adding pieces and parts, resulting in the pattern you see here.

The current incarnation of the Bonefish Junk (and no, I'm still not sure that I'm finished with this pattern, so I reserve the right to add or subtract at my whim) features Super Floss legs and antennae designed to flutter realistically in the water, attractive mono and epoxy eyes, and a carapace mottled to better match up with the variegation of the natural. I can't say that I had any particular species of shrimp in mind for this pattern but instead tried to create a pattern that had general life and movement to it, even when sitting still on the bottom.

Super Floss turned out to be the perfect answer for the legs and antennae as it is much more durable than Sili Legs and takes a marker quite well, enabling me to add specks of color. I believe strongly in mottling things up as this broken pattern seems to replicate a bit of movement. I added a beard of bright orange egg yarn to make a hot spot on this fly as well, with the reasoning that this shot of color would help the fly stand out from a distance on a mottled bottom. The eyes came about after seeing the prominent green orbs on the natural when one jumped into our southbound flats skiff at South Andros, and the development of a process to mass-produce these epoxy-coated eyeballs was a pleasant discovery along the way. And finally I formed the carapace from Polar Fibre, a dense synthetic hair that has a bit of sheen, subtle breathing qualities, and great durability. In this process I lengthened the fly considerably, with the old adage of "big fly = big fish" ringing in my head. While the Bonefish Junk certainly shares its lineage with the Gotcha, I like to think that I've added some major improvements to the original, with more movement and a better silhouette and color.

BONEFISH JUNK

Hook:	#1-4 Tiemco 811S
Thread:	Fire orange 140-denier Ultra Thread
Weight:	Stainless-steel bead-chain eyes, sized to hook
Antennae:	Shrimp pink and bonefish tan Super Floss
Flash:	Pearl Diamond Braid, shredded
Mouth:	Orange egg yarn
Eyes:	Melted mono with painted epoxy ball on each end
Body:	Pearl Diamond Braid
Legs:	Shrimp pink and bonefish tan Super Floss
Underwing:	Pearl Diamond Braid, shredded
Overwing:	Shrimp-colored Polar Fibre
Markings:	Sepia and orange permanent marker

TYING THE BONEFISH JUNK

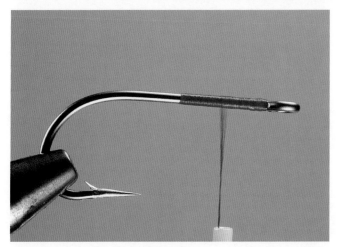

1. Start the thread just behind the eye and build a smooth thread base back to the midpoint on the shank. Return the thread to the 75 percent point.

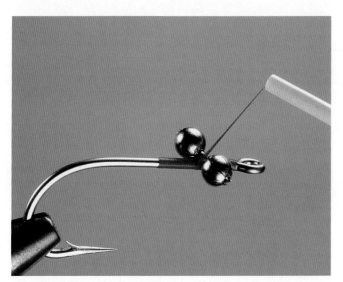

2. Clip off two bead chain eyes from the strand with a pair of dikes. Place the eyes across the hook shank at the 75 percent point and make a half dozen taut wraps of thread over the stem at the center, coming from the back near side to the front far side.

Pry the near eye back a bit so the stem is more perpendicular to the hook (I usually hold it with my thumbnail) and make another half dozen turns crossing the first set across the center. This set of wraps should be going from the front near side to the back far side of the eyes.

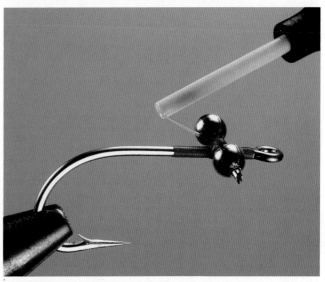

3. Make another set of wraps going each direction while pulling tightly on the thread to anchor the eyes in place. Make sure the eyes are perpendicular to the shank and tied in tightly.

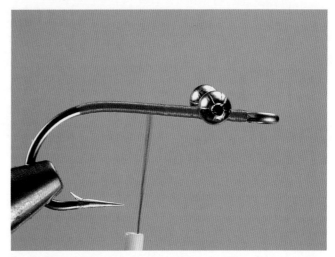

4. Add a drop of Zap-A-Gap to the thread wraps between the eyes to lock them down. Continue wrapping the thread all the way back to the bend, forming a smooth thread base as you go. Return the thread to the midpoint on the shank.

5. Tie in one long strand of pink and one more long strand of tan Super Floss at the center of their lengths at the midpoint on the hook. Just use two tight turns here to hold them in place.

6. Pull the front ends of the Super Floss to the rear of the hook and pick up the other ends in your fingertips. Pull all four strands tight as you wrap the thread back over them to the bend.

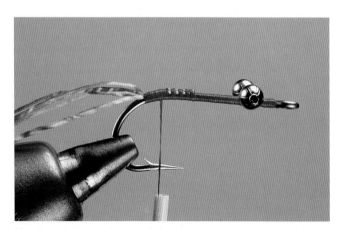

7. Anchor the base of the Super Floss strands down with a smooth band of thread at the bend and return the thread to just behind the eyes.

8. Tie in a 6-inch length of pearl Diamond Braid at the center of its length just behind the eyes.

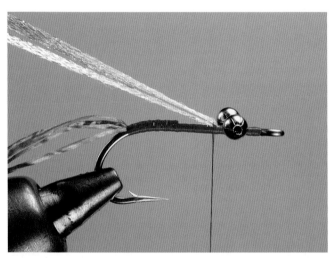

9. Fold the front end of the Diamond Braid back as you did with the Super Floss in the previous step.

10. Hold the braid on top of the hook and wrap back over both strands to the bend.

11. Use a wire dubbing brush to shred the Diamond Braid. Start at the tips and work your way back toward the hook until the strands are all completely separated.

12. Measure about one and a half shanks beyond the bend of the hook and lay your scissors in at an angle to trim the Diamond Braid. Trimming at an angle like this assures that you get a ragged end that is not cut square like a brush. The shortest of the cut fibers will be about a shank-length long and the longest will be about a shank and a half.

13. Clean up the ends of the Diamond Braid if needed by cutting across the bottom of the clump at the same angle. The longest fibers will now be in the middle of the bunch and should extend well beyond the hook bend.

14. Peel a 4-inch-long strand of egg yarn loose from the package and tear off a clump from the main strand so it is ragged on both ends. Do not use the whole strand. Use only about half of what you think you'll need for the fly. You will be doubling this piece of yarn over just as you did with the Super Floss and the Diamond Braid. Fold the yarn in the middle so the tips are about even, yet still somewhat ragged.

15. Measure the egg yarn clump against the hook so the base is just behind the eyes and the ragged tips extend about one shank length beyond the hook bend.

16. Tie the folded clump of egg yarn down right behind the eyes with several tight turns of thread. You can clip any remaining butt ends close now.

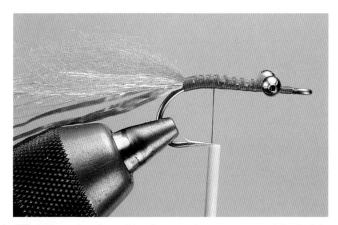

17. Wrap the thread back over the egg yarn while holding it on top of the hook shank with your material hand. Wrap all the way back to the hook bend. Use the wire dubbing brush again to fray the egg yarn into a sparse tuft.

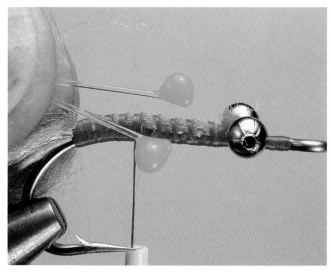

18. Select two of the prepared mono eyes (see sidebar on page 169) and clip their stems so they are about a shank-length long. The eyes are not centered on the mono stalk, so oppose the eyes so they face away from each other as shown.

19. Place one eye on the near side of the hook shank and anchor it in place with a wide band of thread. The eye itself should extend about a half shank beyond the bend and should be facing out away from the hook shank.

Tie the other eye in on the other side of the hook with the same method. The two eyes should be even and facing out from the hook. Bend the mono stalks a bit to angle the eyes out from the hook.

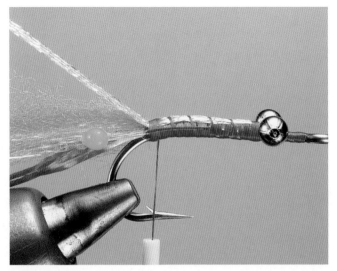

20. Return the thread to the back of the bead chain eyes and tie in a long strand of pearl Diamond Braid. Wrap back over the Diamond Braid to the bend of the hook, taking care to keep a smooth base as you go. Anchor the Diamond Braid at the bend with a tight narrow band of thread.

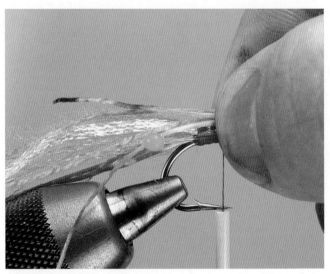

21. Select and cut two strands of tan and two strands of pink Super Floss. Trim them at the top so that they are as long as possible. Place them all in one bunch so the ends are sort of even but not perfectly square. Measure the ends of the Super Floss strands so they extend beyond the hook bend about two shank lengths. They should protrude beyond the ends of the shredded Diamond Braid.

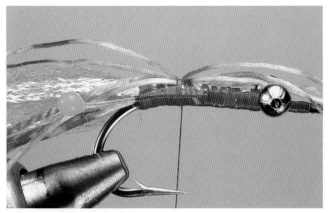

22. Tie all four strands of the Super Floss down just above the hook point, making sure there is space between the tie-down point and the hook bend.

23. Wrap the thread over the Super Floss to about the midpoint on the shank, creating a wide band of thread.

24. Hold the rearmost strands of Super Floss up and out of the way while you begin wrapping the Diamond Braid from the bend up to the front of the tie-down point for the floss. You can hold the floss taut in your thumb and forefinger and use your middle finger to pin the braid against the hook between turns.

25. Lay the front four strands of floss down and continue wrapping toward the eye with the braid. You can slightly overlap the base of the first set of legs with the first turn of braid behind them to help push them rearward. Wrap the braid up to the base of the second batch of Super Floss.

26. Pull the remaining two strands of tan Super Floss toward the bend of the hook . . .

27. . . . and trap them in place by overlapping the braid over their bases. Continue wrapping the braid forward to the last two strands of pink Super Floss.

28. Pull the two pink strands of floss toward the rear of the hook.

29. Continue wrapping the braid forward over the base of the pink floss, pinning them back along the hook shank toward the bend. Wrap the braid right up to the back of the bead chain eyes.

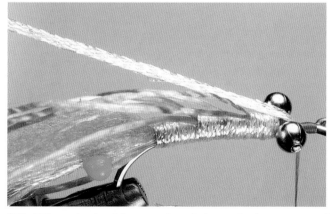

30. Wrap the braid around and through the center of the bead chain to cover the thread. Make one turn from the front near side to the back far side . . .

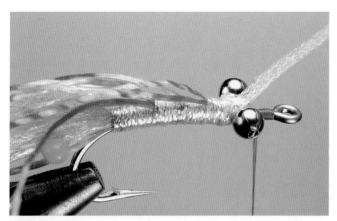

31. . . . and then make another turn from the back near side to the front far side. These braid wraps should cover the threadwork holding the eyes in place.

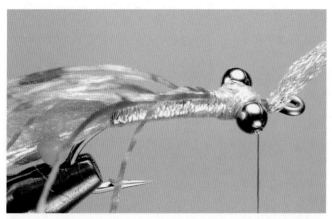

32. Repeat the above X wraps with the remaining braid and tie the braid off just in front of the bead chain eyes. Clip the leftover braid. You should still have about two hook-eye lengths worth of shank in front of the eyes with nothing but thread on them.

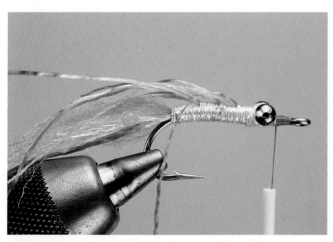

33. Build a smooth thread base over the butt ends of the braid.

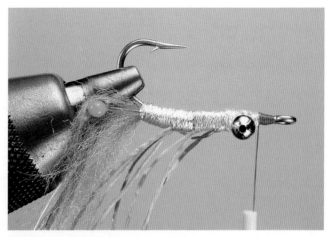

34. Invert the hook in the vise.

35. Measure another six- to eight-inch length of pearl Diamond Braid and fold it in half. I like to leave the ends uneven to save trimming later. We want this to end raggedly as well.

36. Tie the new strand of braid in just behind the hook eye at the center of its length with two tight turns of thread.

37. Fold the front end of the braid back over the hook and bind it in place with a band of thread going from the base of the hook eye to just in front of the bead chain eyes.

38. Shred the Diamond Braid with the wire brush.

39. The ends of the shredded braid underwing should extend to almost the end of the Super Floss antennae.

40. Comb and cut a large clump of shrimp Polar Fibre. Bundle the clump into a nice tight bunch and measure it against the hook so the wispy tips extend to just short of the ends of the shredded braid.

41. Tie the Polar Fibre bunch in on the bottom of the hook shank just in front of the bead chain eyes with a few tight turns of thread. Be sure the wing is centered and in line with the hook point, with half of the wing on either side.

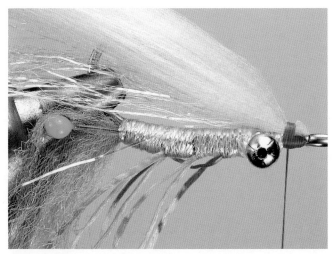

42. Clip the butt ends of the Polar Fibre wing as close as you can behind the hook eye. I try to leave an abrupt step off the ends of the wing to help shape the thread head.

43. Build a smooth thread head over the butt ends of the wing by wrapping from the back of the hook eye up to the base of the wing. Wrapping from the front to the back will make it much easier to work up the tapered base. If you try to wrap from the base of the wing to the eye, the thread wraps will slip down and pile up right behind the eye. Keep the head smooth and well shaped. Whip-finish the thread just in front of the wing base. Clip the thread.

44. Turn the fly over in the vise once more.

45. Pull all the legs up above the shank and run the tip of an orange marker across the strands to create several evenly banded stripes. Remember that you are stretching the legs so you don't want to make these bands too close together as they will recoil once you release the tension on the legs.

46. Pull the antennae out to the side and repeat the banding process on them as well. Be sure to work the bands all the way out to the ends of the strands.

47. You should now have some nicely variegated legs and antennae as shown here.

48. Invert the hook once again and lift the Polar Fibre wing up tightly above the hook. Use a sepia or brown marker to make eight or nine wide bands of color across the top of the wing. These bands will be blurred in the next few steps so don't get too heavy with the marker. Make sure the bands go all the way from one side of the wing to the other, but leave the underside (the side closest to the hook) plain.

49. Use that wire brush once again to comb out the wing, smearing the ink bands. Brush from the base of the wing toward the tips on both sides by pushing the wing fibers into the brush with your fingertips.

50. The brush will fade and blend the markered bands into the wing creating the subtle barring of light and dark.

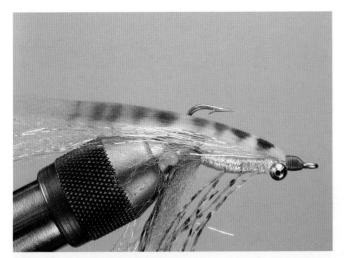

51. Use your dubbing brush to comb the wing down along the top of the fly (the fly rides hook point up, so in this case, the top of the fly is the point side of the shank). Work the Polar Fibre wing down around the hook point and brush it all out to smooth the wing into one unit with a hook point and bend protruding from its middle.

52. You can hold the fly in your fingers for this step, but I am using the vise here for photographic clarity. Trim the legs to random, yet somewhat equal, lengths. I like the irregular length of the legs to encourage differing amounts of movement, just like a real shrimp.

SEVENTEEN

Ragin' Craven

Ever since my first exotic saltwater trip, I have wanted to catch the elusive permit. After tying up tons of flies for months on end, I remember the disgust I had with my guide when he reached in my fly box and selected a big, cartoonish Del's Merkin for me to throw at these incredibly frustrating fish. I had rows and rows of patterns that were carbon copies of real crabs, yet Taku's top pick was an abstract combination of rug yarn and rubber legs. It took me several years

of fishing, and even a few landed permit, to figure out why.

While my immature saltwater mind reasoned that a fish with eyes as big as a permit's would be tough to fool with a fly that was anything less than a dead ringer for crab salad, I finally learned that it's not the exact shape, color, or even the size of the fly that matters so much, but rather how the fly acts in the water. A Merkin doesn't look so much like a real crab, but it acts just like one. The

The Ragin' Craven takes fish all over the United States and Caribbean.

flattened yarn body and heavy lead eyes of this venerable favorite dives quickly to the bottom like the real thing might when confronted by a rubber-mouthed permit intent on grubbing him down.

After throwing the Merkin at hundreds of fish—and even having a few of them close the deal and eat the dang thing—I came to realize that flies that dive for the bottom grab the fishes' attention. Most often I would be instructed to cast close to the fish and sometimes even to hit him on the head. The fly would splat on the water, and one out of every thousand casts or so, the fish would turn quickly and grab the fly and we'd be off to the races, with my knees shaking and adrenaline pumping. But nearly all of those other casts were met with one of two other responses: The fly was either totally ignored, as if it didn't even exist, or the fish would only follow it tentatively. Even if the fish followed, no combination of fast, slow, short, or long strips would close the deal after the fly had touched the bottom. All of the permit that ate the fly did so while the Merkin plummeted from the surface to the sand, but I have never had even one touch the fly after it hit bottom.

Conundrums like this weigh heavily on my mind, especially during the long stretches between trips. I drilled every other saltwater angler and guide I could corner on their theories of why this would happen, and after years of questions and answers, as well as a fair bit of research on permit foods and habits, I cobbled together my own, be it landlocked, theory on the issue.

It seems that permit will occasionally encounter a live crab that is up toward the surface of the water, and the crab, upon discovering his vulnerability, will dive for the bottom only to be promptly sucked into the permit's oversized mouth. Of course, permit will also dig crabs out of the substrate by rooting around, and they will even churn up quite a bit of mud when chasing down their prey. It seems, however, that crabs don't try to run, knowing that they have zero chance of outpacing this predator. Instead, the crab will bury itself in the sand bottom and try to hide, but the permit's wily nose and eyes always find him.

Shrimp, on the other hand, being much better swimmers and capable of quick, short bursts of speed, will sometimes dart away, no doubt trying to get enough of a head start in this potentially fatal game of hide and seek. It seemed to me that I needed a fly that would match up a little of both the crab and the shrimp characteristics so that I could fish the fly on the drop, as well as on the

Bonefish are just one of the many species that will eat the Ragin'.

retrieve with a reasonable chance of fooling the fish one way or the other. And so I embarked on the quest for the next great permit fly, as quixotic as that may have been.

The Ragin' Craven is the pattern that I eventually came up with that would fish well on the drop yet still be realistic, animated, and general enough to be slid, hopped, or dragged across the bottom with some chance of success. My idea involved creating a fly that was both crab and shrimp enough to do the job, but not so much of either as to pigeonhole it in one fishing method. In the process, I developed a fly that works wonders on permit, bonefish, tarpon, redfish, and even striped bass.

A fly as complicated as the Ragin' doesn't come about overnight, and I'm still not quite sure where I got the idea to form the body with a Craft Fur dubbing loop, but no doubt it came at least in part from my frugalities of not wanting to waste the typically discarded underfur from this unusual material. However it popped into my head, I am glad I figured it out, as the loop-dubbed body creates both bulk and volume while retaining various dangling appendages from the ragged long fibers inherent in this material. Adding Merkin-esque rubber legs to the pattern was a given in order to give some reverence to the pattern that had really got permit fishing on the map. The dark bars of color added later, as well as the overall markered makeup job, provided further realism to the pattern and the ability to tailor it to any shrimp or crab species or local variation as needed.

The Ragin' is not a terribly easy fly to tie and it will take some trial and error as well and some adjustments

Craft Fur is similar to but not quite as dense as Polar Fibre. I use the longer guard hairs as well as the underfur to create my Ragin' Craven.

to get it right, but I don't really think of this fly as complicated. I know many folks will look at this huge tutorial and say, "No way," but I urge you to give it a try. Sometimes expanding your comfort zone is all it takes to grow as a tier.

FISHING THE RAGIN' CRAVEN

The biggest asset of this fly is its ability to be easily mistaken for either a crab or a shrimp. Being locked into one imitation or the other seemed to limit my opportunities. With a crab I had the cast and drop option covered, but once that fly reached the bottom, the game was over. With a shrimp fly, you really needed the fish to simply encounter the fly along his path, but then keep it interested with a few longer strips that would sometimes bring them chasing. The Ragin' was developed to be a little of each critter and allow a reasonable silhouette of a diving crab on the drop, but also be shrimpy enough to fish out the cast if need be. The ambiguous shape of the Ragin' seems to cross over well from crab to shrimp and gives me a bit more confidence should the fish either ignore or nose down on the fly after the drop. The waving rubber legs, Krystal Flash antennae, and fur body create some subtle yet lifelike movement, instilling confidence in both the angler's attitude and the fish's likelihood to eat it.

Over the years friends and strangers alike have fished the Ragin' to a variety of different species, all with surprising results. When tied with small lead or bead chain eyes, it has been a great bonefish fly in the Bahamas and Keys, and apparently murders redfish along the Texas and Louisiana coasts. Tied unweighted and in smaller sizes, it cleaned house on Belizean and Mexican bones as well. It has also come to my attention that anglers in the northeast have taken to using this fly for striped bass, a species I really know nothing about and which was never on the intended species list for this pattern, but who am I to complain?

A bit closer to home I have used the Ragin' on both largemouth bass and carp in warm-water ponds and lakes with high-quality consequences. The bulky shape and overall profile of the Ragin' match up well to smaller crayfish found in these ponds, and the fish seem to recognize it with no introduction. I have even caught a few confused trout on this odd little fly in some of our larger reservoirs, where they have developed a taste for these crustaceans.

TYING THE RAGIN' CRAVEN

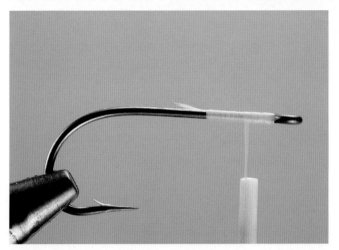

1. Clamp the hook in the vise. Start the thread right behind the eye and wrap a thread base back to just short of the middle of the shank. Return the thread to the hook eye, making a second layer, then return the thread to about three eye lengths back from the hook eye. You want a solid thread base to mount the lead eyes on next.

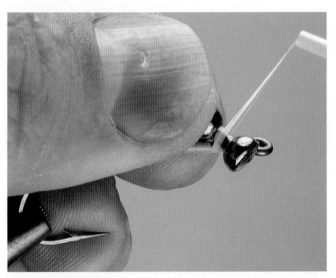

2. Lay a lead eye across the hook shank and bind it in place with several firm wraps of thread from the near back side of the eyes to the front far side. I try to make enough thread wraps to cover the bar between the eyes with thread.

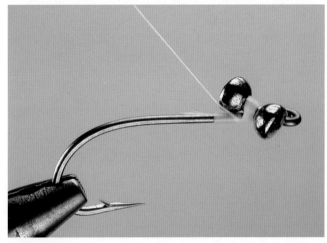

3. Bring the thread to the back of the eyes and make a turn around the hook to prevent a single exposed turn of thread at the front of the eyes.

RAGIN' CRAVEN

Hook:	#1/0-2 Tiemco 811S
Thread:	Chartreuse 3/0 Monocord
Weight:	Lead eyes (medium)
Antennae:	One strand each of black and root beer Krystal Flash
Mouthparts:	Tan Craft Fur
Claws:	Furnace or cree Chinese neck hackle tips
Legs:	Natural latex rubber legs (medium), colored with markers
Body:	Tan Craft Fur spun in a dubbing loop
Eyes:	Black permanent marker
Weedguard:	12-pound-test Mason hard mono
Notes:	For larger sizes, you can use chartreuse or fluorescent green 210- or 140-denier Ultra Thread; use small lead eyes for #2, extra-small lead eyes for #4 and #6.

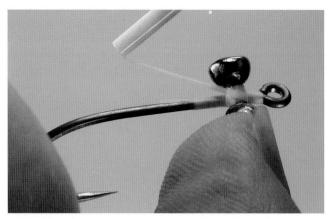

4. Pry the eye on the near side of the hook back so the eyes are now perpendicular to the shank. Bring the thread to the front of the eyes under the hook and make several more firm wraps going from the front near side to the back far side of the eyes.

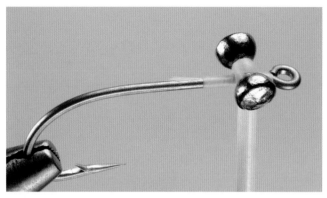

5. Repeat the above process a couple more times, alternating the directions of the wraps until the eyes are firmly anchored perpendicularly to the shank.

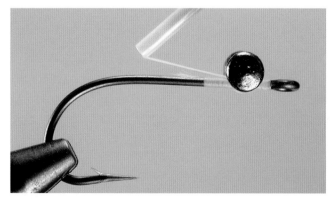

6. Now, make several tight turns of thread around the base of the eyes between the shank of the hook and the eyes themselves. Think of these wraps like you would the turns on a parachute post. These wraps will tighten the previous wraps and lock everything in place.

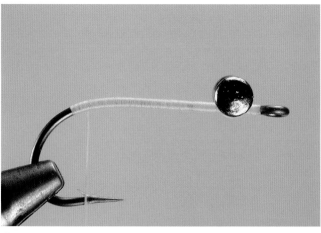

7. Bring the thread all the way to the back of the hook, extending the thread base slightly around the hook bend.

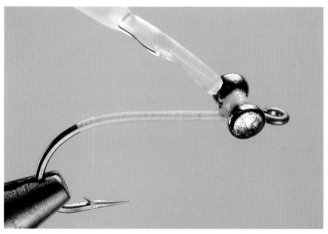

8. Put a light coat of Zap-A-Gap on the thread wraps both on the top and the bottom of the eyes.

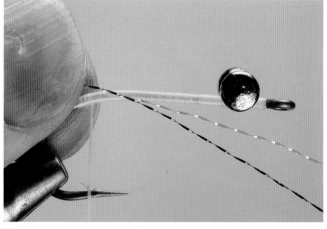

9. After the Zap-A-Gap dries, cut off one strand of black and one strand of root-beer-colored Krystal Flash. You want these strands to be about six inches long.

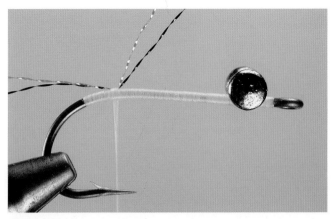

10. Tie both strands of Krystal Flash in at the center of their length just above the hook point. Make just two turns to lock them down. Be careful that the front ends don't lie down on that wet Zap-A-Gap on the eyes.

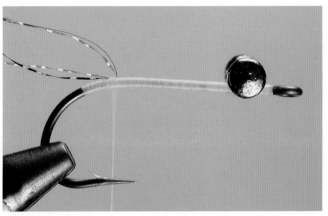

11. Pull the front ends of the Krystal Flash back over the top of the hook, looping it around the tie-down point.

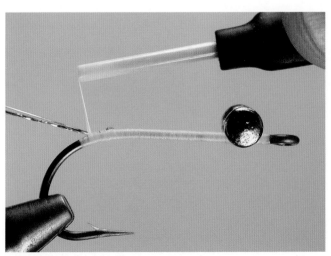

12. Draw the Krystal Flash back and wrap the thread over its base to the end of the thread base.

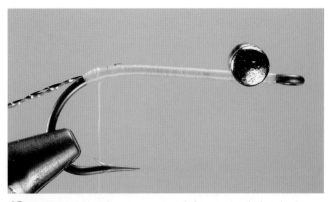

13. Note that I have wrapped far enough back down the hook bend to cause the Krystal Flash to point slightly down. This will be in the up position on the finished fly and you want these strands to be slightly elevated, so at this point, they should be pointing slightly down.

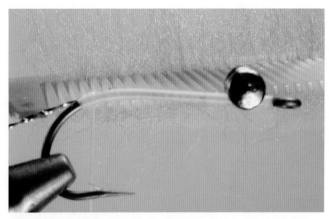

14. Use your bone comb to brush through the patch of Craft Fur and draw out a small clump of underfur to be used as dubbing in the next step.

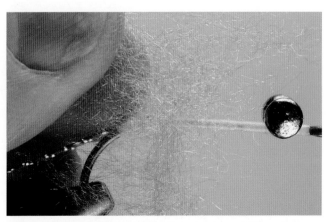

15. Peel the dubbing from the comb and keep it loose and airy, not all matted up like something you combed out of your dog.

16. Twist the Craft Fur underfur tightly onto the thread and dub a small, tight ball of dubbing just past the hook bend.

17. Cut a clump of Craft Fur from the hide, as close to the "skin" as you can. There will be lots of long fibers and some of that softer and shorter underfur in the clump.

18. Peel the underfur from the clump, leaving only the longer fibers in your fingertips. Save the shorter underfur for either the next fly, where you can use it to dub the ball at the bend, or, if you can keep it aligned and in a neat, flat bunch, you can use it in the dubbing loop body.

19. Measure the ragged tips of the Craft Fur bunch against the shank so the clump is as long as the whole hook. Again, beware any remnants of the wet glue at the eyes.

20. Place this measured clump of Craft Fur at the front of the dubbing ball and let your fingers slide it slightly down around the sides of the hook. You want to distribute this fur around the shank, and the thread torque will help with this in the next step, but it works best if you work the hair slightly around the shank first.

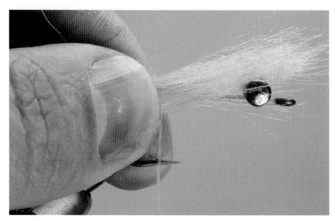

21. Grab the tips of the hair beyond the hook bend and hold them in place just in front of the dubbing ball.

22. Put a loose turn of thread around the fur at the base of the dubbing ball. As you tighten this wrap, the fur will spin and encircle the shank.

23. Let go of the tips and let the thread distribute the fur more as you wrap back over it, forcing the fur up against the dubbing ball so it splays out a bit.

24. Clip the butt ends of the Craft Fur clump just behind the lead eyes.

25. Wrap forward over the stub ends of the Craft Fur to the eyes. Work the thread back and forth over the shank to cover the Craft Fur and smooth the shank. Leave the thread hanging just in front of the hook point.

26. Select two nicely marked furnace- or Cree-colored neck hackles. Even out the tips of the feathers and oppose their tips so they curve away from each other.

27. Measure the neck feathers against the shank so they are just slightly longer than the whole hook. Clip the butt ends of the feathers even and strip about a quarter inch of fibers from the feathers, leaving a bare stem at the base of the feathers.

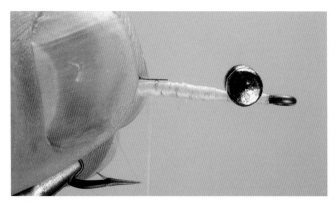

28. Lay the stripped stems of the feathers in right above the hanging thread. Pinch the butts in your fingertips and tie them in place on the top of the shank with several tight wraps of thread.

29. Detail of the feather tie-in. Note that they are centered on the top of the shank and are well ahead of the Craft Fur clump.

30. Tweak the feathers to either side of the shank, so they sweep out along the outside edges of the Craft Fur clump. Be careful to keep the feathers oriented on their edges and don't let them twist out and flatten. When looking at the fly from the side, you want to see the wide side of the feather.

31. Push the feathers down slightly as you grasp them in your fingertips. Hold the feathers in place and wrap back over their bases to the base of the dubbing ball. I try to twist the feathers ever so slightly toward me as I wrap over them to counteract the thread torque and keep them centered on the shank.

32. Detail of feather claws from the side.

33. Detail of the feather claws from the top. Note the wide spread on the feathers caused by wrapping over them up to the base of that dubbing ball.

34. Form a long dubbing loop with your thread by drawing out about fifteen inches of thread. Put your thread hand index finger in the center of the thread strand and double the bobbin back up and around the hook shank. Make sure to lock in both legs of the loop with several tight thread turns. The loop shown in this photo is too short, but it needed to be to illustrate the technique.

35. Draw the two legs of the loop to the rear of the hook and wrap back over them to the bend. Note that the loop is closed at the top where it touches the hook.

36. Move the thread forward to just in front of the hook point. Lay a single 3-inch strand of round rubber across the hook right above the thread with the center of the rubber leg touching the shank.

37. Tie the rubber leg to the hook with a few X wraps just like you used to attach the lead eyes. You do not need many wraps to secure the rubber, so go lightly. The rubber will want to flop and slip all over, but just concentrate on getting the X wraps laid in on it. Once you have a few turns, you can pull and stretch the legs a bit to line them up under the thread wraps so they are perpendicular to the shank.

38. Move the thread another quarter of a shank length forward and repeat the leg tie-in with another strand of rubber. Repeat this one more time about another quarter of a shank forward, being sure to leave space between the last set of legs and the lead eyes.

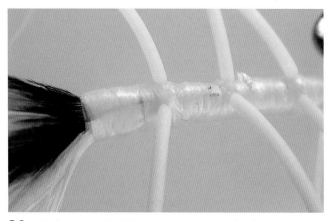

39. Make sure the X wraps securing the legs in place are neatly stacked and tight and that the legs are secured on the top of the hook shank.

40. To prepare the craft fur for the body, start by combing the craft fur flat against the "hide" to align the fibers.

41. Use your scissor blade to lift up a section of the fur at a right angle to the hide.

42. Grasp the fur about halfway down and trim it from the hide as closely as you can.

43. Remove the hair from the hide with it pinched between your first and second fingers. Try to keep your fingers toward the tips of the hair and to keep it lying in a somewhat flat sheet.

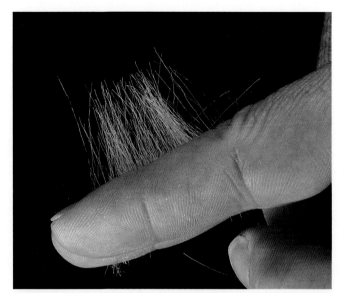

44. Transfer the fur to the other hand by pinching at its base between the first two fingers of your other hand. Pull any extra long fibers out and either discard them or save them for the mouthparts on the next fly. You want just the softer denser underfur with perhaps a few longer straggly strands left.

46. After you clip the fur from the hide, try to keep the clump in a flattened sheet as shown here.

45. Carefully place the Craft Fur clump on the tabletop so it stands upright. Standing it up like this will make it much easier to grab with one hand when you need it.

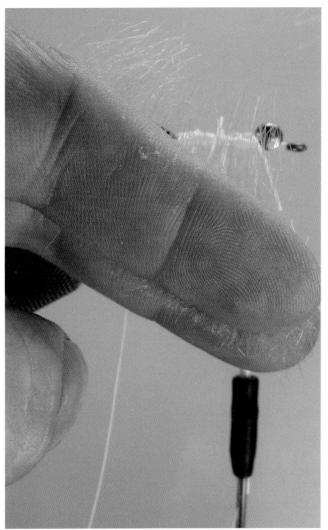

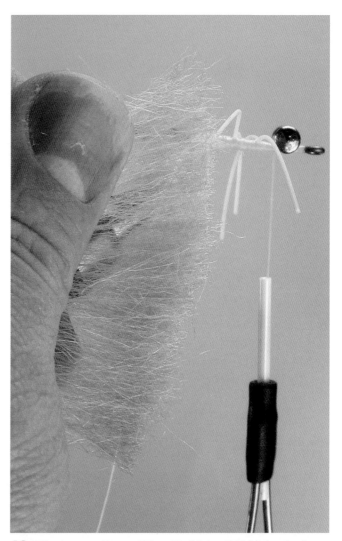

47. Pinch the base of the clump between your fingers as shown here. Holding the fur like this will help to keep it flattened and elongated. Draw the long "guard hairs" from the clump, leaving only the shorter underfur in your fingers. Set the guard hairs aside where they can be used for the mouthparts and dangling appendages on your next fly. Place this clump of hair on the edge of your tabletop where you can pick it up easily and repeat the above process with another wide clump of Craft Fur. You need two good bundles of fur to complete the next step.

48. Place your Dyna-King Dubbing Whirl in the bottom of the thread loop you formed earlier, and let it hang tight. Pick up the first clump of Craft Fur and align it with the tips to the rear and the square cut edge toward the hook eye. Hold the clump near the tips, leaving yourself enough material to hold it together and comfortably in your fingers.

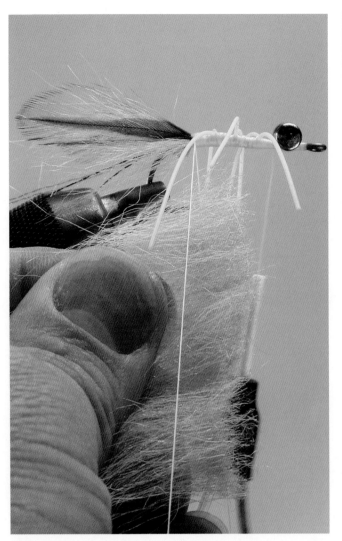

49. Pull the near side leg of the loop toward you to separate the strands and carefully place the first clump of Craft Fur in between the legs of the loop up near the hook shank.

50. Put the second clump of Craft Fur into the loop right below the first. This will be a long loop of thread and dubbing to start with, but it will get shorter and more manageable once it is twisted, so bear with me. Note that the fur is not centered in the thread loop but instead is biased toward the longer tip ends of the fur. This will leave the denser underfur to create the volume for the body.

51. Draw the dubbing loop down and pinch the loop together right at the base of the Craft Fur. (I know the photo shows it being drawn toward you, but my arms are only so long and I have to reach around this camera to do this, so use your imagination a little.) Spin the Dubbing Whirl quickly and let it twist the thread below your fingertips. Once this thread has twisted up, release the pinch holding the strands and draw the tool down to work the twist up the thread through the dubbing in the loop. The twist will jump right up the thread and form the Craft Fur into heavy, ragged, and thick chenille.

52. You should now have a thick strand of homemade Craft Fur chenille. You may need to spin the whirl a bit more to really tighten up the rope, so do so if needed.

53. Draw the legs toward the hook eye while you make a turn with the dubbing loop at the hook bend. Leave the Dubbing Whirl in the base of the loop to act as a convenient handle while you wrap.

54. Make three slightly stacked and overlapping turns of the chenille at the hook bend up to the first set of legs. Use the tips of your scissors to maneuver the legs as needed to keep them from being bound down with the loop.

55. Make three more turns with the chenille between the first and second sets of legs. It helps to stroke the fibers back a bit after each turn, sort of like what you might do with a wet fly hackle.

56. Make two more turns between the second and third sets of legs.

57. Finish with another two or three turns right up to the back edge of the lead eyes. Ideally, you will be out of fur and left only with bare thread at this point, but if you have too much fur, just let the Dubbing Whirl hang and unwind so you can remove the excess fur from the loop and tie off the thread loop strands only.

58. Draw the base of the dubbing loop above the hook and tie it off with several tight turns of thread right at the back of the eyes. Clip the loop from the shank, but don't cut it flush. Leave slack when you make this cut, as the thread is twisted and is under tension and could slip back under the thread wraps you used to tie it off.

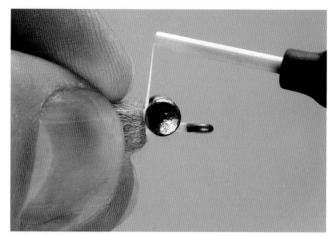

59. Stroke all the fur back toward the bend and build a short collar of thread anchoring the tag end of the loop.

60. Bring the thread under the shank and in front of the lead eyes and whip-finish. Clip the thread.

61. So after all that, you have a fuzzy little ball of crud with some feathers sticking out the back and some rubber bands dangling from the sides. Stand by: things will get better quickly now.

62. Use your Collier Dubbing Brush to comb all the fur back toward the bend. Really get after the fur with the brush to pick out any trapped fibers.

63. The fly should look like this.

64. Trim close across the hook point side of the body, creating a slightly humped shape. The hump is both from the eye to the bend and from one side to the other on the fly. I hold the legs and fur from the edges of the fly down with my fingers to avoid accidentally trimming them.

65. Turn the fly over and while holding the legs out of the way, trim a groove down the center of the shank as close as you can get. Leaving too much material on the bottom of the fly will prevent it from riding properly when fished. Be sure to leave some of the fur sticking out the sides of the fly.

66. Detail of finished bottom trimming. Note that the bottom of the fly (top of the hook shank) is flat, which will help with the fly's hook-up orientation in the water.

67. Press the tip of a black Sharpie marker into the fur at the hook bend to make small dark dots for the eyes. Do this on each side of the hook, just behind the dubbing ball at the bend.

68. Use a sepia marker to make some bands of color across the body of the fly. Of course these bars can be any color you choose or can be skipped altogether. I sort of dab and press the marker across the fly to blot the ink well into the fur.

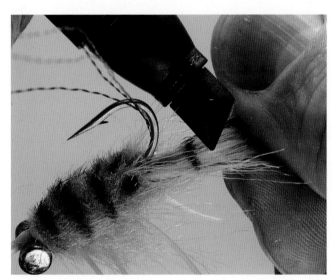

69. Pull the Krystal Flash antennae around the hook point to hold them out of the way and draw the long craft fur fibers at the bend taut in your fingertips. Drag the tip of the sepia marker across the fibers several times, creating narrow bands of mottling.

70. Make the bars as evenly spaced as you can and extend them to as close to the tips of the fibers as you can get. This is a good spot to add a bit more color if needed and you can go back and add some additional barring with other colors. Orange, chartreuse, and even black are all good choices, but don't get carried away. Pull the Krystal Flash antennae back around the hook point. I like to stretch the Krystal Flash at this point by gently tugging on the ends of each strand. Stretching the flash makes it just slightly softer and less stiff, allowing it to wave seductively in the water.

71. Now for the legs: draw all three strands on the near side of the hook taut in your fingers and rub the wide side of the sepia marker tip across them. I sort of roll the legs up and down the tip of the marker to create a nice band of color. You can stretch the legs very tightly and end up with much finer barring or keep them under less tension for wider bars. Do the same thing with the legs on the other side.

72. Detail of leg banding.

73. Use a red marker to color a wide band at the end of each leg just as you did with the sepia marker. I like the red band to be wider than the brown bands.

74. Trim the ends of the legs so they are about a shank-length long. Pull and prod the legs as needed to set them perpendicular to the hook shank. They should be evenly spread and all about the same length.

75. Top view of leg position and coloration.

77. Pinch the ends of the mono with a pair of Tiemco Debarb pliers to flatten the last quarter inch or so. We want to reduce its bulk since it will be pushed up through the hook eye on the next step, and you'll need enough space left in the eye to thread the tippet.

76. Almost finished. If you do not require a weed guard on your fly, you can simply epoxy the thread wraps around the base of the lead eyes and thread head and call your Ragin' done, but if you fish where there is grass or coral, read on to learn how to add a mono weed guard. Place your fly back in the vise with the hook point facing down. Restart the thread right behind the hook eye. Straighten a long strand of Mason 12-pound-test hard mono by pulling firmly on both ends. Cut two strands from this piece and even the ends.

78. Push both ends of the flattened mono up through the hook eye from the bottom. Just push the ends through to where they almost touch the base of the lead eyes.

79. Capture the ends of the mono with several firm wraps of thread between the hook eye and the lead eyes.

80. Move the thread forward to the back edge of the hook eye. The flattened mono still extending below the hook eye should be about the same length as the thread head, or the same length as the distance from the hook eye to the base of the lead eyes.

81. Fold the mono strands back under the shank, making sure that they are lying next to each other and are not twisted up.

82. Begin to bind the mono strands tightly to the shank on the underside of the hook right at the back edge of the hook eye.

83. Wrap over the mono to the base of the lead eyes, and then forward again to the hook eye. Whip-finish the thread and clip it.

84. Invert the hook in the vise and kink the mono upward so the tips extend beyond and above the hook point.

85. Clip the tips of the mono just beyond the hook point, making sure that they are both the same length.

86. Flatten the tip of each mono strand with the pliers. While holding the tip of the mono in the pliers, push the jaws of the pliers toward the eye to kink the weed guard at the base of the flattened portion.

87. You should now have two mono spikes with a sharp bend at their tips that extend slightly above the hook point. This style of weed guard has become my choice for flies like this. It is not so protective to prevent solid hook-ups, but creates enough of a diversion to keep weeds and other flotsam from fouling the hook.

88. Put a light coat of epoxy over the thread wraps and around the base of the weed guard at the head. Be sure to coat the head all the way around, top and bottom. If you use a light coat, the fly should need no rotating, but if you are doing several of these at once, a fly rotisserie is a good idea.

89. Finished epoxy head. Note that the entire thread head and the base of the lead eyes are coated with a durable layer of epoxy.

Index

Advanced Wing Duns, 99
Antron, 2, 70, 71
Arkansas River, 43, 47, 86–88
Autumn Splendor, 156

Baby Boy Hopper
  Chartreuse, recipe for, 138
  Cricket, recipe for, 138
  fishing, 129–130
  Olive, recipe for, 130
  overview of, 127–129
  Tan, recipe for, 138
  tying, 130–137
Barr, John, xiii, 88, 113, 128
Barr Dubbing Teaser, 75
Barr Emerger, 23
Barr Flies (Barr), 88
Barr's Damsel, 78
Bartholomay, Ross, 43–44, 47, 71–72, 86–88
Basic Fly Tying (Craven), xii
BC Hopper, 113, 128
Beanie May, 47
Best Way Products, 4
Betts, John, 99
Bighorn River, 89
Bonefish Junk
  eyes, making the, 169
  overview of, 167–170
  recipe for, 170
  tying, 171–181
Borski, Tim, 170
Brassie, 58
*Bugs of the Underworld: The Natural History of
  Aquatic Insects* (Cutter and Cutter), 13,
  15

Caddistrophic Pupa, xii
  Amber, recipe for, 68
  Cream, recipe for, 68
  fishing, 59–61
  Olive, recipe for, 61
  overview of, 57–59
  tying, 61–67
CDC Golden Stone, 87
Cecil, Marty, 78
Charlie Boy Hopper, 3, 46, 47, 87, 127–128
  Chartreuse, recipe for, 126
  fishing, 113
  Olive, recipe for, 126

overview of, 111–113
  Tan, recipe for, 126
  tying, 114–125
  Yellow, recipe for, 114–125
Charlie's Mysis
  overview of, 69–72
  recipe for, 71
  tying, 72–76
Cheesman Canyon, 3, 97–98
Chernobyl Ant, 112
Collier's Dubbing Brush, 162, 198
Colorado River, 47, 141
Comparadun, 98
Copper John, 13, 24, 33, 47
Cotter, Riley, 128
Craft Fur
  for Bonefish Junk, 170
  for Lead Eyed Gonga, 154, 155, 161, 166
  for Ragin' Craven, 184–196
Craven, Julie, 3
Crazy Charlie, 169
Cutter, Lisa, 13, 15
Cutter, Ralph, 13, 15

Danville Thread, 47, 79, 114, 126, 158
Dave's Hopper, 111
Debarb pliers, 201
Del's Merkin, 182–184
Diamond Braid, 170, 172–173, 175, 177, 178
Dremel tool, 111–112
Dry Magic, 100
DuPuy Spring Creek, 98
Dyna-King Dubbing Whirl, 162, 194, 196,
  197

Elk Hair Caddis, No-Hackle, 106
Engle, Ed, 35

Flash, 1
  See also Flashabou; Krystal Flash
Flashabou, 1, 24, 25, 45, 155
Fluoro Fibre
  for Caddistrophic Pupa, 59, 61, 68
  for Jujubaetis, 25, 29–30, 32
  for Jujubee Midge, 2–5, 8–11
  for Soft Hackle Emerger, 88–92, 94, 95
Franken-Fly, 140
Frying Pan River, 70
  Bend Hole, 71–72

Giambrocco, Mike, 37
Gloss Coat, 140, 150, 152
Gonga (original), 155–157
Gordon Griffith's thread, 25, 32, 47, 55, 56,
  128, 130, 138
Gotcha, 170
GTH (Go to Hell) Variant, 113
  Blue, recipe for, 153
  Lime, recipe for, 141
  overview of, 139–141
  Pink, recipe for, 153
  tying, 141–152
  Wine, recipe for, 153
Gudebrod thread, 2

H&L Variant, 140
Hareline Dubbing, 68
Hare-Tron Dubbin, 61, 62, 68
Heng, Tim, 69–70, 156
Henry's Fork, of Snake River, 104–107
Henry's Fork Hopper, 112
Humpy, 113

Ice Dub
  for GTH Variant, 140, 141, 150, 153
  for Lead Eyed Gonga, 155, 158, 165, 166
  for Poison Tung, 36–42

Jack Flash, 33
Jujubaetis, xii, 44, 129
  Juju PMD, recipe for, 32
  overview of, 23–25
  Purple, recipe for, 32
  recipe for, 25
  tying, 25–32
Jujubee Midge, xii, 13, 23–25, 33, 35, 129
  Blue, recipe for, 11
  Brown, recipe for, 10
  Chartreuse, recipe for, 11
  fishing, 4–5
  Olive, recipe for, 5, 10
  overview of, 1–3
  Red, recipe for, 10
  tying, 3–4, 6–9
  Zebra, recipe for, 10
Jumbo Juju Chironomid
  Bleeder, recipe for, 22
  Blood, recipe for, 15
  Blue, recipe for, 21

Camo, recipe for, 22
  fishing, 14–15
  Olive, recipe for, 21
  overview of, 12–14
  Red, recipe for, 22
  tying, 15–21
  Zebra, recipe for, 21

Kaufmann, Randall, 78
Kaufmann's Damsel, 78
Krystal Flash, 155, 184, 185, 187, 199, 200

Lagartun thread
  for Caddistrophic Pupa, 61, 68
  for GTH Variant, 141, 153
  for Jujubaetis, 25, 32
  for Jujubee Midge, 5, 10, 11
  for Two Bit Hooker, 47
Lagartun wire
  for Poison Tung, 35–37, 39, 40
  for Two Bit Hooker, 56
Lawson, Mike, 112
Lead Eyed Gonga
  Black Gonga, recipe for, 166
  fishing, 156–158
  overview of, 154–156
  recipe for, 158
  Rusty Gonga, fishing, 156
  Rusty Gonga, recipe for, 166
  Tallow Gonga, recipe for, 165
  tying, 158–165
Lime Humpy, 139–141
Lime Trude, 141
Loop Wing Emerger, 98

Mason monofilament, 169, 185, 201
Matuka, 154
McFly Foam, 71
Mercer, Mike, xiii, 43, 44, 47
Metz Magnum, 165, 166
Microfibetts, 88
MicroMay, 43–47
Mirage Tinsel
  for GTH Variant, 140, 141, 143, 153
  for Jujubaetis, 25, 29, 30, 32
  for Jumbu Juju Chironomid, 15, 21, 22
  for Two Bit Hooker, 45, 50, 54–56
Mole, the River, 99
Mole Fly
  fishing, 99
  overview of, 96–99
  recipe for, 100
  tying, 100–103
Morpho Fiber, 59, 61, 66–68
Mugly Caddis, xii, 60, 61
  Olive, recipe for, 110
  overview of, 104–107
  recipe for, 107
  tying, 107–110
Mustad hooks, 79

No Hackle, 98
No-Hackle Elk Hair Caddis, 106

Olson, Bruce, 3

Parachute Adams, 89, 98, 100, 113, 140
Pheasant Tail Nymph, xiv, 23, 47
Platte River Spider, 155
Poison Tung, 4, 141
  Black, recipe for, 39
  Brown, recipe for, 39
  Deep Blue, recipe for, 37
  Olive-Black, recipe for, 40
  overview of, 33–37
  Purple, recipe for, 40
  Red, recipe for, 39
  Tiger, recipe for, 42
  tying, 37–39
  Wine/Silver, recipe for, 42
  wire bodied, tying, 40–41
  Zebra, recipe for, 41
Polar Fibre
  for Bonefish Junk, 170, 178–181
  for Lead Eyed Gonga, 155, 158, 161–163, 165, 166
Prowse, Bean, 47
Prowse, Matt, 47, 60–61, 139

Ragin' Craven, 155
  fishing, 184
  overview of, 182–184
  recipe for, 185
  tying, 185–203
Reynolds, Weston, 128
Roaring Fork Anglers, 69–70
Rollo, Van, 3
Royal Wulff, 139–141
RS2, 23, 88
Ruedi Reservoir, 70

Schmidt, Brian, 128
Schrantz, Chris, 155
Schroeder's Parachute Hopper, 111
Sharpie marker, 67, 114, 125, 137, 164, 199
Sili Legs, 155, 158, 160–161, 165, 166
SLF Dubbing, Whitlock, 107, 110
SLF Prism Dubbing, 59, 61, 66, 68
Snake River, Henry's Fork of, 104–107
Soft Hackle Emerger, 160
  Black, recipe for, 94
  overview of, 86–89
  PMD, recipe for, 95
  recipe for, 89
  Rusty, recipe for, 95
  tying, 89–94
South Platte River, 88, 111
  Cheesman Canyon, 3, 97–98
Sparkle Dun, 98

Stimulator, 113, 140
Superfine
  for Jumbu Juju Chironomid, 15, 19, 21, 22
  for Poison Tung, 39
  for Two Bit Hooker, 47, 50, 55, 56
Super Floss
  for Bonefish Junk, 170, 172, 173, 175, 176, 178
  for Caddistrophic Pupa, 58, 61–64, 68
Super Hair
  for Jujubaetis, 25–28, 32, 44
  for Jujubee Midge, 1–7, 10, 11
  for Jumbo Juju Chironomid, 14–18, 21, 22

Tarryall Creek, 111
Thin Fly Foam, 114, 126, 130, 138
Thin Skin, 13, 16, 18–22, 113
Tiemco
  Debarb pliers, 201
  Dry Magic, 100
  Morpho Fiber, 59, 61, 66–68
Tiemco hooks
  for Baby Boy Hopper, 128, 130, 138
  for Bonefish Junk, 170
  for Caddistrophic Pupa, 61, 68
  for Charlie Boy Hopper, 113, 114, 126
  for Charlie's Mysis, 71
  for GTH Variant, 141, 153
  for Jujubaetis, 25, 32
  for Jujubee Midge, 4, 5, 10, 11
  for Jumbo Juju Chironomid, 15, 21, 22
  for Lead Eyed Gonga, 158, 165, 166
  for Mole Fly, 99, 100
  for Mugly Caddis, 107, 110
  for Poison Tung, 35, 37, 39–42
  for Ragin' Craven, 185
  for Soft Hackle Emerger, 89, 94, 95
  for Two Bit Hooker, 44, 47, 55, 56
  for Wiggle Damsel, 79–81
TroutHunter, 99
Two Bit Hooker, xiv, 129
  Black, recipe for, 56
  Brown, recipe for, 47
  Dark Olive, recipe for, 55
  Light Olive, recipe for, 56
  overview of, 43–47
  Red, recipe for, 55
  tying, 48–55

Ultra Thread
  for Bonefish Junk, 170
  for GTH Variant, 140, 141, 153
  for Jumbu Juju Chironomid, 15, 21, 22
  for Ragin' Craven, 185
  for Two Bit Hooker, 55, 56
Ultra Wire
  for Caddistrophic Pupa, 61, 68
  for Poison Tung, 34, 39–42

Umpqua Feather Merchants, 2, 3, 47, 113, 128
Unique Hair, 4
Uni-Thread
   for Charlie's Mysis, 71
   for Jujubee Midge, 5, 10, 11
   for Jumbu Juju Chironomid, 15, 21, 22
   for Mole Fly, 100
   for Mugly Caddis, 107, 110

   for Poison Tung, 37, 39–42
   for Soft Hackle Emerger, 89, 94, 95
   for Two Bit Hooker, 55
UTC thread, 40
UTC wire, 35–36
   Ultra Wire, 34, 39–42, 61, 68

Web Wing, 113
Whitlock SLF Dubbing, 107, 110

Wiggle Damsel
   fishing, 79
   overview of, 77–79
   recipe for, 79
   tying, 80–85
Wonder Cloth, 100
Woolly Bugger, 78, 155

Zap-A-Gap, 116, 132, 158, 171, 186, 187